Foggy on Bikes

FOGGY
On Bikes

Carl Fogarty
with Neil Bramwell

CollinsWillow
An Imprint of HarperCollins*Publishers*

First published in 2001 by
CollinsWillow
an imprint of HarperCollins*Publishers*
London

1 3 5 7 9 8 6 4 2

A CIP catalogue record for this book
is available from the British Library

ISBN 0 00 711838 4

Design by Terence Caven

Circuit illustrations by John Lawson

Printed and bound in Great Britain by
Clays Ltd, St Ives plc

The HarperCollins website address
is www.fireandwater.com

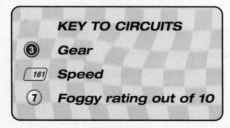

KEY TO CIRCUITS

③ **Gear**

161 **Speed**

⑦ **Foggy rating out of 10**

CONTENTS

INTRODUCTION

I was knackered. We had been riding for a couple of hours and had just reached the halfway point of a really tricky steep section called Walna Scar in the Coniston area of the Lake District. It was more suited to trial bike riding than trail bikes – a slippery gully filled with boulders, and water running off the top of the mountain. I remember once following Dougie Lampkin, the world trials champion, up there and he made it look easy. I had already fallen off three or four times but I still managed to catch a lad called Kevin Moore, who had come past me laughing his head off. He was always pretty quick up that section because he had strong legs from his days playing football for Swansea City, when they were at the top of the old First Division. Sure, you need strong arms for balance, but when you are trying to keep the bike upright and to push off the rocks when your wheels are spinning, all the effort comes from your legs.

I could just about see the dry stone wall, where we always stopped for a break and which served as a finish line for the 'race', and saw a chance to overtake Kevin at the last minute. So I went for the tightest of gaps, he came across and we smacked into each other. I fell off, but he fell underneath me and we were both howling with laughter as we scrambled to pick the bikes up and reach the wall first. For the record, I won!

During the break, the banter was flying round about the exploits on that last section. Another mate of mine, Austin Clews, a director of a company in Blackburn called CCM which makes

Saying hello, or goodbye, whichever way you want to look at it, to the Brands Hatch crowd of 2000 following my accident in Australia.

motorcycles, came round to have a good look at the new bike I was riding, a Suzuki DR400. It was a bit lighter than the other bikes because I was still struggling with my injured arm. Then, before we'd hardly had a chance to catch our breath, someone shouted, 'Right, we're off!'

The next section was also full of rocks and shale, so I decided to try and ride on the moorland grass, thinking I would manage to get up to the top if I got a good enough run at it. By this time the weather had closed in and I could hardly see more than a few yards ahead because of the mist. I just about made it over a little ridge at the top of the slope when the engine suddenly cut out. Every time I tried to start it, it died straight away, and I was getting more and more tired just trying to hold the bike up on the steep slope. It did not have a kick-start, so I was worried that the battery would go flat. Everyone else had cleared off. I could barely hear them, never mind see them.

When the bike eventually fell over, I decided to go back down the hill and try to start the thing on the way down. It would not bump-start because it was sliding on the grass, and even the electric-start would not work. *What the hell is wrong with this thing?* I thought during a minute's rest back down at the wall, staring at the bike in frustration.

Then it hit me: the fuel had been switched off. It must have been Austin when he was examining the bike. I had been left with enough fuel in the pipe to get the bike started and perhaps run it for about a mile on the flat. I flicked the switch back on and eventually made it to the top, falling and stalling on the way up because I was so shattered. I was panting like a dog when I reached them. They had been waiting so long that Austin had actually forgotten he had switched the fuel off! Bastards!

When I smashed my arm at Phillip Island in Australia in April 2000 – the injury which forced me to quit racing – I was more pissed off at having to miss days like this one near Coniston than I was at missing the actual superbike races for the rest of that season. For me, racing in the World Championships was never fun. It was a serious business – I had to win, and people expected me to win. It was hard to enjoy something when there was so much pressure on you to do well.

Most people who own a bike find it difficult to understand that I didn't get a thrill from putting my knee down at a corner. That's part and parcel of the fun of bikes for them. But I can count the number of times I've ridden a bike on the roads in the last ten years on the fingers of one hand. I took my enduro bike out onto the roads a couple of times, just to get a feel for it and run it in for a few miles before taking it up to the Lake District. One of the other few times I have been out on the roads was when travelling between the hotel and Misano for the World Superbike round in Italy in 1999. As at most circuits on race days, the traffic approaching the track is bad. So, rather than have fans banging on the window while I sat in a hot car in a traffic jam, I decided to use one of the Ducati scooters to ride to and from Cattolica, where we were staying. I've seen Eddie Irvine do the same thing, and it's quite funny watching people's reactions when they realise who it is flying past, especially in Italy where I have a huge following because of my association with Ducati. They just about manage a 'Ciao, Foggy!' before I'm off down the road, riding like a typical Italian.

The bikes I keep at home are also used more as ornaments than as functional bikes. The 996 Ducati on which I won the world title in 1998 is mounted in my hallway in front of a mirror. There is also a replica of that bike, given to me by Ducati, in the new office and trophy room we designed at home. Then I have a Ducati 900 Monster, also given to me by Ducati. That bike has been fettled to make it a 960. It has a different exhaust, pistons, barrels and heads. My intention was to ride it on the roads occasionally, but I've had it for two years and never taken it out. There's time yet, though as you've probably guessed I'm not really a fan of riding bikes on the roads. And that's not unusual for racers. I guess it's a bit too much like taking your work home with you.

The bike I probably use the most at home is my KTM 250cc motocross bike – at least until the arm injury prevented me from using it on the small track I built in a field behind the house. I also bought two Honda XR100s from America to use at Fogarty Park, so that I could find someone to race against – and beat. Then Malaguti gave me a scooter, after they did a deal with Ducati to produce a series of Foggy replicas. It was sprayed up in the same colours as the bike on which I won the 1999 championship. That has also done zero miles! I bought Danielle a Yamaha TTR90 for her ninth birthday, and the girls also have a little quad bike. And I've got a Birel four-wheeler, which has a steering wheel and a four-stroke lawnmower engine. The manufacturer also sprayed that red, put some Ducati stickers on it and sold a few on the back of the fact that I owned one. It was useless for riding on grass because it had slick tyres and would not have had enough grip, but I did ride it around the paddock for a while because it looked different and a bit freaky – the Volkswagen Beetle of the biking world.

I also have a 90cc Honda Cub field bike, probably best suited to teenage lads, which I bought for £500 from a shop in Burnley

> **FOGGY FACTOR**
>
> 'Whether I'm riding a CCM 600 up a mountainside or throwing my Honda XR100 over jumps at home, I always go for it 100 per cent.'

in 1996. Don't ask me why. I used it as a paddock bike when I was with Honda in 1996, and it's a good bike for pulling wheelies as it has a lot of low-down power. You can get the back wheel up pretty easily, as long as you keep one finger on the back brakes to stop it going over! Finally, there's the mini-moto, which lives in the lounge area of the kitchen. These are actually raced in Italy and are really difficult to control, as the engines are really 'wick'. It's not like a little four-stroke that just chuffs along. Danielle is already very confident on it.

But, while my own are used mostly as toys, bikes still play a major role in my professional life. I'm still very busy on the World Superbike circuit. I've retained close ties with Ducati and they want me to help develop their young Spanish rider, Ruben Xaus, into a world title contender. And I am currently trying to attract sponsorship to set up my own race team. But as far as riding goes I'm happy to stick to the 'rideouts' in the Lakes, supermoto riding or mucking around on the motocross track in the field at the back of our house.

My approach, though, is always the same. Whether I'm riding a CCM 600 up a mountainside or throwing my Honda XR100 over jumps at home, I always go for it 100 per cent. And I'm in my element when someone makes any sort of a ride into a race. Then, as always, it's win at all costs.

That's probably why I was pushing so hard at a track at Anglesey in North Wales when I suffered my latest bad injury in September 2001. I'd been booked to ride for CCM in a big supermotard race in Belgium and was keen to put in as much practice as possible, as I would have been up against people like Jamie Whitham and Ruben Xaus. I also wanted to give the regular supermotard guys a proper race. But I high-sided on a gravel section and snapped my tibia and fibula on landing. The weird thing about it was that the circuit is an absolute dead ringer for Phillip Island. It's situated at one end of Anglesey, the sea surrounds the track, and the bend where I went down exactly matches the one where I crashed in Australia in 2000.

The first operation to reset the joint wasn't successful so I had to stay in Bangor Hospital over the weekend in order that the doctors could have another go. I had plenty of time to think things through. As much as I like riding competitively, I can't afford to get injured again. So I will have to stop. I'm 36 years old – not 20 any more. I don't bounce like I used to or heal like I used to. And I do have to think of other people as well – like Michaela because she has to look after me and hump me around when I'm in plaster. But there's no looking back, and I have no regrets.

It was that desire to push myself to the limit that made me the best superbike rider of all time. Four world titles are proof of that fact. Sure, a lot of the other riders had the talent, but not the same hunger for success. That is something that cannot be taught. It has to be there inside you. But there are certain techniques, practices and principles that can give you an edge over the next guy. I was never a textbook rider; I had my own distinctive and aggressive style around the track. It was the same in my early days in motocross, not to mention on the road circuits where I won another three world titles, before clinching my first world title on the track with the World Endurance Championship in 1992.

It goes without saying that much of the advice contained in this book is not best suited to safely riding your own bike on the country's roads. But after reading about the secrets of my success – as well as the scrapes, problems and laughs along the way – every rider, whether a world championship contender or a weekend plodder, will be able to get even more performance and enjoyment out of his or her machine.

Section 1

WHAT MAKES A WORLD CHAMPION

'I've always admired Carl as one of the world's best motorcycle riders of the 1990s, regardless of whether you're talking 500cc or superbikes. Carl won four World Superbike Championship titles and no one gets lucky four times. He worked hard, he had talent and determination, and he deserved all the success that came his way.

'Our careers had a lot in common. Both of us won our first world championship in 1994, and we each had more than 50 race wins in our respective categories. Unfortunately we were also both forced out of the sport by injuries from crashes within a few months of each other.

'So what makes a world champion? To be honest, there's no secret recipe. Every rider is different and so much depends on your team, the support of the manufacturer you're racing for, the level of competition, tyres, plus a slice of luck here and there.

'I went to quite a few World Superbike races over the years and Carl seemed to have a good relationship with his team and Ducati. He also had a strong attitude, and the right level of self-confidence that you need to win — a bit like Eddie Lawson had when I first went into 500cc.

'Sometimes both Carl and I were called ruthless when we were racing. What people don't always understand is that on race weekends the main priority is getting yourself in the best possible position to go for the win on Sunday afternoon. Winning gives you the most satisfaction, and Carl did plenty of that.

'Over the years I've lost count of the number of times I've been asked, by the British in particular, how I think Carl would have gone on a 500. I'm sure he would have been very competitive, but he had a good, long-standing relationship with Ducati in superbikes, like I had with Honda in 500cc, and he may have felt better off staying where he was. You spend years building up working relationships, and it's a big risk going to another team, or category. That's one of the reasons I stayed with Honda throughout my 500cc racing.

'At the end of the day Carl didn't have to race 500cc to prove he was a good motorcycle rider. He'd already done that in superbikes. He was a great champion and role model for young British riders. Above all, he was someone who knew how to win.'

Michael Doohan
Five-times 500cc World Champion

WHAT MAKES A WORLD CHAMPION

1: Tools for Success

Ever since I was a small boy, I hated losing. At school, I could not stand losing at football. Nobody else seemed to be all that bothered. I did not take part in athletics because I knew I wasn't good enough to win. Looking back, that was the wrong attitude to have because I missed out on a lot of fun – but then again, the boy who thought coming second was pathetic turned into one hell of a winner.

Bike racing was the only thing I knew I would be good at. But even when I started racing, I had a fear of what people might say if I did not win a race. I imagined them laughing or pointing at me behind my back. So, as a boy, I was always more comfortable flying around the fields on my own or racing against a few mates who had hardly ever ridden before, situations where I knew I would come out on top. Some of my mates were able to do tricks, like pulling wheelies, better than me. I did not seem to have that natural feel for a bike. But I hated it if they didn't tell me I was faster, and I would really get off on it when they did.

We even tried to do wheelies on a step-through Honda 50 – a 'plastic chicken' as they were called, because of their shape. I never really knew who owned that bike because it was just left at our house, and it soon became a total wreck. One day, when

Riding a Honda 250, not the fastest Honda in the world, to fourth place in the 1987 Junior TT on the Isle of Man.

me and a friend were bored, we decided to trash the thing by throwing it in the stream at the bottom of my house, then setting fire to it. A couple of weeks later, a lad who lived up the road called round to ask if anyone had seen his bike. 'Nope, I've no idea where it is,' I said, knowing it was a heap of molten metal.

All this time, I had an ambition to be the next Kenny Roberts. But, looking back, I wasn't exactly doing a lot to make that dream come true. I wasn't training every night or riding my bike around the fields when I came home from school. The kids of today who want to make it in racing are out riding mini-motos from around five or six years old. My nine-year-old daughter Danielle is already pretty confident on a bike, whereas I didn't even get my first bike until my ninth birthday, so I was a pretty late starter.

By the time I did start racing motocross at the age of 15, I had already missed out on a lot of development. When you look at the successful riders today, they all started around the age of 10. I really wished my dad had pushed me into proper racing at an earlier age, though I would only have gone kicking and screaming. Had I started earlier, I can't help thinking that I would have been an even better racer than I turned out to be.

To me, there are only two reasons for riding bikes: to win or to have fun. Right from the start I was always desperate to win, but in the early days, when I travelled around England with my cousins, I guess we also had a lot of fun. The higher I climbed up the racing ladder though, the less fun it became and the more anxious I was to learn and improve. It was probably only at the age of 20 that I thought *Shit, I can be really good at this and make a good living*. It was around that time that I really put my mind to it and improved as a rider more quickly than at any other period in my career. By the age of 23, I was a world champion.

In some ways I suppose I was lucky because alongside the determination to be the best I also had natural talent. There were those who had as much, if not more, talent, but there were never many with the same hunger. The Australian Anthony Gobert was a case in point. He could do things on a bike I could never do. Gobert had the ability to slide a bike going into or coming out of a corner like nobody else. But I'm mainly talking about playing around on a bike outside races. For instance, he could stand up and pull a wheelie with one hand and one leg off the bike. In my mind, there's no doubt that he had the talent to become one of the best riders there has been, but talent alone is never enough. Gobert did not put in the hard work that is necessary to make it to the top. Instead, he went off the rails a bit.

> ### FOGGY FACTOR
>
> 'As a boy, I was always more comfortable flying around the fields on my own or racing against a few mates who had hardly ever ridden before, so that I knew I was going to be faster.'

It's also one thing to have the determination and motivation, and another to stay at that same level year after year. The American Scott Russell was another rider blessed with a lot of talent, and for a couple of years he wanted to win races and the World Superbike Championship just as much as I did. But he lost the will to win – just like that. When I beat him at Phillip Island in 1994 he made a gesture to me as I passed him which said that he was throwing in the towel, and from that day on it seemed as though he was out there just to get paid and pick up the odd result. In fact, I think the only major races he has won since then have been at Daytona. There was no way I could have gone through the motions like that. Had injury not ended my career, I would have known when to call it a day: the minute I stopped having the motivation to win every race.

Not every rider wears his heart on his sleeve, though, like I do. Troy Corser, my team-mate in 1998 and 1999, always reminded me a lot of the Irish riders, who seemed very laid back about it all. He's another who can do all the tricks, but when it came to

I was wearing a borrowed helmet in this club race at Darley Moor in 1985 because there had been a fire in our caravan.

riding round a track for 25 laps, he wasn't as good as me. And the bottom line is that I would always rather be great at racing than good at tricks.

Track

1   *Assen*

There is no doubt that Assen was my favourite track. More than anywhere else, this circuit suited my riding style of being able to keep good speed through the corners. It's a real rider's track, with a lot of camber on the corners. And my record there is second to none. Towards the end of my career I was virtually unbeatable. From 1993 onwards I won 12 out of 14 races there, which is pretty amazing, including five double wins.

The Van Drenthe circuit dates back to 1925, so it has a rich history. I started racing there back in 1988 in the F1 TT World Championship – my first race experience abroad. Right from those early days, the omens were good. At that time, the rest of the more established Formula One teams were using quick fillers to force the fuel into their tanks and make pit-stops as quick as possible. Our lot was not that sophisticated; my main mechanic, Tony Holmes, hadn't even travelled with us. Towards the end of the race, my mate Gary Dickinson, who wasn't really a race mechanic at that time and was only there for a laugh, had worked out that we needed only another four litres to finish the race. While the others were filling their tanks with these contraptions, we used a jug and funnel, saved loads of time and I ended up finishing ninth, which I was pretty chuffed with. The others must have finished with half a tank full of fuel. It also meant I won £600, so for once I was able to pay our way home instead of relying on the money my dad had given us. Needless to say, we spent most of it by the time we got back to Blackburn!

Things hadn't really run as smoothly as that, though. For a start we were placed over in the lepers' paddock, way over on the other side to the Grand Prix teams, who were at the same meeting. There were only three of us, so whenever the weather changed we had to load different tyres onto a pole and I had to cart them over to the pit-lane myself. It was real low-budget racing.

Earlier at the same meeting, we had been warned that we wouldn't be able to race until we controlled the noise of the bike, which was way over the protected limit. Another racer, Roger Burnett, told us about a way of getting round it by taking off the silencer and inserting a washer in the exhaust. All of a sudden, my bike went from the noisiest thing on the track to the quietest, so the stewards, who are as strict at Assen as they are anywhere, knew something was up. When they found the washer and started bollocking us, I went mad. 'What do you want us to do? We're just starting out and can't afford all the stuff we'd need to meet your standards.' They eventually let us off with a warning.

Gary must have had a thing about the stewards at Assen. Nearly 10 years later, when he was working for Sean Emmett, there was a big argument on the grid. Neil Hodgson's bike had got some air in the clutch and the officials allowed him a minute to bleed it. Gary's team thought he was getting special treatment, so they decided that when the time came to leave the grid, they would leave it as late as possible. When they tried it on, one of the stewards, a massive bloke, picked up Emmett's front stand and hurled it over the barrier. The red mist came down over Gary and he smashed the bloke with his torque wrench. The following year Emmett was not allowed to race until he paid a £600 fine for what Gary had done the previous year!

Here's a description of my flying lap around Assen. I would go through start–finish in second gear and move up to fifth through Timmer Bocht at the end of the pit-lane, where you run across a white line and a hump that can sometimes upset the bike, and straight-line it through the kink. Then I drop down two gears for the proper turn one. I enjoy this third-gear corner. You go in quite hard and then just let go of the brakes while the camber of the track holds you tight into the corner and helps you turn in. The other riders seem to keep braking all the way round. As soon as possible, just after going into the

Worst crash:
Never had one!

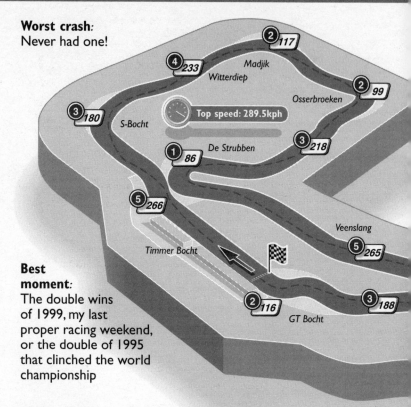

**Best
moment:**
The double wins
of 1999, my last
proper racing weekend,
or the double of 1995
that clinched the world
championship

Closest finish:
Kocinski came past me going into last corner, ran wide
and allowed my Honda back underneath. Kocinski also
allowed Corser into second

Best other rider:
Frankie Chili. He has come
from 250cc GP's and so
has a similar style to mine

Worst moment:
Being splattered by a
bluebottle and losing to
John Kocinski in 1997

ASSEN

NETHERLANDS

Rating **10**

"All circuits should be
like this! I won 12 out
of 14 races here."

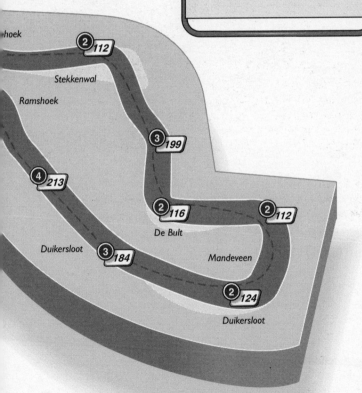

hoek

2 112

Stekkenwal

Ramshoek

3 199

4 213

2 116

2 112

De Bult

Duikersloot **3** 184

Mandeveen

2 124

Duikersloot

corner, I'm onto the gas and using all the room on the exit before going up through the gears to fourth and moving side to side through a couple of slight kinks left and right. This section is called Witterdiep, but they cannot really be called corners.

The next turn, Madjik, is possibly my favourite corner in racing. I go down two gears to this straightforward right-hand corner, with plenty of room going in and plenty coming out. As soon as I exit, I'm straight on the gas and can feel the bike sliding at the rear, which is a really good feeling. Then it's up through the gears and through another dog-leg kink before getting hard on the brakes for the tight, well-banked, second-gear Osserbroeken. I exit that in second gear, climbing over the bike as I change up into third and go through another kink and under a bridge before shutting off the throttle and keeping it in third around the right-hander. More often than not I will try to run the bike in second gear through the De Strubben horseshoe, but I used to go down to first for the slowest corner on the track. That was a bit too low and upset the bike too much on the exit.

FOGGY FACTOR

'Madjik is possibly my favourite corner in racing.'

Then you are onto the back straight, the fastest part of the circuit, although it's not technically a straight as you're switching from one side to the other while veering slightly left all the way along. That's characteristic of the Assen circuit. I short-shift through the gears before the first kink and get on the limiter – I never used sixth gear at Assen – before getting hard on the brakes into Stekkenwal. You have to be leaning slightly over to the left while braking, which has never been my favourite thing to do. As soon as you lift the bike up for the tight right-hander you go down into second, throw it in and exit in the same gear. I'm quickly up to third before another straightforward kink and into the banked, tight, second-gear De Bult left-hander. This is another nice, smooth corner. A few people are caught out going too fast through here and lose their front end but I have never had a problem with it. In fact, I have never ever crashed here, which is another very unusual fact.

I can then just get away with leaving the bike in second before the Mandeveen turn. Occasionally I went up into third, depending on the state of the race and whether I was trying to save the engine a little bit. I stay in second for that double right-hander. The first part is pretty straightforward before I lift the bike up a little bit, move it up to third and push it back in again into Duikersloot. It's a bit tall, but by the time I come out into the long run towards start–finish, third gear is fine. I will leave it in fourth through the Meeuwenimeer, a very fast right-hand dog-leg. You cannot get through there flat out, you have to shut off the throttle and then move up into fifth gear through the Hoge Heide dog-leg.

The last section is all left-handers, and I move down to third through Ramshoek, although it's hard to move quickly down through the gears here because you're always going from one side of the track to the other. I pick up speed mid-corner through this long left-hander before the final GT Bocht chicane. This was possibly my fastest part of the circuit, a good place on the track for it. If you can get through this section quickly then you're in a good position to get up someone, like Chili, through the chicane. Most people will run through this in first gear, I use second really well. I passed Troy Corser while in second gear in 1999 and I could tell he was still in first. However, if I have to protect my line by braking a bit later, I use first gear at this point. On the exit of the chicane I am back all over the front of the bike trying to keep the front wheel down and running across the kerb on the inside to straight-line it through start–finish.

WHAT MAKES
A WORLD
CHAMPION

2: Starting to Race

As a general rule, girls and bikes don't mix. I'd be far happier if
my two daughters, Danielle and Claudia – and Michaela, who
has just passed her test – did not become involved. There are
women who give it a go and do okay, though. The German racer
Katja Poensgen has just become the first woman to compete in a
250cc Grand Prix and she seems to be beating a few of the men,
which is some going.

I think it's great that women
get involved. For a start, Katja's
an attractive girl. That's probably
one of the reasons why she has
got to where she is, because sponsors know they will get a lot of
exposure for their team. If she
was a pig in a wig, things might
have been different! But there's
no question she can ride a bike,
and I have seen her go very fast at
times. I remember once winding

*Danielle gets to grips with a Foggy
replica scooter.*

up Karl Harris about her when he was riding Superstock in 1999. I asked him at a meeting how he was doing.

'I'm doing pretty good, up there in fourth,' he replied, forgetting to mention that Katja was second quickest.

'What are you talking about?' I came back. 'You're letting a bird beat you, you silly sod!'

I laughed, and Karl went out for the next session and went quickest! But I hope Katja does well because she has been around the World Superbike paddock for the last five years and gets on well with everyone.

There are quite a few women who also race at club level, although I'm not sure exactly how many because I don't follow club racing. My old mechanic Anthony 'Slick' Bass's new girlfriend, Juliet Manning, is part of a four-woman team racing at that level. There they are not so much at a disadvantage because on a 125cc or 250cc strength does not play a big part. There used to be a Finnish female rider, Taru Rinne, who was very fast in the 125cc GPs and probably finished in the top 10 on a few occasions in the late eighties. I think she even qualified in pole position once. It's a different matter on a superbike or GP 500cc bike, though. There will never be a successful woman in those series, although I would like to be proved wrong. I don't think they could ever have that aggression or 'bastard' attitude that some of the men have.

But it has been interesting to watch my girls starting out on bikes. Danielle has a little Yamaha TTR90 and Claudia has an old Yamaha quad that I've been servicing. I ordered a new plug, an on/off switch because the old one was broken, put some air in the tyres and changed the oil. When I stripped it down, and all the parts were lying around the garage, Michaela took one look at it and said, 'Well, that thing will never run again.'

She was wrong, but she had a point. In all my time in racing, I never really had to be the one who bothered about making the bikes work, but once I had started on one bike, I tried to get a few of the others that had been standing around for years to start. The Birel had done about 10 miles at the most, yet the lawnmower-style pull-start would not work. I pulled and pulled at it until my arm ached. I took the plug out for a check, but that looked okay.

Leading Michael Doohan in the Czech Grand Prix of 1990, while standing in for the injured Frankie Chili.

I then checked there was fuel coming through, but that was fine too. I began to get really pissed off. Then, after I had charged up its battery, the Honda Cub kept cutting out after running for just a second or two.

Why is it that when machines are left for twelve months they will not start? Maybe the fuel had gone a bit shitty after sitting in the carb for so long. I wanted to ring someone in Japan and drag him over for an explanation. It made matters worse that my kids were watching me fail – miserably. I don't really have the patience, or the time, to mess around for too long before giving in and taking them down to the local bike shop. I'm not too bad on simple things like cleaning the filter of a two-stroke, but anything more complicated than that and I'm soon out of my depth.

It took some time for Claudia to gain confidence on the quad, which was strange because she is usually the one who will have a go at anything. We had to buy her a crash helmet the last time we went skiing because she goes so quickly. At one point she started crying because we wouldn't let her go down a black run. I thought she would enjoy messing around on the quad, but she is much happier on the back with Danielle driving. Maybe it's just that she's not happy around machines.

Danielle was very confident on the quad, and she was soon asking if she could have a bike of her own. I wasn't sure whether that was a good idea, but I got her the Yamaha anyway. I don't really know where it's all leading. After she had been on it a couple of times, I asked whether she wanted to continue on it or get a new quad, but she was adamant that she wanted to carry on riding the Yamaha. She's actually very smooth on it, even though it's probably a bit too heavy for her with its fat 90cc engine, which can be difficult to move around. Sure, she could get hurt on the quads, but being automatic and having four big chunky tyres means they are a lot easier to have safe fun on. And it's an easy way for children to start riding because the throttle has a restrictor that puts a limit on how fast they can go. As they become more confident, the screw can be loosened so that the quad can reach higher speeds. With bikes it's a different matter, and there can very easily be tears. If we had a little boy, there would be no problem with him tearing around, falling off and collecting a few scars. It's a different matter with girls, though.

> **FOGGY FACTOR**
>
> 'There will never be a successful girl racer at world level, although I would like to be proved wrong. I don't think they could ever have that aggression or 'bastard' attitude that some of the men have.'

Michaela is also pretty confident riding the bikes around the field. And she was full of herself recently when she passed her road test. Mind you, she was wearing my lucky green T-shirt, so what do you expect? Seriously, though, I was convinced that she would fail because she was due to take the test on a 500cc when she had been learning on much smaller bikes. I thought that was a pretty stupid way of going about it. I sent her instructor, John Stone, a note saying, 'Thanks for putting up with her.' So I couldn't believe it when she rang to say that she had passed first time. I was really proud of her. She knew she would never have been able to live it down in and around the World Superbike paddock had she failed, and said the whole experience was worse than giving birth. She won't be going out riding on the road, but she might buy a 125cc or 250cc trail bike and come enduro riding in the Lakes. I'd be quite impressed if she could do that, although she wouldn't be able to do the really tough stuff and would have to stick to the fireroad sections. But it just wouldn't be her, somehow. She's better suited to playing tennis or shopping in Manchester!

I remember the very first time my dad sat me on a bike quite clearly. He had bought me one for my ninth birthday, a bike made up by a Honda dealer called Ken Martin. It was basically a 'monkey bike', with a Honda 50cc engine and a chassis made up from different parts. It was a case of crash and learn. At one point, having fallen off a few times, I was convinced I would never be able to change gear. So we started again by dad putting the bike in second gear while I got used to the throttle. I opened it up and shot off down the drive, out of control! There were a couple of ornamental statues at the bottom of our garden, but they didn't last long!

Dad let the other kids at my birthday party have a go, and one lad shot off the back when he opened the throttle too quickly. The bike did not have much to speak of in terms of top speed, but it accelerated pretty quickly. It seemed a long time before I was riding with my feet on the footrest instead of sticking them out in case I lost balance. Maybe I tried to go too fast from the start, because Danielle never seemed to have the same problems when she was learning. Perhaps she had more sense and took it more slowly, realizing she could get hurt if she fell off. Bikes do need to be respected.

The next step was obviously learning how to shut the throttle off while changing gear. But for my next birthday I was given an XR75, a four-speed bike with a clutch. I couldn't get the hang of the clutch at all. When a bike revs loudly, or stalls, or jumps in the air, it puts you off trying. So I thought *I don't really have to use the clutch. Dad will put it in second gear and I can just let the clutch out once and ride around forever in second gear.* The bottom line is confidence, and it takes a while for anyone to learn

I had fifth place in the British GP of 1992 in the bag at Donington until my Harris Yamaha hit coolant that had leaked from John Kocinski's bike.

how to ride a bike. I certainly didn't take to it like a duck to water. In no time, however, I was pulling wheelies with the older boys, my dad and his mates, and all my early problems were quickly forgotten.

The hardest thing for me was making that step from mucking around to actually entering my first race, which I did at the age of 15, a schoolboy motocross 125cc event in Carnforth. I was not that good at motocross but I did win every now and then, and within two years I was up against senior riders. That summer of 1983, I went to the Isle of Man, as usual, to watch Dad in what was to be his last ever TT meeting. Immediately I realised that I had been wasting too much time in motocross and that my heart lay in road racing. This was what I knew I could be the best at. All it needed was for dad on my behalf to apply for a novice licence and enter me in a race meeting at the nearest club – Aintree, in Liverpool.

Anyone can do this by approaching their local branch of the Auto Cycle Union. Novice riders are forced to wear an orange jacket for 10 races so that the better riders know to stay clear for

Riding the Honda RC30 on the way to my second World Formula One title in 1989, with one of the Nortons in the distance.

their own safety, but all the novices have probably been brought up riding bikes and know the basics. It would never be safe for someone to come off the street and race without any knowledge of bikes, even if they were wearing the orange jacket. When those 10 races are complete, you are free to enter club races without having to wear that jacket. It was a bit different with me, though, because I was beating people who weren't novices from the word go.

The other way to get a head start is by going to a race school. I have just set up a Carl Fogarty race academy in conjunction with Brands Hatch and Ducati. The aim is to get riders, especially those between the ages of 12 and 18 who cannot get track time due to licence requirements, up to ACU licence stage five. That way there should be opportunities for riders to get cheaper bike insurance, and some of the best pupils will get a chance to test with Ducati's race team, as well as British superbike support teams.

For the first level of training, riders must have some experience of bikes or scooters and be able to balance without aid, steer, and be able to stop and start the machine. Specific points will include the need to look ahead, throttle control and how to build a rhythm through a slow start. To test their skills, they will have to perform an extra-slow slalom, another slalom at 30mph so that they begin to appreciate weight shift and balance, and a triple hairpin to develop steering and balance control with braking and accelerating. The second level is really an extension of these disciplines for the slightly more advanced young rider. The third, though, takes on board other disciplines such as pit-lane and circuit entry, overtaking, braking, gear change and body position in corners, for riders with a full licence. Riding dynamics will be tested, as will braking performance, and in addition to another slalom course there will be riding in a circle to examine position on the bike. Again, the next level, four, is a refinement of these disciplines to get riders ready for racing in level five, after which I'll be giving them individual tips.

It all sounds very straightforward, but sitting on a racing bike seemed like the strangest thing in the world at first. I had been used to having the handlebars sticking straight out on a motocross bike. To suddenly find myself in this strange, cramped racing position took a lot of getting used to.

Track 2
Brands Hatch

Brands Hatch has always held a special place in my heart because of the amazing support I received there, but it wasn't a circuit on which I really enjoyed racing. I was either very good or very bad there. It's a typical British track, where a rider is on the go all the time. I could never feel relaxed at any point, as it's not a track that flows smoothly. It's a very demanding and challenging circuit where people really struggle on their first visit, so the British riders tend to do quite well there.

The local support is like nowhere else, and that includes Italy. The event in 1995, when I won both races in front of around 60,000 people (which was the biggest crowd at a British event for a long time), was one of the highlights of my career. And to race in front of the 120,000 fans who turned up for the 1999 round was an unbelievable feeling. That day, though, was probably one of the lowest points in my career. I desperately wanted to send everyone home happy but tyre problems ruined my first race and I had to use a different tyre for safety in the second race. The grip was awful, and I felt I'd let everyone down. That included a group of fans who would sit opposite the pits from the crack of dawn cheering my every move. It's probably one of the worst places to watch the action from, apart from the start of the race.

I only used to touch fifth gear for a second coming through that start–finish position before braking at around the bridge before Paddock Hill. It's a corner I enter quite quickly, running over a white line at the exit of the pit-lane to get my line. From there I drop it down two gears to third and keep the bike in tight because the corner drops away sharply, so the last thing you want to do is turn it in late. As soon as I'm over the kerb, I take the weight off the front by getting on the gas and driving down Hailwood Hill and up the other side in third gear. There might have been the odd occasion when I shifted up to fourth before dropping quickly back down.

On a clear flying lap I enter the next corner, Druids, in second, while riders who don't carry as much corner speed take it in first. That made it difficult for me to pass people on the entry to that corner, because you obviously have more chance of overtaking in first. If anyone was ever holding me up, I would use first gear to spoil their line and get past them, even if that meant I was slow around the corner. And the line of the corner was so tight that they would struggle to come back past me.

I was leading the race in 1997 when it was stopped after Graeme Ritchie was killed. After the restart I got stuck behind Neil Hodgson and John Kocinski, both of whom were holding me up at Druids. I was getting really frustrated. At one stage I tried to get on the gas too early exiting the corner and I brought the rear right round on myself so quickly that, although it didn't high-side me, it did drop me down on a low-side. I took Simon Crafar with me when he hit my bike and Chili missed running over my hand by half an inch. I felt as low as I'd felt in my first-ever superbike race, when I was leading at Donington and crashed. I had been all set to win both races in front of a massive crowd.

You sometimes run out of road and get onto the rumble strips on the exit of the next second-gear left-hander at the bottom of Graham Hill. I try to leave the bike in third gear going along the straight behind the pits, although it will get close to the limiter for fourth gear. The next second-gear corner, Surtees, is pretty difficult because there are a few different lines. Some riders will go wide while others come up the inside, and a few bumps make it even trickier. On the exit, you're accelerating hard up the hill to get on the back straight

FOGGY FACTOR

'If anyone was ever holding me up at Druids, I'd use first gear to spoil their line and get past them, even if that meant I was slow around the corner.'

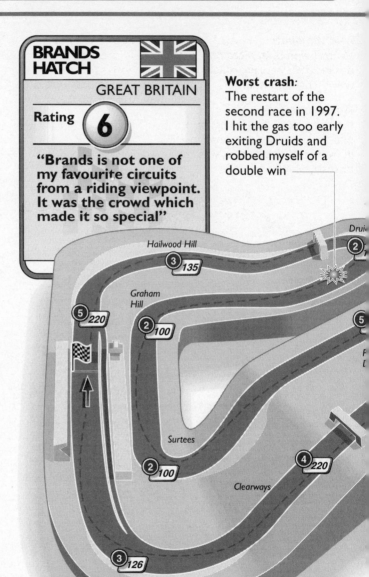

BRANDS HATCH

GREAT BRITAIN

Rating 6

"Brands is not one of my favourite circuits from a riding viewpoint. It was the crowd which made it so special"

Worst crash: The restart of the second race in 1997. I hit the gas too early exiting Druids and robbed myself of a double win

Hailwood Hill

3 135

Graham Hill

5 220   **2** 100

Drui

2

5

Surtees

2 100

4 220

Clearways

3 126

Clark Curve

Closest finish:
In 1998, Troy Corser opened a three-second gap but I had to hold off Jamie Whitham and the two Hondas for second place

Best moment:
When I won both races on a red hot day in 1995, virtually clinching the world championship

Worst moment:
I've been either hit or miss at Brands but the tyre problems I had in 1999, in front of 120,000 fans, was the lowest point

Best other rider:
Giancarlo Falappa won both races in 1993 by a mile in the worst rain I've ever seen

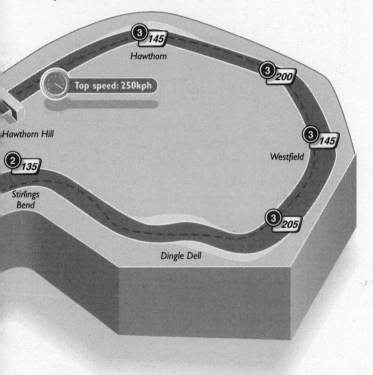

Pulling the bike over to the right before the dog-leg, going over the rise onto the back straight at Brands, while trying to keep the front wheel down at the same time.

and it's very hard to keep your front wheel down. You could sometimes see me, crossed up and leaning over to the right, trying to keep the front wheel down while changing to third gear.

Before you brake for Hawthorn, you hit a dip at the bottom in fifth before the track shoots you back up the hill. There are some markers at the side of the track, numbered three, two and one, which helped me to decide when to brake and drop quickly down to third. Late in the race, when the tyres have gone off, you get a lot of movement on the exit of that corner. Then I usually stay in third gear along Westfield Bend, a fast downhill right-hander, before the track opens up to Dingle Dell in fourth.

I aim for a tree as a peel-off point for Dingle Dell Corner, and when I hit that point I look away and start to turn in because you can't see the corner, which I take in third. It's almost a straight line through, touching two corners on the inside and the middle one on the outside. The bike is light and nervous at that point because you're also on the top of a brow. It's quite spectacular.

Then I hold the bike at half revs in third gear before dropping to second for Stirlings Bend, which is a corner I don't like. The camber of the track doesn't seem to turn you into the corner and you have to push hard to hold the front end in. I crashed there in 1996 when I lost the front end of the Honda. It always seems to be the corner that catches you out on cold tyres, and it's probably my least favourite corner at Brands.

When you go under the bridge before Clearways in fourth, it feels like you're entering a stadium, with a massive crowd on the left-hand side. I like to get into the corner early, although there are a few preferred lines again, and accelerate into Clarke Curve in third. On the exit there's a pretty bad bump which can upset the bike. On the Honda, I had to take my backside off the seat when the bike hit it because the back end of the Honda always seemed out of control. On the Ducati in 1995 I short-shifted into fourth to keep it nice and smooth through the bump and stop it wallowing down the straight. Then it's through the start–finish straight, which typifies Brands because it's not really a flat straight as it slopes down towards the pit-lane.

Section 2

RACING
TECHNIQUES

'Carl Fogarty the person and Carl Fogarty the rider are two different people, but his personality has a lot of influence on his riding. Sometimes, he had to be aggressive off the track because it was the only way he knew how to transmit his personality. When he is with other people he sometimes looks uncomfortable if he doesn't know them. Carl is still a bit shy, even after all his success.

'In the beginning he was a bit hard to manage because I had first to try to understand him. Then I was lucky because we found a very good feeling together. It's not so difficult to read him. It means looking him in the eyes and already knowing what he needs and what he wants, or what he wants to say. Also, he understood that I was often already doing what he was going to ask for.

'Carl was very aggressive on the throttle, so we needed to set the bike up hard on the rear. Especially when he thought the grip was poor, he would turn the throttle so quickly that it was difficult to set the rear suspension. But, at the end of the day, you could always say that Carl would ride round any problems with the bike. He would try hard during qualifying but we always knew that he would put in IIO per cent on race day.

'His body used to move a lot on the bike and he would use his weight to adapt to different corners. And if there were problems with the bike, he would use his own body to solve them by hanging off at different angles. He would not hang off as much as someone like James Whitham, but just use his bodyweight to hold the corners. In that way he could carry high corner speed, a big part of his technique.'

Davide Tardozzi
Ducati factory team manager

RACING TECHNIQUES

1: Positions

Hideous. That's the only word for my style when I first started out on the race track. It was probably something I had picked up from watching my dad so often during his racing career. I had a horrible tucked-in style, a bit like Mike Hailwood. That's not to take anything away from the achievements of Mike. In his day there was no one better. It was just that racing was starting to enter a new era. I guess Kenny Roberts, who grew up on the dirt tracks of America, is the one man credited with introducing the style where riders were hanging off their bikes and sliding the rear end round corners. But Roberts himself will tell you that he picked the style up from Finnish rider Jarno Saarinen.

At the start of my road racing career, around 1984, I used to listen to a friend of my dad called Bill Ingram, who tuned engines. He told me to alter the bars on my bike so that they were pointing in, almost as far as possible, which meant that my riding style was totally tucked in – but as I later discovered, that did not suit my riding style at all.

It was a year later when I finally said, 'I don't like the bars like this. It's really uncomfortable.'

'Well, why do you have them like that, then?' my dad asked.

'Because I was told to have them there,' I replied. That was typical of me at that time. I was not confident enough to stand up for myself, even if I thought there was something wrong. 'So I can put these bars where I want, dad?'

'Yeah, course you can!'

As soon as the bars were moved so that they were a lot further out, I realized immediately I could ride a lot better. Until that point, probably towards the end of 1985, I had been a very slow learner. And I didn't realize how much more room there was for improvement until I started studying videos and pictures. It wasn't just the top international racers I learned from. Even the good national racers, people like Niall Mackenzie, were hanging off the bike a lot more than I was doing at the time.

It was clear that I had to start getting my knee down and to throw the bike around more at the corners. Nowadays, there is just no way a rider can stay upright through a corner without falling off. The sheer size and speed of the machine means that the bike has to be tossed from side to side. And it stands to reason that the more a bike tilts over in a corner, the less grip you are going to have as there is less of the tyre in contact with the track.

I found the Honda CBR600 hard to handle when riding in the British Supersport championship in 1991. For one thing, the footrests were too low.

So the more you lean off the bike and put your knee down on the surface, the more upright you can keep the bike.

There was another position I'd also become more aware of: the financial position in terms of my dad's support of my career. Dad had sounded a few warning bells at the start of the 1986 season.

'Look Carl, we can't keep putting money into this unless you start winning. This is going to have to be the last year our company can fund you unless something happens,' he said.

It was obvious that I was going to have to shape up or spend my life working on a factory shop floor.

By April, I had gone from winning club races to winning internationals against 250cc Grand Prix riders like Donny McLeod and Alan Carter. It was as though I'd missed out a step on the ladder – winning national races. You often see a similar leap of form in athletes; someone who has finished third throughout one season suddenly starts winning at the start of the next. Footballers are the same. A season off through injury can make them stronger and wiser. Neil Hodgson suddenly came back a better rider in the 1999 season after time off. It appeared the previous winter had had the same effect on me.

But a bad crash later that year set me back a bit. I came off at Oulton Park during practice and smashed my femur pretty badly. Still, I used that winter, laid up at home and feeling sorry for myself, to study other people's techniques even more. I was determined to put what I had learned into practice on my return to racing in 1987. But my leg was still causing problems and, during that 1987 season, my tibia snapped because of an infection around the pin that had been inserted to help mend the femur fracture. At the start of 1988 the discomfort of my leg being cramped up on smaller bikes made me switch to the bigger superbikes. I could then really put my theories into effect, and I was soon well on the way to winning my first world championship: the Formula One TT world title.

This is the case with all riders, though. Nobody jumps on a bike and keeps the same style from the start of their career to the finish, although most will probably have a smoother learning curve than I had. Mine was very steep during that period from 1984 to 1988, only flattening off around 1990. And it was not the only thing that flattened off.

I was always altering things to try and squeeze that little bit extra out of my bike. For instance, it was around that time that I noticed that the bars of American rider Fred Merkel were almost totally flat. The superbikes in those days were more like 'sit up and beg' street bikes, not like the superbikes of today, which are more like the Grand Prix bikes of those days. So it was more natural to have flatter bars. Merkel looked really cool and comfortable on his bike and I wanted to give it a go.

I tried it first in wet weather conditions at Kouvola in Finland in 1990. If you are going to fall in the wet, you usually lose the front end of the bike, and in those days I was a lot harder on the brakes coming into a corner. I wanted to be as upright as possible so that I was not pushing on the bars as well as putting pressure on them through braking. And with the RC30, which I was riding that year, you could slide the bars off, turn them upside down and slide them back on so that they were pointing slightly upwards. My mechanic, Dennis Willey, thought I was mad, but I felt as though I had loads of control in the wet, even though it looked an unnatural position. It had been dry during the practice sessions in Finland but it pissed down for the race itself – my last ever TT F1 race – so I decided to give it a try. I won the race easily and lapped everyone up to second place, although it has to be said the competition was probably not the strongest I have ever raced against. I never repeated this feat, because that style was probably more suited to street racing than the track, where you have to hang off even more.

My friend Geoff Hopkins owns a Foggy replica which he rides on the road. A couple of years ago he was complaining that his back was hurting. I suggested that he tried turning the bars upside down so that he was sitting more upright in the saddle and not hunching his back as much. My old mechanic, Slick, was staying with us, and after he had turned them over Geoff agreed that it was much more comfortable. I bet there are thousands of riders out there who would benefit from this advice.

When I signed for Honda in 1991, I told Dennis Willey that I wanted the angle of dip to be changed from 15 degrees to around 5 degrees because I felt too cramped. I could not make up my mind whether or not I liked the new position – and my results

The more I hung off the bike, the more it stayed upright. Somebody like Michael Doohan might have put the bike down more, perhaps losing a bit of corner speed but picking up an advantage exiting the corner.

were not very good that year. I assumed it was the bars and went back to the 15 degree position for the rest of the year and for the next couple of years, but I still had this nagging feeling that the lower the bars were, the more hunched forward I was. So in 1994 I asked Slick to move them back up to a 10 degree dip on my Ducati 916 – a kind of happy medium. I felt that it made mid-corners more comfy, because the riding position is not a natural one for your body to be forced into for 25 laps. I was also that bit more upright when I was braking, and it seemed to be less painful on my knees.

At the end of my career, the angle of dip had probably crept back up to around 5 degrees, probably less than for any of the other riders, who preferred it at around 8.5 degrees. There are those who like their handlebars at around 15 degrees, and a lot of the Grand Prix riders had an even bigger angle of dip. One year in Japan, for some reason, we were using the older style bars with a bigger angle of dip. I simply came in and said, 'I can't ride this. I want to go back to the 5 degrees.'

I always wanted to be on top of the bike as much as possible so that I could throw it through chicanes, where I was always very fast. I did not feel able to do this if I was crouched down. Body strength was never one of my strong points, so that was perhaps another reason why I needed to be on top of the bike, giving myself as much chance as possible of throwing the machine effectively from side to side.

There are two other things to take into account when positioning the handlebars. The main one, as I mentioned from earlier, is that as well as up and down you can change how the bars are angled into or away from the bike. And as my style was all about hanging off the bike as much as possible, I always thought that the further I was tucked in, while remaining comfortable, the more I could hang off in corners.

I think this is why people used to say that I looked big on a bike. I was often told that I looked a lot smaller in real life than I did when I was riding. The press have written things like, 'Never has someone so small made himself look so big on a bike.' A lot of small riders look lost on a bike, and I'm a small guy at 5 ft 8 in, but it's because I hung off the bike and moved around the saddle so much that I appeared bigger. Again, if the bars had been angled further out from the bike, I would have been straining forward, with my weight too far over the front.

At some tracks, with a lot of right-handers, I would angle the left-hand bar a bit further into the bike than the right. As I hung off the bike, the movement of my left arm would be limited by the bike's tank; moving that bar in a few millimetres gave me the chance to hang further off to the right without that left arm catching on the tank. I probably first did this in 1997 when I was struggling with the line of my Ducati, especially at tracks like Donington where I was having difficulty at corners such as Redgate, McLeans and Coppice. Albacete was another track where I sometimes felt the need to do this in order to maximize the contact patch of the tyre and find the best possible grip.

When I asked Slick to do this in Spain, he presumed I wanted the right-hand bar moved inwards as well, and got to work.

'What are you doing that for?' I said when I saw he was working on both bars.

'Well, I presumed you wanted them both doing. You couldn't ride to the chippy with it like that,' he replied.

'Just leave it with the left-hand bar,' I insisted.

Other riders tended to prefer more of what I would call a motocross style, where the bars are sticking out more in the manner of Fred Merkel. That helps them carry more speed into the corners before braking and sliding the back end round, a bit like a speedway rider but obviously not so exaggerated. It allows them to use the strength in their arms more easily. The riders who are very good at this are Noriyuki Haga, Chris Walker and

Anthony Gobert. That was never my strong point. My style was all about carrying speed at mid-corner and my position was perfect for that. One thing the angle of my bars was not perfect for, though, was storage. The mechanics could never get my bike into the transport crates because of the bar positions!

The second thing to take into account when setting the bars is the positioning on the fork-legs. Like every other rider I know, my bars were as high as possible, touching the bottom of the yoke. Again, that was just a comfort thing – I did not want to be crouching any lower than I had to.

The other things that have to be decided on when trying to get the best possible position on a bike are the location of the footrests and how much padding to have on the seat. Much of this was actually forced on me because of my injuries. I had lost a lot of flexibility in my right knee because of the two bad breaks early on in my career. Obviously, on the bigger superbikes there was not the same pressure on my knee to bend as much as there was on a smaller 250cc. But even on superbikes, I could still try to make my racing position as comfortable as possible. The key was to have my footrests a bit further forward than other riders. When Troy Bayliss first sat on my bike after I had crashed in

> **FOGGY FACTOR**
>
> 'Nobody jumps on a bike and keeps the same style from the start of their career to the finish.'

Australia, he could not believe how far forward they were. By moving the footrests forward, though, I stopped my legs being cramped up and also stopped myself from leaning any further forward than I had to. Again, I think some riders like to have their heels as far back as possible to help them slide into corners. That was the last thing I ever wanted to do. I wanted to ride smoothly through the corners and keep the wheel turning forward, so moving the rests back was not something I was bothered about.

At the end of the 1995 season in Australia, after I had agreed to ride for Honda the following season, I asked Slick to check the height difference between the top of the seat and the footrests on the Ducati that I had been riding. I was worried that the Honda was not going to be as comfortable, and when I first sat on the Honda it turned out that the difference was about an inch less. The footrest position seemed okay, so we had to add foam to the seat until the height difference was the same, otherwise I would have been in a lot of pain – the last thing anyone wants to be worrying about during a race.

Tall riders often struggle. A lot of people think Colin Edwards is pretty tall, just because he is slim, but he's actually not much taller than I am. It's the six-foot riders that really have a problem, and there just aren't that many about now. You don't see many six-foot jockeys, either. My old Kawasaki France endurance team-mate, Terry Rymer, was a big lad and his height must have hampered him. We always had to compromise when setting the bike up because it was a big, bulbous bike – a tank of a thing. The bars had to be angled further out to accommodate Terry, and as a result I really struggled to hang off it.

One more way in which my preferred position meant that my bike differed from a lot of other riders' bikes was in the size of the screen. Most riders like big screens, but when I'm in a corner I like to see nothing but the track in front of me. If you study pictures of me riding around corners, I'm hanging so far off the bike that the screen just does not come into my line of vision at all. If I'd had the same size screen as other riders –probably about 20 per cent bigger – I would have been cricking my neck trying to look round the side.

At tracks with long straights, however, such as Hockenheim and Monza, I did not have a choice in the matter. Gaining top speed down those straights was so important that I had to use a bigger screen to improve the aerodynamics of the bike. I didn't like that at all because whenever I came to a bend, the bike did not feel like my own. It always took me a long time to get used to that change. Even so, I still didn't use as big a screen as the other Ducati riders, probably going for half the normal difference between the two sizes.

When I started out, of course, these alterations were not an option. You had what you had, and you had to make do and mend. Or at least that's what I thought. When I look back now, I think, *You thick bastard! Why did you not make some brackets so that the footrests could have been moved forward after your broken leg?*

Even with all the expertise available to me towards the end of my career, I never stopped questioning things. After I had struggled with Honda in 1996, I expected everything to be perfect when I returned to Ducati for the 1997 season. But something did not quite feel right. In fact, I still believe that I lost the world title that year because the testing hadn't been right for the bike. This niggling feeling lasted all the way through the 1998 season, when I regained the World Superbike title but was still struggling to hold my line through corners.

'I still can't seem to hang off the bike like I used to in 1995,' I told Davide Tardozzi, my team boss at Ducati. 'The tank seems to be getting in the way.'

'Well, Carl,' he replied, 'the tank is bigger than it used to be. You need more fuel for a race now.'

'What do you mean? Nobody bothered to tell me!'

The information just crept out like this because there had been so many changes in personnel at Ducati. The bigger tank certainly

Everybody said that I made myself look big on a bike because of the way I moved around in the saddle, as this shot at Kyalami in 2000 shows.

Flat out in the tuck position at Brands in 1999.

explained away a lot of my problems over the previous couple of years. The outcome was that they altered the tank for me and Troy Corser for the 1999 season. The shape and size had to be kept the same, but they managed to take some of the bulk off the top and add it to the bottom. We used it for the first time in pre-season tests at Misano in February. I tested for one day with the old tank, but when it was swapped for the new one I loved it from the word go. I equalled my best time for the test straight away, and that was on old tyres. Troy didn't like it to start with because he didn't hang off the bike as much as I did. If only someone had told either me or Slick about the new tank when we returned from Honda, things might have been a lot different in the 1997 season.

This experience taught me never to stop questioning even the smallest things. At the start of my final season, before the crash in Australia, I was convinced that something had changed with the gear lever.

'Are you sure the rubber isn't thicker this year?' I asked. 'Are my boots any different, then? Because something doesn't feel quite right.'

When I went to the first test in Valencia, I changed the position of that gear lever so many times. The riders have this lever in roughly the same area on their bikes, because you never get the chance to ride other racers' bikes, I'm not sure whether my preference was much different – it is not as noticeable as the position of the bars or the footrest – but for some reason I just couldn't get comfortable during this test. I seemed to be hanging over the front of the bike and didn't seem able to get my foot under the gear lever to go down through the box and change from third or fourth back to first. You cannot alter the position on the splines, because there would be too big a gap. On a factory racing back, the gear lever bar is egg-shaped and swivels around so that it can either be under your foot or away from it. At this track, though, as I said, I could not make myself comfortable, for no real reason because the lever had not been altered. It was either too high when I was changing up through the box or too low when I was coming back down and had to put my foot underneath it. Perhaps it was because that circuit is hard on the brakes, with almost every corner taken in first gear. And you had to change so quickly down from fourth to second that the position had to be spot on.

Whatever the reason, it just goes to show how many things are going through a rider's mind, especially that of a perfectionist like me, when he is racing and testing.

RACING TECHNIQUES

2: The Perfect Line

The credit goes to the Honda RC30. When Jamie Whitham and I rode for Honda in 1990, we both had a lot of problems with the front end of the bike. Jamie hated the bike more than I did. He hung off the bike a lot, but not in the same way as me. His style seemed to be led more by his neck, and his knee did not touch the floor as much as mine did. When I felt the front end going, I could actually try to catch it with my knee and try to push the bike back upright, and I have never worn out my knee-sliders as much as when I rode the RC30. Jamie was not able to do that and spent a lot of the year on his backside.

In some ways, though, I had those problems to thank for a lot of what happened in the future. Because I struggled for so long with that front end, it prompted me to take a tighter line so that I didn't feel as though I was going to make things worse by sweeping in from the outside after braking late.

In the last few years of my racing career, I was always tighter going into corners than any other guy. It felt so much better for me. For someone who carried a lot of corner speed, you would expect the opposite to be true, that I would prefer to take a wider line, but I always thought that if I had been peeling in from way out while carrying so much corner speed I would have felt as though I was going to crash the front end all the time. It was almost as though I did not have the confidence to be out as wide as the other guys. So, at the point when all the riders were starting to brake, I would probably be a couple of feet nearer the inside kerb.

This was obviously more exaggerated on the slower corners. For the very fast corners, such as from Redgate down to Craner Curves at Donington, the line is pretty much the same for everybody; for the slower corners, though, the other guys would try to maintain maximum speed for as long as possible before hitting the brakes really hard and very late. But by that time, I was probably starting to run through faster. Even for the faster corners, I tended to brake that little bit earlier and then let go of the brakes to run in with as much speed as possible. The other riders would leave the braking until the last minute and then start to slide the back end round a little bit while scrubbing off speed. If I was behind any other riders, they would hold me up in the middle of the corner because by then I would definitely be carrying more speed.

The result of that extra speed was that I had to hang off the bike that much more than anyone else to hold the line. If anyone

I'm slightly tighter than Colin Edwards and Troy Corser going into this turn.

There's probably only a foot difference in it but I am holding a tighter line into the corner in 1999.

were to compare pictures of me with almost any other rider at the same point on the same corner, the other rider might have his knee on the ground and his arse hanging off the bike. With me, my head and shoulder were also nearly touching the ground. For a right-hand corner, my left arm would basically be totally locked out so that I could reach over as far as possible.

At somewhere like Assen, one of the faster tracks, my line would be pretty much the same as anyone else's. I might just have turned a little bit earlier into corners, but other riders, like Jamie, turned in a lot later than the rest. He was always a hard opponent to get past because he would brake so late and so wide. You would think you were about to get past him when he'd come *whoaaaa!* right across you. I was always glad to get past Jamie whenever he got away in front of me at the start of the race. But it was no surprise that he lost his front end so often by braking so late on such wide lines.

The rider who probably had a similar line to me was Pier-Francesco Chili, who also enjoyed Assen. Colin Edwards is also similar in a lot of respects. But riders like Garry McCoy, Noriyuki

Haga and Chris Walker are in some ways all about a lot of action going into corners and being a big handful coming out. That's fine if it suits their style of riding, but that was never my style.

So, once I had turned early into a corner, I wanted to get all my body weight hanging off the bike as early as possible. That way I could hold the tightest line and open the throttle mid-corner. At a track like Assen, where there are more fast corners than average, no one could live with me because the other riders did not open the throttle until they were coming out of the corners. It's no coincidence that Chili was one of the few exceptions.

Turn one at Assen is a perfect example. You approach very fast in fifth gear and then, suddenly, it's *brmm-brmm* and you're down to third gear while going hard on the brakes. While the other riders were still on the brakes, scrubbing off that speed, I had swooped in, picked up on gas, taken the weight off the front end and accelerated out. When I was injured in 2000, I had to smile to myself when I was watching the race. You had riders like Haga and Bayliss going hard on the brakes with their back ends kicking out all over the place. I thought to myself, *Guys, that's not the way to go round Assen*. The secret is to keep it smooth. Because Assen used to be part of a road circuit, the camber of the track banks right for the right-hand corners and also helps you to keep the bike tight into the corner.

On the slowest corners however, like a chicane or a hairpin, I could be

FOGGY FACTOR

'I always felt that if I had been peeling in from way out while carrying so much corner speed, I would have felt as though I was going to crash the front.'

as hard on the brakes as the best of them. There is no way you can carry corner speed through these anyway. Albacete, for instance, has a lot of first-gear corners, so there was no way I could rely on the style that suited me at places like Assen.

One track I never liked, and which did not suit me at all, was Laguna Seca in the States. The camber of the track almost falls away from you at the first corner, and the rest of the circuit is flat, so there were certain parts where I found it impossible to carry any corner speed. The front end always seemed to be pushing and

Wrestling with my Honda in the 1990 British Superbike Championship.
You can see that I was trying to hang off, but keep my line.

I tried to hang even further off to try to keep the line. I even found myself trying to turn the bars to try to keep the bike in. Before I knew it, the front end was tucking in and I was in trouble. That circuit was just not built for the way I ride a bike, even though I handled the Corkscrew, supposedly the hardest part, as well as anyone. The Corkscrew is a tight chicane with a steep drop which requires the bike to be quickly flicked over from one side to the other, and I was always good at that because of my slightly more upright position on the bike. I also attacked it more aggressively than the other riders, because I was not as physically strong as some of them. I've even thrown the bike over too hard at times, kicking the back end out as a result. And sometimes I've tried to pull the bike over too quickly, almost losing the front, and I did slide off really slowly once in practice.

The next corner at Laguna Seca is also banked, one of the few on that circuit where I could actually carry some corner speed. I always found myself catching up in the last part of a lap there. In 1997 I was passing people on every lap in that section and riding it as well as anybody, only to lose the race in the last couple of laps to John Kocinski. The first part of the circuit was a different matter, all about hard braking, sliding in and sliding out. I tried a few times to maintain my corner speed, only to find myself in the dirt. It probably took me a couple of years to figure out that the track just did not suit me. Then it became a matter of trying to hold people off. I probably rode as hard to finish fourth or fifth at Laguna Seca as I did to win somewhere else a couple of weeks later.

Track
3   DONINGTON

Donington Park has been one big high followed by a big low. I didn't get off to a good start because in my first race there at a club meeting in 1984, I crashed at Redgate. But it was at Donington that I first realized how much British success meant to all the home fans. In the 1990 Grand Prix, I was pushing too hard at McLeans and came off. The look on the faces of the fans said it all, and I knew I would have to deliver one day.

I also crashed in the first race of the World Superbike round in 1992. I was the leader by three seconds going into Goddards but I tipped the bike over a bit too far in a pathetically slow crash. I tried to get back on before noticing that the footrest had been knocked off. It was a real kick in the teeth because I had just bounced back from a difficult year in 1991. All I could do was slump over the bike and burst out crying. But, typical of Donington, I didn't have to wait for long before there was a high. I won the second race of the day, the biggest win of my career at that point.

Of course, there was another low on the horizon. In that year's 500cc British Grand Prix, I was lying fifth on a privateer Harris Yamaha. All of a sudden, going into Redgate, I joined Doug Chandler in the gravel while Kevin Schwantz frantically waved a marshal's flag to try to get the race stopped. John Kocinski's bike had expired, spilling coolant on the track. There was nothing I could do about it.

The following year was a similar story. After coming a close second behind Scott Russell in the first race, which was over two legs because some oil had been deposited on the track, I had probably my worst crash at the track in the second race.

It is beginning to sound as though I could never stay on at Donington, but that was the last time I crashed there, although the sequence of highs and lows kept on going. I was in for a big high in 1994, when two World Superbike rounds were held at the circuit. At the start of the season I was first and third, only to be brought back down to earth in the wet at the end of the year when I could only manage 14th and 5th. So now I was due for another high, and it was probably one of the highest points in my whole career when I won both races there in 1995.

The races at Donington in 1996 on the Honda were crap, as they were practically for the whole of the year; with all the fans' expectations weighing heavily on me, I could only finish ninth and seventh. Things picked up in 1997 when I won my first race back on a Ducati and then my results were bad again the following year. So it was only right that it all ended on an upbeat note when I won in 1999. It was so weird how the results always managed to fit perfectly into that sequence.

This is how, without fate playing a part, I would try to ride the perfect lap there. I'm in fourth gear through the start–finish; I always tried to set the gearing up so that I didn't have to change up to fifth on that straight, because I didn't want to have to change down three gears into second for Redgate. This is a good place to pass by going up the inside of another rider and spoiling his line. There are a few different lines into the corner and riders tend to peel in from different angles.

> ## FOGGY FACTOR
>
> 'I stayed in fourth down the start–finish straight. That was because I didn't want to have to change down three gears into second for Redgate.'

Then it's hard on the gas as the track drops down through Hollywood and through the Craner Curves section before you hit a heart-stopping downhill left, the fastest corner on the circuit, in fourth gear. It's a classic spot where people are often caught out. It's often cold at Donington for a start. That's normally good news because otherwise the track is hard on the tyres and they can easily overheat, but for the first few laps the tyres aren't working properly on the left-hand side when you flick it over into that fast bend. In fact, on a 125cc bike you're flat out all the way through and it's not much of a corner. I've crashed there flat out in fourth gear and I don't recommended it.

Worst moment:
Hitting Kawasaki's coolant
in the British GP when I was
up there with the best 500cc
riders

Worst crash:
When I came out of the Cran
Curves, leading the second ra
1993. It was fast but
I wasn't hurt

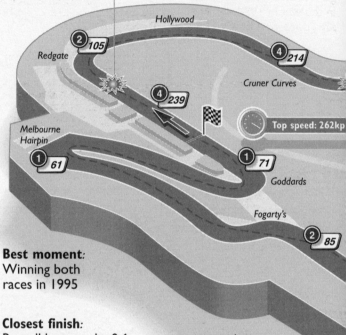

Hollywood

Redgate ② 105

④ 214

Cruner Curves

④ 239

Melbourne
Hairpin

① 61

Top speed: 262kp

① 71

Goddards

Fogarty's

② 85

Best moment:
Winning both
races in 1995

Closest finish:
Russell beat me by 0.6s over aggregates times
in 1993 when the race was stopped. I thought
I had won because I was 1.0s clear going into
the second part of the race

Best rider:
Me! Apart from me, Scott Russell always seemed to go well and was very good in the wet in 1994. Corser also does well here

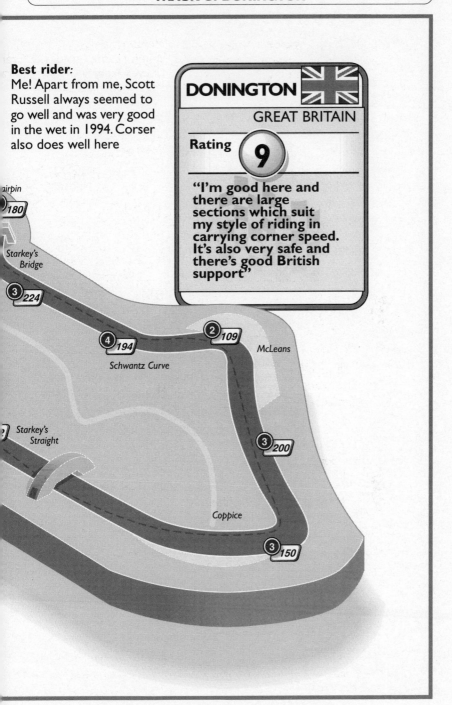

DONINGTON

GREAT BRITAIN

Rating **9**

"I'm good here and there are large sections which suit my style of riding in carrying corner speed. It's also very safe and there's good British support"

airpin

180

Starkey's Bridge

3 224

4 194

2 109

McLeans

Schwantz Curve

3 200

Starkey's Straight

Coppice

3 150

When I crashed there in 1993 I was leading the race – another fall which probably cost me that year's title. This was a case of the tyres not warming up properly by the third lap. When I threw it to the left, the rear came round on me, so down I went. It flicked me off so quickly that the bike carried on in a straight line. When I stopped sliding, I started to run after the bike but when I got there it was mangled and covered in mud. Having said all that, I'm usually one of the quickest through that section and I'm usually in a position to get up the inside of riders going into the Old Hairpin.

This is a right-hand third-gear corner which is downhill until the apex, when you start to go uphill again and change to fourth. If the bike's set-up was good I would try and keep it in fourth gear under Starkeys Bridge, which is a flat-out left-hander for which I might roll the throttle slightly before getting straight back on the gas again. I might just touch the limiter for fourth gear through the long, sweeping Schwantz Curve and into McLeans. It was touch and go whether to change up to fifth, but I always tried to leave it in fourth all the way round Schwantz. My line into McLeans, a second-gear right-hander where the front end is often upset by a few bumps, might be a little bit tighter than the others, as I like to get in early and use the whole of the road on the exit to the corner. Then it's hard on the gas uphill to Coppice Corner, which is a blind corner on the brow of the hill.

I change up to third well before Coppice and leave it in that gear for the corner. I know a lot of other riders didn't do that, instead changing up to third halfway round, but I like to keep it smooth. It might mean it's a bit long through the corner, but by the time I pull out onto the straight I am at maximum revs, right up someone's backside and can pass them without much of a problem.

There is a bit of a leap along Starkeys Straight, just as you reach top speed under the bridge before the track drops away. Then it's back on the brakes as I shift down from fifth to first for the best corner on the track – Fogarty's! I opened that section in 1999 but I wish it had been called Foggy's. This was another place where I could pass people, and I was always pretty good on the brakes here. It's hard to keep the bike stable going into

Accelerating hard out of the Melbourne Loop at Donington, with so much power that it's hard to keep the front wheel down during my 40th WSB win – the first back on a Ducati in 1997.

Fogarty's as the downward slope means that the back end is up in the air. So, again, I leave a small gap between third and second so that it's not too much all in one go. It's a pretty straightforward chicane, but you have to be careful not to go too silly on the exit as it's slightly uphill again, and as you change up to second gear it's quite hard to keep the front wheel down. You would often see me clambering over the front of the bike to keep the weight forward.

Then it's up into third and I just touch fourth before going over the hill and dropping down to the Melbourne Hairpin on the brakes. It's easy to spot the rear end of the bike sliding around here when a rider is changing down to first. Obviously I always tried to keep it stable but it was very difficult, and even my rear would sometimes slide at that point. The track again slopes uphill into another first-gear hairpin, Goddards, another point where you can try to pass up the inside if you've got a good drive coming out of Melbourne. My line tended to differ here: I preferred to keep the bike tucked in whereas others peeled in from the outside or the middle of the road. It is without doubt my least favourite corner on the track because it's a bit bumpy and off-camber. A lot of people have high-sided there and I often struggled to get on the gas and usually lost a bit of drive down the finishing straight.

RACING
TECHNIQUES

3: Braking

The last thing you want to do, having just stepped off the overnight ferry from Heysham to Douglas on the Isle of Man without having had a wink of sleep, is to throw a bike around one of the most dangerous circuits in the world. But that is the kind of thing you have to put your mind and body through if you want to give yourself the best possible chance of finishing the TT course in one piece.

It was 1985 and I had already been to the Isle of Man the week before the Manx Grand Prix – the first time I raced on the island – just to drive round the course in the car. Then we returned to the mainland and raced at Mallory Park, where I finished 11th in an ACU race. We probably arrived in the Isle of Man at around 4am, absolutely knackered after a three-hour drive from Leicestershire and a four-hour ferry journey. But I had to make the most of the time available by doing that extra couple of laps early on the Monday, when the roads were closed to the public.

The fact that I was the favourite to win the newcomers' race made my preparation even more important. After an hour and a half I was dead on my feet, and at 6.30 in the morning I went back to the hotel to try and grab a few hours' sleep before more practice, even though I always found it difficult to get to sleep after riding early in the morning.

One of the main things to learn on a new circuit are the braking points for the corners. We had of course driven round the course in a car the previous week to get a feel for the track, but it's a lot different when you put your helmet on, jump on a bike and produce some speed. It's also a lot different when riding a road bike because the brakes are obviously better for race bikes. And in a road race there is no margin for error. If you run on at a corner, you hit a wall – and that's not advisable. At the North West 200 circuit in Northern Ireland, there is a first-gear corner at the bottom of one of the longest straights I have raced on, probably two miles long. You are braking at 190mph and, because it's a road circuit, you feel as though you're braking on manhole covers. Luckily, at that particular point the road does carry on while the riders turn off to the left. So it's essential that a rider gives himself every chance of getting to know the circuit before the race itself to learn things just like that.

For every corner on every circuit, I picked a marker where I would brake. It might have been as I passed under a bridge, something on a board next to the track or even just a bump in the earth. Towards the end of my career, I walked, jogged or did a few laps on a scooter – depending on the length of the circuit – before tackling a new track. I learned some tracks more quickly than others; one on which I struggled was the Nurburgring. I felt lost there for a while, whereas the other guys went quickly straight away. And until then I had always thought I was a quick learner. It's a big track with a lot of corners which all look the same, so I found it difficult to pick out which were going to be quicker than the others. When I first went to Sentul in Indonesia it was new to everyone, but within the first five minutes Doug Polen and Scott Russell had left me for dead. 'Are you sure they haven't been here before?' I asked. But by the end of the first session I was quicker than they were.

Obviously, the first time you ride round any track you brake a bit earlier than you would normally have to. The next time you brake a bit later, and so on. But the faster the corner, the harder they are to learn. For instance, a chicane is pretty straightfor-ward, whereas a third or fourth-gear corner will take a bit longer to learn. That's because there is a bigger chance of getting hurt if you get it wrong, so you take more care. If you run wide on a slow corner you can run off and get away with it.

Another of the first decisions to make at any track is the size of discs to use, and this can be a frustrating choice during practice. The harder the track is on the brakes, such as somewhere like Donington, the bigger the discs that are needed. But bigger discs mean that the bike is harder to move around, because they are obviously heavier, and the less weight you have low down on the bike the better. In recent years there have been just two sizes, 290s and 320s, although they are testing a new 305 size for use at Daytona.

The smaller the diameter of the disc, the less the gyroscopic effect. That basically means that it is easier to steer the bike with a smaller, lighter disc. But at the tracks that are harder on the brakes, like Donington, these will heat up too quickly. At Donington in 1998, one race was split into two parts because of rain, so for the second leg I tried the smaller discs. But even after just 14 laps they were knackered at the end (although I did win that second leg of the race). Had it been a full 25 laps, I would

The rear axle on which the back brake disc is mounted. I have never used the back brake in all my years of racing.

not have got away with it. Also at Donington, we used to run discs that were 6.5mm thick instead of 6mm. Again that was just to improve heat dispersion.

The brake pads are also made out of different materials. Now they are called performance friction, and are carbon-impregnated. As they wear down, they stick carbon onto the disc so that you effectively have carbon to carbon. The ones before that were sintered. They did a similar thing, but more aggressively and so didn't wear as well. We used to be able to use carbon-fibre discs, but they were banned at the end of 1994. The view was that the privateers could not really afford to use them at £800 a disc, so it was an unfair advantage for the factory boys. I don't see why they cannot be allowed again because the hotter the carbon-fibre discs got the better the brakes were. The opposite is the case with metal discs.

The material for the Brembo carbon-fibre discs was actually too soft for the brake pads, and we were wearing out the discs rather than the pads. I shouldn't really admit this, but at Albacete in 1994 we only had two sets of discs and one of those was already worn out with tramlines with two sessions of practice remaining. We didn't want to use the new set because we wanted to save them for the race, so we got the old discs and glued some emery cloth to the brake pads. Then we started the engine up so the back wheel was spinning and Slick suddenly hit the brakes. Carbon dust flew everywhere in the garage, which is not the best thing for your lungs, but at least the discs were back flat again and we could use them for practice. That's not how the Brembo engineer saw it, though. He was freaking out.

Ideally, and particularly at tracks you know will be hard on the brakes, you want to heat them gradually. So it always made sense to go a little bit easy on them in the early stages of a race, but I have always found that difficult to do when I know there is a race to be won. My attitude has always been that I try to get to the front, and if there's a problem later on, I'll ride round it.

At Kyalami in 1999, I had problems with the brakes of the second bike sticking on all weekend. It was a similar problem to the one Aaron Slight had struggled with for a couple of years. We racked our brains as to why I was suddenly having this problem, which effectively meant that I only had one bike to use for the whole weekend. I kept returning to the pits, shouting, 'It's stuck on again! Do something about this!' I was seriously pissed off because we were wasting half a session doing stupid things like cleaning the brake pads. I had tried going softer on the brakes and this hadn't seemed to work. It didn't help that it was the first meeting of the season and I desperately wanted to get going.

Whatever I was doing differently, it was heating the brake pad up so much that it was locking inside the calliper. We changed the pads from performance friction to sintered, but still had the same problem. Then we tried changing the forks and yokes – still nothing. So we had to machine the end of the brake pad to give it more clearance. Instead of 0.6 mm we made it 0.8 mm so that it was now rattling around inside the calliper. It did solve the problem, although we never really understood why it had suddenly occurred – and on just the one bike. Slick's theory was that it was because I was using the brakes a lot harder as soon as I was coming out of the pits. After the second round, the guy from Brembo, the brakes manufacturers, found a permanent solution by increasing the pad clearance. That never used to be checked, and maybe it had changed, but it is now one of the things that is checked as a matter of course.

Another problem we had in 1995, when we were forced to ditch the carbon discs, was that the brakes were more inboard of the wheel and the mudguard came further over. That meant that the air struggled to get to the brakes to cool the calliper down. The first idea was to get more air into the standard radiators, then the team decided to cut holes in the mudguard and cover it in gauze to stop dirt getting through. Straight away, the calliper temperature dropped from 130 degrees C to 90 degrees C.

The Brembo guy would always come round to ask if everything was okay, but I never found him that useful. If things were going wrong, there never seemed to be much anyone could do about it. The problems were at their worst during my year with Honda in 1996 when I had to break in new discs at every meeting, wasting half a practice session through having to brake nice and gently. Eight times out of ten I would have to come into the garage and say, 'The brakes are juddering again.' It should have been someone else's job to do something like take the bike out onto the

Hard on the brakes and changing down to first. My arms are almost locked and I'm pushing my body backwards, trying to stop my weight from going over the front end.

road to run the new brakes in. I didn't like to mess around and be constantly experimenting. Once I had found something that worked, I preferred to stick with it. And this would normally be done at a special test session, not during practice and qualifying for the races, when I wanted to concentrate on tyres and set-up.

Even so, I would say that in nearly every race I have competed in over the last few years I have had to adjust the brakes during the race. I like to have the brake lever quite hard and tight, while some riders like to pull it in quite a long way before it bites. At tracks that are hard on the brakes, the lever would often work its way in towards the bar and become spongy, meaning I couldn't apply enough force on the brakes. So a small adjuster wheel was fitted which I could turn a couple of clicks to move the lever back out to its normal position. At another circuit, though, I might never have to use the adjuster.

I'm also unusual in that I have never used my back brake, on the right footrest. If you ask ten riders, six probably don't use it and four do. I think that if I had ever tried to use it, I would have lost time. And the position I rode in meant that when I was braking hard I was so far over the front of the bike that I couldn't feel what was going on at the back brake. It's more of a psychological comfort for me, knowing it's there should anything go wrong with the front brake. Then again, even if that were the case the back brake would hardly slow you down at all because it needs to be used four or five times to get some heat into it.

A few people change their back brake to make it a thumb lever on their left handlebar. Michael Doohan started all that when the injuries to his leg meant that he couldn't feel the back brake any more. I tried having one on during 1997, but found that I didn't use it and took it off for the following year. I guess it's the guys who go into corners scrubbing off speed who tend to use the back brake more than others.

If you are riding a four-cylinder bike and you go down through the gearbox quickly, you tend to lock the back wheel up anyway, and a lot of riders like that. A Ducati, however, is not as easy to slide into corners because the engine braking is so different. It does not stop some Ducati riders doing it, such as Troy Bayliss and Neil Hodgson, but the four-cylinder riders seem to be able to do it a lot more easily. When I was changing from fifth to first, I tended to go down a couple of gears and leave a very small gap before going down another couple. That helped me keep the bike as stable as possible and not have the back end weaving all over the place. You never seem to see guys riding twin-cylinder bikes out of shape as much as the four-cylinder riders.

However much preparation is carried out on getting the brakes right, things are bound to go wrong. One major problem is the discs overheating, especially at circuits where you can't generate enough speed to cool them down – again, like Donington. I have had problems with warped discs, when the lever starts pulsing in your hand, and with bits of shit getting onto the discs and affecting their performance.

FOGGY FACTOR

'If I was changing from fifth to first, I tended to go down a couple of gears and leave a very small gap before going down another couple. That helped me keep the bike as stable as possible and not have the back end weaving all over the place.'

At Monza in 1998, my brakes were absolutely knackered and warped in the first race because of all the heat that is generated in the discs around that circuit. I was lying third behind the two Hondas, which were much quicker than my bike that year. But on the final few laps I couldn't outbrake anyone because they were juddering so much, so I ended up dropping down to sixth place. And there have been lots of times, especially when braking too late while trying to do one fast lap for qualification, when I have run on at a corner. Again, that happens more at the fast circuits like Monza and Hockenheim, at the bottom of fast straights.

The first corner at Monza was changed in 2001 to suit Formula One cars, but it became tighter and therefore more dangerous for bike riders. At the old corner it was possible to have three or four riders braking together and very often one ran through the gravel and back onto the track because he couldn't slow down in time. There have been a few hairy moments there, but none worse than that involving Jamie Whitham during practice a few years ago. He came into that first corner at 180mph and his front discs just shattered –a huge chunk went missing. He was travelling so fast that the gravel wasn't able to slow him down and he just managed to pick a line that avoided the wall. He admitted that he had absolutely shit himself!

Another time when riders tend to overshoot is when they have been slipstreaming someone down a straight and are approaching the corner a little bit faster than they would normally. The trick is to brake hard, but obviously not so hard that you lose the front end. Very often you have to run round the outside and come back onto the track.

I have never really considered myself to be someone who is especially good on the brakes, but I've still won races by outbraking riders into the final bend. I beat Chili in 1998 at Assen when he fell off, and I won my first race on a Honda in 1996 by outbraking Aaron Slight at the end of the straight at Monza. The following year I did the same to Neil Hodgson. He was pushed outside the racing line where there is a lot more dust and dirt on the track, and he ran on at the next corner. Clearly, the more a track has been used, the more rubber there is down on the surface and the better the grip is. If you try to brake hard on the loose stones and bits of loose rubber, the chances are that you are going to go down.

The idea is also to keep both tyres on the track. There is footage of me going into corners and braking so hard that the rear wheel is off the ground. And I'll never forget the time during my first TT win in 1989 when I was having a real battle with Steve Hislop, bunny-hopping at the bottom of the hill entering Governor's Bridge in the 750cc production class because I was braking so late and so hard.

So, at the right sort of corner, and if it means winning the race, I can certainly be as good on the brakes as the others are, but obviously people have occasionally got the better of me. In one of my last ever races, at Hockenheim in 1999 after I had clinched the world championship in the first race, I got myself into a position to win the race entering the last corner where all the braking is done. I underestimated how hard Chili had gone on his brakes and he came underneath me to win the race. Luckily I wasn't too bothered because I'd already won the title.

I'm usually better braking into the slower corners, but this wasn't the case in Austria in 1997 on a very slow first-gear hairpin corner. John Kocinski had just taken the lead from me and he broke really late because he knew I was going to come back at him. I knew I could outbrake him so I hit the brakes as late as I could – too late on this occasion. I was in two minds whether to run through and knock him off (he was a big rival) or to run wide. There was a split second's hesitation and panic before I ended up running into the back of him, taking myself out of the race while he went on to win.

To actually pass someone on the brakes you have to be right on their back wheel going into the corner. Sometimes you have to let go of the front brake, enough to run past the other rider, and then brake later in the corner again. That would have meant spoiling my line as well as John's and scrubbing off some speed, but it's worth losing three tenths of a second off your lap time if you get past another rider. It might also mean taking the corner in first rather than second gear, so then you are using a combination of the front brakes and engine braking.

RACING TECHNIQUES

4: Tyres

We must have looked like four Michelin men, except for the fact that we were using Metzeler tyres. It was my first trip to Japan, with my dad, my mechanic and a guy called Lew Durkin, who came everywhere to help out. We were still on a pretty tight budget, so we couldn't afford to pay freight charges. A bike had been lined up for me to ride in the 1989 Formula One World Championship round in Sugo, but we had to bring out our own gear – including tyres.

So each of us checked in for the flight with a tyre on each shoulder, along with all the other stuff we needed. But that was nothing compared to having to find the right train when we got there and then to carry this lot all the way to Sugo. We arrived to find a disgrace of a bike. There was oil all over the place and the brake pads were knackered. We'd also heard that Joey Dunlop was not going to make the trip. So there was a RVF sitting there doing nothing while I, the reigning world champion, had to make do with this heap. There was no way, though, that they were going to let me use that bike.

It didn't matter for one practice session because Metzeler produced a fantastic rain tyre and I was easily the fastest when it rained. We had loads of Japanese hanging round the garage trying to see what kind of tyres we were using. There was probably no one else in the world using Metzeler tyres on short circuits because Metzeler couldn't afford to travel to places like Japan. We had to do all the work on the tyres ourselves, although they advised us on pressures and the like before we went.

I had a crap race, finishing 13th but picking up a few valuable points towards my next world title. But the 'fun' did not stop there. Dad didn't know we had to phone ahead to secure reservations for the flight home, so when he tried it was fully booked. They eventually found us some seats but told us we needed to pay a penalty for having too much weight; we had to carry a one hundredweight toolbox on board as hand luggage. Luckily we had left all the tyres at the circuit – even though we had ended up not even using them for the race – because we couldn't be bothered to lug them all the way back to Tokyo.

In those days, we used Metzeler tyres because they were free and we couldn't afford Michelins. They weren't that bad, especially on road circuits. Everyone else in 1989 was running 17in Michelin rears on the Honda RC30, while I was running 18in Metzelers. It was all a bit 'pre-war', but I loved it. People thought I was mad, and they were a bit hit and miss. At some circuits, such as Thruxton and Mallory, the Metzelers were crap, but at others they were great. The previous year at Donington when I was going for my first F1 world title, there was no way the Metzelers were going to work, so I bought a Michelin, scrubbed the name off, stuck some Metzeler stickers on and came fifth to clinch the championship. Michelin were not too happy when they found out, of course; while Metzeler didn't know what to think. They were too busy celebrating the win anyway. Then, again at Donington in 1989 the Metzelers were brilliant. Niall Mackenzie had returned from the Grand Prix circuit and thought he would clean up in all three races. He didn't, but I did. From then on, after signing for Honda in 1990, I was on Michelins for the rest of my career, apart from one year on Dunlops in 1992 as a privateer, when we had to negotiate a special price.

There didn't seem to be the same tyre sponsorship available in those days as there is for young riders today. Nowadays, the methods of selection are a bit more sophisticated, but the need to go to any lengths to get the right tyres on the bike is even more

important. Tyre selection is perhaps the most crucial part of qualifying and practice. When I started out in racing there was not
too much choice. Everyone pretty much ran on intermediate
Michelin tyres – a bit like today's cut slicks, which have grooves
sliced into the rubber by a machine, but straight out of the
mould. If it rained, there was a wet tyre, so there were only two
choices. Even by 1995, the choice of tyre never seemed critical as
they all seemed to work on the best bike I have ever ridden.

I wish it had been like that towards the end of my career. Now
there are different compounds, different sizes and different shapes
to take into account when trying to decide which tyre to use for
a race. In 1996, when I was riding for Honda, finding the right
rear tyre was an absolute nightmare. I guess it's because the bikes
are getting faster and more powerful, so there is less and less grip
and more and more heat in the rear tyre. From that date onwards
it was almost as though you would win the race if you could find
the right tyre – as simple as that.

The size of the tyres when I started out was 18in. That size
then dropped to 17in and now 16.5in tyres are sometimes used.
When the 17in came out in 1985, it looked really good. Although
it was an intermediate tyre, the sides almost looked as though
they were slick, with no tread. Maybe it was just a psychological
thing, but I loved it.

Everybody seemed to be using Michelins in those days,
although a lot of racers and motocross riders have now switched
to Dunlop. It was always pretty well accepted that Michelin produced a better tyre for superbikes and Grand Prix bikes while
Dunlop made tyres more suited to the 250cc and 125cc series.
But the balance has shifted because Dunlop now produce a very
good superbike tyre. In the few races I competed in 2000, I
noticed that Dunlop had made big strides during the winter.

But there have been a lot of changes recently. In the last dry
races of my career, at Kyalami in South Africa in 2000, I rode on
a 16.5in front and rear tyre for the first time in my career. It felt
really good, although I went back to a 17in at the front for the
second race because I was struggling to change direction a little
bit. The smaller the wheel, the fatter they are, and because my
shoulder was already injured for those races I found the steering

really heavy. Although I was going really quick and set the new lap record, I kept losing the front because the 17in tyre at the front was a bit narrower and would not hold the track as well. I was given a few warnings when going over bumps, but I guess I ignored them and down I went.

For the rest of the year, all the riders on Michelins used 16.5in tyres at the front and rear. It's strange because in my last six years of racing, I had tested 16.5in and 16in front wheels but never liked them. I always asked for them to be changed back straight away to 17in with a 5.75in rim at the back and 17in with a 3.5in rim at the front. The steering on the others always felt heavy and they didn't give me any advantage. The only problem with the 17in tyres was that their grip would drop off very quickly towards the end of a race. But a 16.5in rear, while not providing the same grip at the start of a race, would be better towards the finish.

So deciding on the size of tyre was never really too much of an issue. Most of the debate centred around what was the best compound for the conditions and circuits, especially at the rear, where all the drive comes from. I would go so far as to say that finding the right rear is the most critical part of racing. More often than not I would find a front tyre I was happy with early on and then stick with it. But, particularly in 1997 and 1998, not being able to find the right rear tyres cost me a lot of races. When Davide Tardozzi became my team manager in 1998, we started to ride race distances on a Saturday to make sure that we found the tyres which would last the 25 laps and give good grip.

With so many different options in the choice of compound or profile – there might have been between eight to 15 choices available – it was easy to miss the best tyre during testing. It might have been tested and ruled out, for instance, during practice on a Friday, when the grip of the track was not as good. Come race day, when there were a couple more days' worth of rubber on the track, it might have performed a lot better. And that choice was even harder if there was a sidecar meeting. After the sidecars had been on the track for two days, the choice we had made on a Friday might be completely useless by the Sunday because side-cars deposit a lot more rubber than bikes, and the more rubber on the surface the better the grip on most tracks. The hard work of 1999 paid off though, because seven times out of ten we chose the right tyre.

Michelin have always got a pretty good idea of what to use when we arrive at a meeting. The obvious starting point is to return to what was used the previous year. My tendency was always to go for as hard a tyre as possible at the outset, and try the softer ones later if necessary. As I carried a lot of corner speed, I wanted a tyre which would hold together well mid-corner when I was leaning over as far as possible. So my rear tyres always tended to be that bit harder than those of other riders. That wasn't always the case, because Ducati had always got away with using a softer compound than Honda until 1995, but come 1997 we started using a harder compound because the engine had become so aggressive that it had started to destroy the softer compounds. So, around then, we started to lose an advantage over the Hondas. Softer tyres are not always ideal, though. If they get too hot they can grip too much and then the bike can chatter because it starts to grip-slip, grip-slip, grip-slip.

Even for Superpole, the one-lap shoot-out that decides grid positions, my qualifying tyres tended to be that little bit harder. But it has generally been accepted that Dunlop produce a

FOGGY FACTOR

'I would go as far as to say that finding the right rear tyre is the most critical part of racing.'

better qualifying tyre than Michelin, and Troy Corser confirmed that with his move from Michelin to Dunlop when he rode for Aprilia in 2000. That didn't bother me because Michelin produced better race tyres, which was far more important. Superpole was never my strong point, yet I still finished second in the Superpole standings for the season behind Troy in my final full year in 1999. Had I been fourth instead of fifth at Sugo, I would have won the competition – a competition I didn't even know existed.

The only other people I could compare my choices with, apart from my team-mates, were the Honda riders, who were also on Michelins. During 1999 they consistently managed to use a softer

Most of my body is off the bike, trying to keep it as upright as possible and increase the contact patch of the tyres and so increase the grip.

compound than us. Everybody considered that to be strange, because the four-cylinder bike can rev quicker and spin up more and so should have put more pressure on the rear. Misano proved a classic case of this, so during the warm-up on the Sunday morning I asked to try the hardest compound available. The team didn't want to give it to me because Michelin had told them it was too dangerous in the cool early-morning conditions.

'I think I can use it for the race and I want to go out with it now,' I insisted. I eventually got my own way, so the last thing I wanted to do was make a fool of myself by crashing. I took it easy for two or three laps, yet still managed to set the fastest lap of the warm-up a couple of laps later. 'It's perfect, that's the one I'm using,' I said.

The first race was quite close between me and my team-mate Troy Corser, because the bike kept jumping out of gear. The suspension was also a bit soft, and when the tyre went off towards the end of the race there was a lot of sliding around. Troy had a reputation for being very good at setting his bike up, yet he would often be the one copying what I had done. After we sorted the gearbox and stiffened the suspension slightly, I won the second race by a mile. Had I had the right set-up for every race, nobody would ever have beaten me.

The climate was always something that had to be considered, but that didn't always mean the hotter the country, the harder the tyre that was needed. The surface of the track had to be taken into account too. One of the worst tracks for tyre wear was Phillip Island in Australia, where the weather could be either very hot or very cold. The place was a nightmare and people would regularly blister their tyres there. All the corners are on the left side where you are driving the bike really hard and putting a lot of heat into that side of the tyre, which never has a chance to cool down. When you felt the back of the bike vibrating and juddering, you just knew that bits of the outer tread had come off and the tyre was knackered. One year, mine were so bad that the bits hanging off smashed the telemetry shaft at the back. If you were halfway through the race when the tyres went, it would effectively be over unless you pulled into the pits for a change, which is something you don't often see at a race track.

The classic case when it all went wrong was at Brands in 1999. It was either that there simply wasn't an ideal tyre available, or that we failed to identify it during qualifying – because you cannot physically test them all in the time available anyway. I was convinced that we should have been using one particular tyre – I think it was an 'M' tyre – but Ducati and Michelin persuaded me to change my mind and use the 'P' tyre that Troy had used on the Saturday. I had not gone all that fast during qualifying, but that was more down to me than the choice of tyre. Sure enough, the 17in rear we used for the first race just got too hot and blew out. A big chunk flew off and I had to pull into the pits to change it. That pit-stop was a disaster. The team looked like the Keystone Cops, mainly because they weren't expecting me in at a track like Brands where we'd never had too many tyre problems before. At circuits like Phillip Island and Monza the engineers would have had an airgun and a wheel at the ready just in case, but normally I would try to wobble round instead and finish third or fourth.

Whenever a wheel change was needed, most of the time would be lost entering and exiting the pits, not actually in the act of changing the wheel. This wasn't the case at Brands. I was sat on the bike, desperate to get back out, and I started thinking, *This is taking a bloody long time!* The mechanic had got the stand underneath, put the bar in to lock up the wheel, leaned on the rear wheel to undo it and broken the stand. So he had to rush inside to take the rear stand from the other bike, stick this under my bike and carry on undoing the wheel. All this in front of 120,000 fans. I was not best pleased. I could only manage 19th place after that, but at least it meant I finished every single race that year. That's pretty unusual.

Troy had suffered similar problems, but only on the last lap, so he was able to nurse it round. But Haga had used the 'M' tyre and finished third without any problems, so for the second race the Michelin tyre expert said, 'Look, this 16.5in will get you through the race. John Reynolds used it for the first race and finished fourth, although his times were not as good. We don't think the grip will be fantastic, but it will get you through the race.' The grip was terrible from lap 1 to lap 25, although I still managed to finish fourth. The thing that pissed me off was that Colin Edwards won both races with exactly the same 'P' rear tyre I had used for the first race. *What am I going to do now?* I thought as we tried to figure it out. For some reason Honda managed to run a softer tyre than we did throughout the whole of that season. Yet we had both run the same tyre the previous round at Laguna Seca and both teams had had the same problems.

It was something that bugged me all that winter. One theory was that Honda were able to get away with softer compounds because their bikes had double-sided swinging arms – the metal projections which hold the wheel in place. Maybe that was helping to balance the heat across the rear tyre, or even making the suspension work better. When I rode for Honda in 1996, their bikes had single-sided swinging arms. I didn't win the world title that year because I couldn't get any grip mid-corner. In the middle of the 1997 season they changed to a double-sided arm. Over 1998 and 1999 it became clear that they were getting better grip because they were consistently running softer tyres. I was behind Aaron Slight a few times in 1998 and couldn't believe the drive he was getting out of some corners when my tyre had gone.

I started asking Ducati for a double-sided swinging arm in 1998, but we were only allowed to test it twice during the winter before the 2000 season. The conditions for the tests were not perfect, but at Phillip Island in January I was able to do a back-to-back 15-lap comparison with single and double-sided arms, and to be perfectly honest there was very little difference between the two. The Ducati hierarchy was not keen on the double arm because they felt it spoilt the look of the bike. I was not convinced by this, and neither was Davide Tardozzi. Had there been a big difference, they would have had to go with a double arm, but at the end of the day it was all about selling road bikes, so I couldn't blame them. We tried to test it again at Valencia but I had a big fall, knocking myself out, and we didn't get the chance to do another back-to-back because I didn't test on the second day.

Obviously the riders can make a difference. Maybe I was a bit too aggressive on the throttle at Brands Hatch and put too much heat into the tyre because of all the weight of expectation on my shoulders – there were 120,000 fans desperate to see me win. Yet it's never easy to draw conclusions like that. If you look at the qualifying session for the round that clinched the world title for me that year at Hockenheim, I did the race distance on one tyre and didn't have a problem. I then did the race distance on another tyre and it started to vibrate, so I pulled in before it blew out. There was no question which one I should use. Troy opted for the same one as me, and he had major blistering problems in both races. Two riders on the same bike with the same tyre with completely different outcomes. So I suppose there is a bit of luck involved, although that's a tiny factor compared to the rider's skill and the importance of getting the set-up right.

Sugo was another track on which Michelin riders seemed to struggle. Usually, I am one of the riders who can still get results, even if the tyres have gone off. That was probably the difference between me and Troy in 1999. Once my tyres had gone mid-race I would brake a little bit later or come off the gas and lift the bike up a bit if I felt it starting to slide. Or I could hook it up another gear a bit earlier so that the bike was always driving forward and not spinning the tyres even more. I would do anything I could to get that bike home in second, third or fourth place if I knew I couldn't win the race. Troy seemed to drop further down the field when he had a problem. But, in the last race of 1999, with the world title already in the bag, my tyres went off in such a big way that from leading the first race with a few laps to go I ended up finishing second.

I noticed during 2000 that a lot of riders had started to run softer compounds. For the first time in years, someone on Dunlops had a realistic chance of winning the world championship going into the 2001 season. Ben Bostrom, although he was riding a Ducati, was fastest in the final test for 2001 at Valencia. Neil Hodgson is another rider who has always preferred Dunlops because they tend to slide round corners a bit easier, and he was fastest in the first test at South Africa.

The thickness of the tyres was also a factor that had to be considered. Often we would run a thinner tyre, probably by about a millimetre or two, for the really fast tracks. That did not make sense to me, but apparently the theory is that because there is not as much rubber there to get hot, the tyre stays cooler. There was always a base setting of inflation with nitrogen, again to keep them as cool as possible.

While I never minded trying out new compounds, or different tyre thicknesses, I was never that keen on experimenting with the profile of the tyre. Some are flatter, some more pointed at the apex. I always felt happier when somebody else was testing that kind of thing. Yet in Assen in 1999 I tried a new, more pointed tyre which had been tested on a 500cc bike on that circuit. Troy tried the same tyre but felt it was chattering all the time. I had felt it chattering a little bit too but I decided to stick with it, while Troy went his own way for the first race. I won the first race, and Troy decided to give it another go. I also won the second. I guess Troy was a bit shocked to learn that I was as good, if not better, at setting the bike up as he was. On reflection, throughout the year I made the correct tyre choice more often than Troy. The only time when his choice was better than mine was at Laguna Seca, when he gambled correctly for the second race.

I changed a lot as a rider in that year as I had started to think a lot more about set-up. I had stopped just looking at the TV monitors and thinking, *So and so has just done a fast lap, I'd better get straight out there and beat it.* Troy did that a lot in 1998, using a qualifying tyre very early on in the session to rattle the other riders, who would start swapping their tyres to try to match him. But you just have to ignore that kind of thing. In 1999, all I was bothered about during qualifying was putting in consistently fast lap times so that I could find the correct race tyre, and it paid off.

It was Davide Tardozzi who got me focused on finding the right tyre instead of being so bothered about being on the front row of the grid. Halfway through 1998, he began to say, 'Look, you have to forget about doing these fast laps and concentrate on finding the right tyre. That's how you will win the races.' And I got faster and faster as the year went on, all the hard work paying off in the final round at Sugo, where I chose the right tyre and was the first rider home on a Michelin in the final and deciding race. I ended up beating Aaron Slight by some way, which hadn't been happening earlier in the year, when his choice of tyre had been better.

It's so daft, though, to think that I was only learning about something as important as tyre choice at such a late stage of my career. But until 1995 it had never really been that much of a problem because the bikes were not as powerful. At first, I hated doing race distances on the Saturday, thinking that I would be knackered by the time it came to the race on Sunday. It was for my own benefit, though. If I had worked with the team as hard in 1997 as I did in 1999 to find the right overall package, I would have won the world title in that year as well, there is absolutely no question about that. Some of that was my fault, but a lot of the fault was also the team manager's, Virginio Ferrari, who did not push me to do things.

One of the aspects of tyre work that has hardly ever entered my head is tyre conservation. Other riders will say that they go easy on their tyres in the early part of a race so that the grip is better in the later stages. I think that's a load of shit. When I saw that green light come on, I went as fast as I could to win the race. Just about the only time I did go easy was at Phillip Island in 1998 when I had a good lead and I knew there were going to be problems later on in the race. As I came out of corners I tried to short-shift through the gears and go easy on the revs and maybe pull away at 10,500rpm instead of 12,000rpm so that the bike could pull nicely out of the corners. But when you are in the heat of the battle with two or three guys it's very hard to think about saving your tyres, unless you are behind someone and in their slipstream for a couple of laps. I've heard riders in interviews say, 'Carl won the race because he saved his tyres better than I did.' That's just an excuse because the guy who has come second has to think of a reason why he has not won the race.

It's not just the fast tracks that can cause problems. One of the slower circuits is at Albacete in Spain, where trying to get good grip was a nightmare. The last time I was there, in 1999, I finished third in both races because I couldn't match the acceleration coming out of corners of Akira Yanagawa and Colin Edwards. I was sliding all over the place. So it just goes to show the importance of tyre choice at every type of circuit.

The setting of the suspension obviously plays another big part in terms of whether the tyres will survive a race, but this was my weakest point throughout my racing career. I could never understand pre-load, damping or compression. It was my own fault, but the guy from Ohlins used to say that there was no need for me to understand it, as long as I could tell them what was wrong. I tried really hard around 1995 to learn and understand it all by drawing diagrams and sitting down with the suspension guy, but if I had a problem with front or rear ends chattering all I really needed to do was tell them and they would come in to fix it. It generally meant that the tyre was moving around at the end of a race, when it had gone off. So they would stiffen the suspension before the second race so that it wouldn't be as sensitive.

When we started having tyre problems in 1997, Slick always maintained that we were not concentrating on the right area of the bike by constantly changing the suspension and things like that. He said that a smoother motor would help the tyres last, through having a heavier crank that would produce a less aggressive acceleration. The factory did test a heavier flywheel once in Misano, but only for about five laps, which didn't prove anything one way or another. It's like the difference between a motocross bike and an enduro bike. An enduro bike will have a heavier crank and accelerate less aggressively, so the wheel does not spin so much.

You might think you are going quicker on the motocross bike because of the sound of the engine, but you'll actually be going faster on the enduro bike. The same principles apply.

As the bikes get more and more powerful every year, tyre choice becomes more and more important. It's fine having the most powerful engine, as long as your tyres aren't worn out after 10 laps, because you're not going to win races like that. In 1998 the inlet box was shortened and the airbox enlarged, which gave a much better feel from the throttle to the back tyre. Those two things work hand in hand. You have to get the power delivery to work with the tyre as you only have a tiny

FOGGY FACTOR

'Tyre selection is perhaps the most crucial part of qualifying and practice.'

contact patch on the track. That point was proved in one testing session at Misano when I set my best time despite engine problems. The tick-over of the engine was set at 4,000rpm. That way, the bike was not as aggressive when I opened the throttle. It meant that when shutting off coming into a corner the revs were still quite high, but on opening the throttle on exit it was very smooth instead of delivering one big 'crack'. This was all good for the tyres. Raising the tick-over is not the ideal solution, however, as it creates other problems. For instance, I would have been going into corners a bit too fast as there was less engine braking. And, if I had sat on the line for too long, the bike would have over-heated. Slick felt the longer-term answer was changing the injection system and the mapping.

Another thing that might have helped combat tyre decay was to have a stronger wheel spindle, as these would flex in first or second-gear corners when there was a lot of power going through the back wheel. If you could stop that moving around, the wheel would not move around as much. One way to achieve this was to put a bearing inside the magnesium hub, which is inside the swinging arm. When you press a bearing in, it expands, but I often complained about chatter from the rear wheel, which meant the bearing was too loose. That was a problem towards the end of 1999, and you could almost move the wheel around on the stand after I had come in. This was later solved by using bigger bearings.

Shutting the clutch off really hard so that there is a lot of engine braking will cause the back to come round and scrub the tyre. That was the last thing I wanted, and it happened quite a bit in 1997. Now they make clutches that slip more, at a 14-degree angle rather than at 9 degrees. Where some bikes had three pins, Ducati made it with six.

All the planning in the world can go out the window, however, if it rains on race day. Then there's no point worrying about the choice of compound, although of the three different compounds I would always want to be on the softest possible to give me confidence in the grip. The only other thing you have to decide then is what the weather is going to do. If it looks like raining throughout the race, you use wet weather tyres. But, as happened at Phillip Island for the first race of the round when I suffered my arm injury, it was impossible to guess what the weather was going to do. We opted for cut slicks in the front and rear, while Anthony Gobert gambled on wet weather tyres.

Michelin did produce an intermediate tyre, but I hated it and preferred to have cut slicks. I always felt as though the bike wanted to go straight on their intermediate and I had to really pull the bike over at the point where I wanted it to lean. That's not what you want to do when it's a bit damp or wet. But on this occasion, I was unhappy with the front tyre as soon as they took the warmer off on the grid. *There's no way that's cut enough*, I thought to myself. I almost fell off, and had both my feet down on the sighting lap and had to tiptoe my way around in the early stages. At one stage, it looked as though we had made the right choice because the track started to dry and I was catching up Gobert with every lap. Then it rained again so he was able to clear off. That's the benefit of having knowledge of the local conditions.

Another option would have been to use a cut slick at the front and a slick at the back. That combination is usually used when it's a bit damp and likely to dry out because you always have more chance of losing the front in the wet, so that's where you want the most grip. If you have a few slides with the back tyre, it's not usually as big a problem as you have more of a chance of catching the bike. But the choice is really a lottery. You would try to see what the other guys were using, especially if the race was at the end of the season and you had to beat one person in particular. That's when you see teams trying to hide their choice until the last possible moment.

Obviously, you try to keep the tyre warmers on for as long as possible, which was no fun for Slick. He would regularly get big electric shocks from the warmers, especially if it was damp outside and his feet and gloves were wet because these particular warmers did not have a protection circuit. If I spotted him trying to take them off because of that, I'd shout, 'Put my fucking tyre warmers on!' Slick would shout back, 'You bastard!' as he got another belt, punching the tyres while I sat there pissing myself and drinking my tea.

I definitely made the wrong choice of tyres at Donington in 1994. I could have clinched the world championship that day had everything turned out okay, but it rained for both races, although for the first I thought it was going to stop. 'Put the hard rear wet tyre in,' I said. I had no idea how different it would be to the soft wet. When the rain came down the grip was horrendous. It was incredible to think that it was just the compounds that were different, not the tread pattern. On the last lap, going into Coppice on the brakes, the back came right round on me and I just got my feet down in time. I did my best to keep it upright but dropped right back through the field and finished 14th for a point. Scott Russell won the race and brought himself right back into contention for the world title. Needless to say, we used the softer compound for the second race, and I finished fifth.

It's strange that in the last few years I never felt confident or safe when racing in the wet, whereas it was completely the opposite early on in my career. I won a Formula One TT race in some of the worst conditions ever seen in Finland, lapping everyone up to second place, and won some big races in Ireland in the wet. In those days you'd always catch me wandering around with a big smile on my face when it rained, because I knew I was the fastest guy out there in the wet. It also helped because, after my bad leg injuries, I knew I would not have to hang off the 250cc bikes as much in the wet, so there wouldn't be as much pain in my leg. Maybe it was because I wanted to win so much as my career progressed that I lost sight of where the limit was in the wet. Towards the end of my career I would generally only finish around fourth, although still there was probably nobody as consistent as I was at getting the bike over the finish.

Obviously, wet weather conditions did not suit my style of riding in hanging off the bike as far as possible. It was better suited to the motocross style of rider, whose backside would hang off while the bike stayed more upright, allowing for better drive out of the corners. Yet one of the fastest riders I know in wet weather is Pier-Francesco Chili, whose style is more similar to my own. Perhaps that's because he was a bigger lad and doesn't have a problem getting his knee on the floor, although that makes him more likely to crash. Getting my knee down was always something I struggled to do in the wet. Eight times out of ten I failed to get the balance right between leaning as far over as possible and dropping the bike. When I did get it right I could beat the others. For instance, in my last full wet race in Austria in 1999 I beat Colin Edwards, another rider who is regarded as very good in those conditions.

Probably my most enjoyable ride in the wet was at Monza in 1997. I was following Jamie Whitham on the sighting lap and could not believe how hard he was braking. When it came to the race I decided to give it a go; usually it would take a lot of time for me to build up enough confidence to reach the limit. I ended up leading the race until Jamie came back past me, so we ended up in a dice. Jamie had suffered some bad results so he was desperate for the points. For some reason I was totally relaxed and loving it, and when I took him again I started to flick the 'V's at him and was standing up off the bike waving my arse at him. We might have ended up behind Chili and John Kocinski, but it was good fun.

RACING
TECHNIQUES

5: Suspension

I'm the first to admit that I never really knew all that much about the technical side of the suspension set-up. For me it was all in the feel of the bike. Although I couldn't talk the same language as our suspension experts, they learnt to translate my descriptions of how the bike felt into practical adjustments.

Our suspension guy, Jon Cornwell, who worked for Ohlins, said it was always a struggle to extract information from me, but he also said that it didn't matter what I did to the bike's suspension because I could have ridden round on a couple of steel bars instead of a rear shock had I wanted to. If we did get to the point where I was constantly struggling with the set-up, I would often just look at the lap times and say, 'I'm close enough. We'll keep it as it is instead of constantly messing around with it and confusing things. Don't worry about it, I'll ride round the problem.'

There were times, though, when it wasn't quite that simple – at the A1 Ring in 1998, for instance. Although I had struggled with the tyre in the first race and was having trouble exiting corners and following the lines of other riders, I was still third in the race and was just pipped by Aaron Slight at the death. But the bike was feeling doughy. So we decided to change the shock absorber, stiffening it up to allow me to hold tighter lines yet keep my corner speed up. In the second race when the tyre went off, it didn't pogo around as much and I finished second. I was never the type to praise the mechanics for the sake of it, but this time they had been spot on and I told them so.

There were also times when other Ducati riders, perhaps Frankie Chili or Troy Corser in 1998, were going a bit quicker than me and I made the mistake of bothering too much about their set-up. A year later I would have ignored it, because even if I had got round to trying what they had, it would not end up working for me anyway. More often than not I knew the feeling I was looking for, but they didn't have the set-up and I wouldn't even enter into a discussion about it. The key thing was that I knew how hard I had been riding to achieve any particular lap time during qualifying; the rest of the team didn't know that. So while it might have looked as though I was going a bit slower than other riders, I knew where I could make improvements and any other reasons why my lap times might have been off the pace.

I know that Jon and the other guys found it really rewarding when they made a set-up change and, after struggling for a session, everything suddenly clicked into place and I could relax again. But I think they knew that more often than not it was as much down to what was going on inside my head as the changes made to the bike. When other riders were having problems with their bikes they might back it off a notch during the race and complain, but I would try to get as much out of the bike as I possibly could.

A race bike is set up pretty solid and rigid and gives a lot of feedback to the rider. But I never liked to feel the bumps through my hands, or even for the bike to react over bumps in the first place. I wanted bikes that were stable and comfortable to ride; and I didn't want too much sensation from the actual road surface. That way I found it easier to judge whether the tyres were going to last the race. If it was chattering at the front or moving around at the back, I couldn't do what I wanted to do. Jon would say he could tell when things were not right because I would sit more upright on the bike and not lean off as much into corners. When a bike was more aggressively and rigidly set up, it would not allow me to flow through corners as it would not be forgiving enough.

The way to get the bikes to react less harshly over bumps was to use softer compression damping in the front forks and softer spring in the rear shock absorber. The other important thing would be to change the ride heights around. My bikes were always higher in the front and lower in the rear and more softly sprung than any of my team-mates' machines. I have been told that one other Ducati rider has a similar set-up, and that's Troy Bayliss. But Ruben Xaus, the young Spanish rider who I am trying to help a bit, likes to have the bike set up like a rock. The other Ducati rider for 2001, Ben Bostrum, is somewhere in between those two styles.

When I returned to Ducati after my year with Honda, I used to alter the set-up all the time from track to track. The bike's engine had changed a lot since 1995 and we were having a lot of problems trying to keep the bike stable on corner exits. I couldn't open the throttle mid-corner because there would be much too much of an early hit from the engine. It had not affected Corser as much during 1996, while I was at Honda. He had seemed able to adapt to that style of power, although the 1996 bike was nowhere near as powerful as the 1997 version, especially in the mid-range of revs. But through 1997 I could see John Kocinski becoming more and more confident, while I was losing confidence in the bike. So we had to put a lot of spring on the rear plus a lot of compression damping to make the bike more biased to the front. That way the bike would stay down in the front and carve the corner. Before those changes, every time I opened the throttle it would sit down and run wide.

It was at a test in Albacete to try to finally solve the problems that I told Ducati I wanted my 1995 bike back. When they caved in and allowed me to use it, it was, admittedly, a bit slower. But the engineers could see that it was a lot easier to ride, and I certainly knew it was easier. So Ducati shifted their attention away from pure power to driveability. Still, the problems continued into the following year. The engines were better but we struggled to find a set-up I liked.

Halfway through 1998 we were still forever tinkering with the bike's geometry and everything else during the course of a weekend. I'd had enough. It had got to the stage where I didn't know what bike I would be riding at each meeting. I said: 'Look, I don't want any more changes.' So we then started with the bike set up exactly the way it had been the week before, whether I had been happy with it or not. Then I might just question a couple of things and maybe make it slightly more like a meeting where I'd done well, such as Kyalami, where I'd had two second places. That would act as a baseline setting until the end of the year, when I won the championship at Sugo.

We took that baseline into 1999, but by then we had changed the front fork design and the rear shock design by – I'm told – opening up the oil channels in both the front fork and rear shock absorber and going with a much larger cartridge in the front fork. That took away a lot of the sharp hits and the aggressiveness of the suspension and produced a smoother feeling with less feedback from the road surface. Some of the other riders didn't like it at first and needed a lot of convincing, but I won both races at Kyalami in the first round of the year, by five and six seconds respectively. Obviously I liked the changes. The front fork was firm enough to stop the bike from pitching, or suddenly transferring the weight to the front. Even if there were problems with pitching we would lower the back or raise the front to make the bike more neutral around the centre.

> **FOGGY FACTOR**
>
> 'I wanted bikes that were stable and comfortable to ride and I didn't want too much sensation from the actual road surface.'

I would always have half a degree more head angle – the angle at which the forks sit in relation to the ground. Most bikes will be set at around 22 to 24 degrees; I was at the top of that range, at 24 or even 24.5. The tighter the head angle, the quicker the steering is supposed to be. A more shallow head angle would be slower, but more stable. And because I have relatively short arms, I didn't want to be reaching for the bars. It also meant that as an aggressive rider I could pull the bike more without it bucking and weaving. At a 23.5 angle there would be less tugging and pulling but it would tend to shake more.

I also had a couple of millimetres more offset – the distance between the centre line of the steering head to the centre line of the forks – than anyone else on a Ducati. That made it easier to turn quickly into the corners. Other riders tried it but had to stick with it for some time before agreeing that they liked it. They would complain that they couldn't brake as deep into a corner – but that wasn't the idea. The plan was to get off the brakes early, roll the thing on its side and get on the throttle. I didn't want to trail the brakes to the apex of the corner like the others. That's even more difficult to do on a Ducati than on other bikes because the bike always wants to stand up. Maybe that's one of the reasons why I have always felt so comfortable on a Ducati.

The other thing they did was to go to a flat linkage ratio – the difference between the wheel movement to the shock movement – with three per cent progressivity. When you have a more progressive linkage, as the wheel goes into the stroke the shock speeds up and gets harder. So progressivity is how much the ratio changes from the beginning to the end, and three per cent was going more towards linear. That meant I could get on the throttle a lot earlier and drive the thing out of the corners. Before that, when I opened the throttle there was almost a big 'bang' before the bike sat down hard and ran wide. That kind of set-up needed harder springs and compression damping and would use the tyres up quickly – not rider-friendly.

So, as usual, I had been right all along: the bike was easier to ride once we had returned to a set-up more like the one in 1995. The standard link was harder, and we ran that at Brands occasionally to get over the problem of the exhaust hitting the surface as you went downhill before the hairpin.

Track
4 *Hockenheim*

Hockenheim was the scene of my last race win, when I clinched my final world title in 1999. The plan was simple: I had to beat Troy Corser. That was the only thing which occupied my mind. He started off in the leading pack and I felt a bit unsettled because of what was at stake. When I pulled myself together, I took the lead and started to put together fast lap after fast lap. That split the pack up, although I took Aaron Slight with me. This track can be hard on the tyres because of the speeds generated, but we had done a lot of laps in practice and were sure we had the right tyre for the race. I knew Slight was going to come past me on the last lap because his bike was quicker. There wasn't much I could do about it and it didn't really bother me, because as long as I beat Troy the title was mine. When Aaron came past, I looked behind me and could see there was nobody there, so I cruised around the last few bends and the celebrations started.

When I got back to the pits I found out that I'd won the race because the red flag had gone out on the very last corner of the last lap. I hadn't seen it, but it meant that the positions from the start of the last lap, when I was winning, stood. It was a bonus, but no big deal, although Aaron didn't think so. He refused to take his place on the podium.

Hockenheim is a very similar circuit to Monza, although it's a bit more dangerous because the 'straights' aren't exactly straights but have a slight curve. I go through the start–finish in fourth gear and drop down into second for the first right-hander, where I've never felt 100 per cent comfortable. Maybe that's because it was a bit ripply. Coming out of it, you use the entire road and more, right over the rumble strips. It's another spot where you're clambering over the bike to try to keep the front wheel down on the track, as there's a slight rise. And you want to build as much speed as possible down the downhill straight section, which is probably the fastest point on the World Superbike circuit.

So then it's straight into the tucked position and up through the gears to sixth before getting hard on the brakes for a straightforward chicane. You have to be careful not to hit the gas too hard when you flick it to the left because, especially in the first couple of laps, the left side of the hard rear tyre is a worry. I crashed big style there during practice in 1996 on the Honda, which didn't half hurt. I thought I'd broken my wrist but it turned out to be just bad bruising. I'd also just lost Slick as my mechanic, because he wasn't getting on too well with the Honda mechanics.

To finish only fifth in the first race that year did not improve my mood. And, just when I thought it couldn't get any worse, my daughter Danielle started having a go at me during the break between races.

'What's the matter with you, daddy? Why aren't you winning races any more?'

'I don't know, love. It must be the new bike I'm riding.'

'It's not the bike. It's you!' she snapped.

And it seemed to do the trick because I went on to claim my first win on a Honda in the second race of the weekend. We had changed the bike round a bit after the first race and I got a good start in the repeat. It was the first time I'd been away with the leaders all year and I just grew in confidence throughout the race. Approaching the end of the race, I just knew I was going to win.

Coming out of that chicane, where second is a bit low but third is slightly tall, is possibly my weakest point on the track. I never could seem to stop the bike, either a Ducati or Honda, from po-going out of it. The next section is very fast, although I always tried to run only five gears, but if you get into someone's slipstream you pretty much have to stick it in sixth. This is a very fast corner and one of the places where I'm not as brilliant at going in quickly as some of the other guys, so it wasn't a place where I would often pass people.

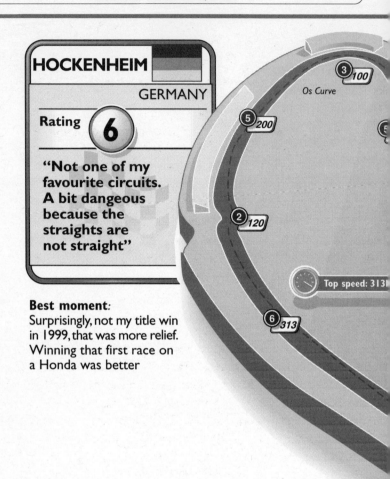

HOCKENHEIM

GERMANY

Rating **6**

"Not one of my favourite circuits. A bit dangeous because the straights are not straight"

3 *100*

Os Curve

5 *200*

5

2 *120*

Top speed: 313

6 *313*

Best moment:
Surprisingly, not my title win in 1999, that was more relief. Winning that first race on a Honda was better

st moment:
s at a real low after
ing fifth on the Honda
996, before Danielle's
vention

Worst crash:
The mysterious fall during
practice in 1994 when I broke
my wrist

est finish:
y race is a close
1. It's a toss up
een the second
s of 1996
1997

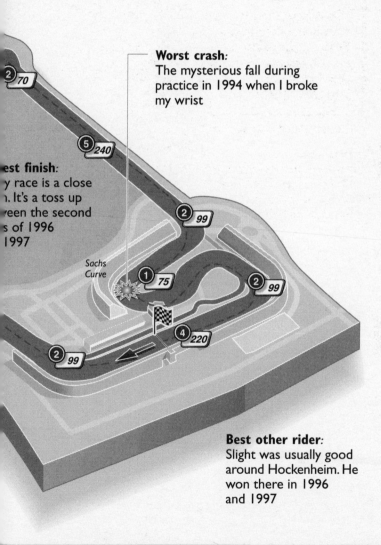

Sachs
Curve

Best other rider:
Slight was usually good
around Hockenheim. He
won there in 1996
and 1997

By the time I get to mid-corner, I'm really fast. There were a few times when I actually passed people on the outside around this corner in third gear. The same applies down the back straight in that I would normally be happy to leave it in fifth, unless I was slipstreaming someone, in which case I would have to use sixth if I was right on the limiter.

For the last chicane it's on the brakes and down into second gear. On the last lap you want to be exiting in second place. Third is okay and still leaves you with a chance, but second is better. Then you draught up the next straight into the last corner entering the stadium – the last chance to get past on the brakes eight times out of ten. This is where all the action takes place. It's also where I won my first race on the Honda, by outbraking Aaron Slight and John Kocinski. The following year I got past Hodgson and Yanagawa and again won the race. Probably the only exception was in 1999 when, after I had won the world title in the first race, I left it a bit late and Pier-Francesco Chili got me there because I had under-estimated him. It's a second-gear corner and you use all the road coming out. If you get into the stadium section at the end of that straight in first place, you're going to win the race.

Once I'm through that flat-cambered corner, I stay in second gear with a quick squirt for Sachs Corner, which is steeply banked on the inside. It's the only real left-sided corner and it always takes a while for the tyre to settle there. I broke my wrist there in 1994 and have never liked it since. The crash, on the second lap of the Saturday practice session, remains a bit of a mystery to this day. Some people say there was oil on the track, but a picture of the crash shows a bit of smoke coming out of the back of the bike. My hand seems to get caught on the bike, and it was probably the awkward position the hand was forced into that broke the bone. The strange thing about it was that Michaela only ever used to watch from

FOGGY FACTOR

'On the last lap you want to be exiting the chicane in second place. Third is okay and still leaves you with a chance, but second is better.'

the pit-wall, but for some reason she had wandered round to Sachs that particular afternoon. She was the first person I saw when I picked myself up from the fall.

Providing you're still on your bike, it's then up to third, through a quick-flicked chicane and onto the double apex final corner in third gear. Going into it, there's a bit of a dip and then a rise before the final part of the corner, where third is again a bit long.

As there are few places to pass and it's hard to pull away from anyone, it often means there's a close finish at Hockenheim. In 1993, I entered the final bend with Giancarlo Falappa and Fabrizio Pirovano, but came out third best. About the only time I wasn't involved in a dice at the end was when I cleared off and won both races in 1995. The closest, though, was probably the second race in 1997, when I outbraked Neil Hodgson to win. I got up the inside of him and he didn't give up, finally coming round the outside into the crap. He ended up finishing eighth after losing his head.

RACING TECHNIQUES

6: Engine

By now, it's probably no surprise for you to read that my bike was geared differently to other riders' machines. Take the years when Troy Corser was my team-mate, for example. My gearing was always lower and, if anything, the bike was slightly under-geared. The thinking behind that was when the tyres went off towards the end of a race, the lower gearing would help me to keep a tight line through the corners, and, again, to carry more corner speed than other riders. If I had gone into a third-gear corner at only 8,000 or 9,000 revs, the bike would have run away with me. By keeping the revs up nearer 11,000, the grip of the bike improved.

There was perhaps only half-a-tooth's difference, although it's not an exact science because both the diameter of the sprockets and the number of teeth on them had an effect on the gearing ratio. If Troy was using a 38-tooth back sprocket, I would use a 39. This meant that my revs were always nearer the top end of the range, as the limit for every gear was that little bit lower. It also meant that as the tyres were wearing, engine braking would be easier with the lower gearing. Again, that helped me to hold the line better and there was less chance of losing the front end by braking too hard in higher gears.

When going into hard-braking corners, I would try not to drop down from fifth or sixth to first gear one after another. Instead, I would drop down a couple of gears and leave a small gap before dropping down another couple into third. That way, both wheels continued to turn and the back wheel did not slide into the corners. Other riders who didn't carry as much corner speed would drop down through the gears in quick succession.

For doing one-off fast laps, my gearing wasn't ideal. That was one of the reasons why Troy was often faster than me in qualifying. If I had wanted to match him, I would probably have used the same gearing, but I felt that my choice of gearing suited race conditions, especially after 10 or 11 laps. I always felt I could ride round other problems, but you still need all the help you can get and there is no doubt that it worked for me.

My dad could never get his head round this at all. The priority when he was riding was to gear the bike for the straights and make sure you achieved maximum speed there, rather than in the corners. Even in the later years of my career he still tried to argue that his way made more sense. He just could not believe that I rarely reached maximum revs in sixth gear, apart from at Monza and Hockenheim. At all the other circuits I was more likely to use only five gears.

It is a very important part of the bike set-up, though, and something I was always messing around with. Apart from tyre choice, this was possibly what occupied my thoughts most during qualifying. Although I didn't really understand all the telemetry and graphs, I would look at the computer readings which would help me to identify where other Ducati riders were opening the throttle and what their revs were in certain gears on different parts of the circuit, and to compare their performances with mine. This was especially the case if we were running out of time, especially on a Saturday afternoon, and were still not happy with the set-up.

Rather than make me try to decipher all the squiggly lines, the technicians tried to produce a map of the circuit showing what gear I was using at every corner and what revs I was pulling at each part. It was usually information I was already aware of but, at times, it was helpful to show where I might have been losing time on specific parts of the track. I would often sit down with my chief mechanic – Slick or, later, Luca Gasbarro – and talk him through the circuit, just trying to make the sounds the bike was making in areas where I thought I was struggling. To do that, though, and to get your message across, you have to have a very good relationship and understanding with your mechanic.

It sometimes means your mechanic has to be very understanding too! A typical dialogue when I got back to the pits might start with me saying, 'It's too hard' or 'It's too soft' or 'It's chattering'. It was then up to the mechanics to find the problem and solve it. Slick likes to tell the story of how, during 1997 when I was really struggling with the bike, I came into the garage during qualifying.

'Fix it!' I said.

'What bit do you want me to fix?' Slick replied calmly.

'I don't give a fuck. Just do something to it. I'm not bothered what it is.'

'Whatever.' Slick just shrugged his shoulders and got on with it.

The scientific approach was unheard of when I started racing. Now it's a whole new development and very difficult, even for a team manager like Davide Tardozzi, to know exactly what is going on in every area of the bike all the times. Telemetry didn't really become a major factor until the mid-nineties. Until then, I had one mechanic and that was pretty much it. Now you can have up to six guys, each responsible for his own specialised area. The bottom line, though, is that the most important thing is the rider's feel for the bike, and I only started to use telemetry around 1998 and 1999, and then only to decide whether I was right or wrong in what I was asking for. I always found it more useful for suspension problems, because the gearing was more to do with the rider's own preference. For instance, when the Ducati riders tested at Valencia before the 2001 season, Ruben Xaus was in second gear at a lot of corners whereas Troy Bayliss and Ben Bostrum were in first.

The graphs might also prove useful for gearing when I wanted to look at the next option available. For example, I might suggest going down half-a-tooth, but the telemetry might show that the next available option was 0.8 or 0.9 and I would know instinctively that to drop down that far would be too much. It might have helped on some corners, but you have to balance it out around the whole track. The bike is never spot-on in every single gear around every single corner of the track, so you might try to make sure that the gearing is right for the corners where you would be looking to overtake, or where you are likely to lose more time if it's not right, and be prepared to lose a little bit of time at the less important corners.

At the start of 1999, Troy and I had a meeting with Ducati to say that we both felt first gear was a bit short. We asked them to make it longer, but that was easier said than done because the factory had a lot of engines to prepare for the start of the season. But Ducati did say that once they were committed to this, there would be no going back. For much of that season we had two engines, one with a longer first gear and one that was standard. On a number of occasions I actually used the standard one and Troy used the longer one, yet I still managed to beat him. Luckily, most of the time we did want different types, otherwise both of us would have been fighting over the same engine.

With a Ducati, it is impossible to change gearbox ratios like you can on other bikes. With other manufacturers, it is possible to take the gearbox out and put a lower first gear in without altering the rest of the gears. The Ducati engine is not designed to change gears that way. It would have been nice to be able to do that, but the Ducati, being a twin engine, has a lot more torque and a smoother rev range over a broader power band. That means it can still pull at the lower to middle range of a gear, while the other bikes might struggle with drive at the lower end of a gear's range.

> ## FOGGY FACTOR
>
> 'The bike is never spot-on in every single gear around every single corner of the track. So you should try to make sure that the gearing is right for the corners where you will be looking to overtake.'

The maximum power for a Ducati comes at around 12,000 revs. Down the straight, you would perhaps have the revs at about 11,500, but when changing up to fifth or sixth you would be at the limiter in order to keep the revs up and keep the bike punching through the air. At somewhere like Hockenheim or other fast circuits, where the bike is pulling a very tall gearing, if you changed at 11,500 you would drop too many revs. So I would rev a little bit over 12,000 and try to change gear as quickly as possible to stop the revs from dropping down.

When I rode for Honda in 1996, the option of changing single gears made everything very confusing. At Sentul in Indonesia I managed to convince the team to make third gear lower by a few hundred revs on the Saturday night before the race. They had to strip the engine down to put a new third gear in and, but as soon as I went out the next morning I realized that I had got it completely wrong. If I had not made that change I believe I would have won both races because I was second in both but lost so much drive coming onto the start–finish straight. Third gear was revving its nuts off! That's the kind of mistake you would not make if you had time testing at the circuit, but we hadn't had the chance out there. And there is no time to change something like that before the second race.

It was another Ducati team boss, Raymond Roche, who first introduced me to the importance of gearing. It happened when I won my first ever World Superbike race at Albacete in 1993, my first year on a factory Ducati. I was still learning how to ride the thing at the time. It wasn't like riding a normal four-cylinder bike, where you just revved the tits off it. Raymond had seen me struggling a bit early on in the weekend and came over for a chat.

'Just try this,' he said. 'I only used four gears around this circuit last year and it worked for me. Go on, try it.'

The engine of the factory Ducati on which I won the world title in 1998.

I wasn't sure at first, but it was perfect. As we had put a small back sprocket on and were only using the four gears, the first was very tall, which is not what I usually liked, but because Albacete is a tight and twisty track it meant that I could use first gear for nearly every corner. If we had geared the bike for five gears, I would have been out of first and into second in next to no time. That was probably the first time I had ever started to think about the right gearing for each track. Davide Tardozzi was similar in his approach, in that he would try to explain things while trying to help me, whereas my other Ducati team boss, Virginio Ferrari, preferred to let these things look after themselves.

In 1998 we had problems with the mapping of the bike. This is a kind of 3D map that charts the throttle, the rpm and the amount of fuel going into the bike. It is all done on a computer. You can change the fuel delivery just by plugging something into the bike and typing the information into a computer. Later on, on my bikes, you could change both injection and fuel maps. So, for instance, you could take a lot of advance out of the ignition to make it more retarded, with less power, and at the same time add more fuel. This would make the bike a lot smoother when you initially opened the throttle. The idea was to make sure the engine wasn't running either too rich or too lean on fuel. The method of fuel injection also changed. In my last year there was just one injector over the throttle bodies, an idea that had been adapted from Formula One motor racing. In the past there had either been two or three injectors.

To make a map for an engine from scratch is very difficult and takes weeks and months of development. Once you have that base, though, you can adapt it for each engine and for rider preference. If a rider wants to be harder or smoother on the throttle, you can make the map work for him. My map was quite aggressive, but not as much as some riders like Scott Russell, who was very aggressive on the throttle. Troy Bayliss, on the other hand, is very smooth. I would get the throttle on earlier than Troy Corser, but although he was later he would then pull it straight through. Maps are used more, though, for trying to take some of the power away from a bike, for example, rather than to suit a particular rider's style.

Ducati have to bring out 200 bikes each year to homologise the bikes they sell with the race bike, as superbikes is all about the fact that the race bikes are on sale to the general public. In 1998 those 200 bikes were the Foggy replicas, one of which is standing in our office at home. We had been a million miles from Honda that year. We knew on the start line that we were only going to finish third at places like Monza because we were 10mph slower than their top speed. To solve the problems we had been having in 1998, they built the Foggy replicas and included a bigger airbox, which was needed on the racing bike. They also shortened off the inlet ports, which made the bike more responsive to the throttle. That halved the difference between the top speeds of the Ducati and the Honda.

But at the end of the day, modern engine performance assessment comes down to the computer, and I was never a big fan of the 'new' science. To me, all telemetry readings did was complicate what I could tell the mechanics simply in my own words. All I could see were squiggly lines everywhere. If I was in a bad mood, I would ask, 'So what exactly does all this tell me? All I want to know is what is wrong with the bike and why it's chattering in turn three. Show me where it says that on here.' Someone would then point to the relevant place on the telemetry chart. 'Okay, all that does is confirm what I've just told you. But how do we fix it?'

The very first time I came across telemetry was on a Grand Prix bike when we were testing in 1993 at Mugello. We could not get the bike to run at all, all weekend. Raymond Roche summed things up. He stood in front of the computer and said, 'I know what the problem is. You take off all this shit here, and you put it in the bin there.' That might have pissed off all the top people at Cagiva, who had paid for all the equipment, but he was right in a lot of ways. At the end of the day, they found out that the battery had been flat. Give me a good old rev counter clock any day!

Telemetry also measures things like air temperatures, revs, wheel spin, travel speed, fork and shock movements, water temperature and pressures. It was first used on one of my bikes in 1994, but only on one because Slick didn't want to put it on the other as it was taking too much of his time away from concentrating on the bike's actual problems. From 1995 we always had telemetry but it has never really helped my career. As far as I was concerned, someone was paid £40,000 a year just to piss about on his computer. It was only really in 1999 when it started to make just a little bit of sense to me, and so began to be of value.

Slick, too, eventually found it good for comparison. He could see the differences between the two bikes I was using and could make adjustments if one was faster through a certain section. He could also compare two different laps on the same bike, again highlighting any parts of the track where it was possible to make up time. The team could also compare two team-mates. If one was faster or slower around a certain section, they could see, for instance, whether his bike was sitting higher or lower than the other on the suspension. If it was lower, you could end up running too wide, but if it was sitting too high it might be a bit nervous, although you would be able to steer it more quickly.

Maybe, before 1999, I had just turned my back on the new technology and didn't make enough of an effort with it. I was perhaps just caught between two schools of thought, the old and the new; you either made an effort to learn all about it or you stick with what you knew best. But I still believe that the rider knows best what is wrong with the bike. Telemetry is more of a toy for the engineers of today.

RACING
TECHNIQUES

7: Conditions

Once upon a time there was a young rider who, whenever it was raining, used to walk around the paddock with a big grin on his face. But, as the years went by, that smile turned to a scowl if he had to race in the wet!

I don't think there's any simple explanation for this, although I suppose it all boils down to confidence. When I started racing, I always felt I could win in the wet and I had some great results at club and national level. Maybe I got overconfident on the 250cc bikes because I ended up crashing in wet weather at Silverstone in 1987, which resulted in me snapping my tibia and fibula where the bone had been weakened by an infection following a previous break. It was a year when I wasn't really in with a shout of winning races in the British championship unless it did rain, as I was struggling for movement in my leg because of a bad fracture of my femur the previous year. In the wet, I didn't need to lean as far off the bike so it was nowhere near as uncomfortable. I had won both races in the first round of the British championship by a mile, riding round the outside of Gary Cowan, who went on to win the championship. During the second round I was reeling them in and had got up to second or third when down I went. That injury must have put me off wet weather conditions a bit because I never had the same success on superbikes as I'd had on 250cc bikes when everyone was on the same wet weather tyres.

Rain is just about the only thing that has ever stopped me from going out to win a race. In superbikes, whenever there was a world championship at stake, my priority in the wet was always just to finish as high up the field as possible and collect as many points as I could. My mind was fixed in 'finish' mode rather than 'win' mode. In 1998 I had some of the worst results I have ever had in the rain when I was 13th in both races at the Nurburgring. But that was due to a back injury more than anything else. I was also ninth at Albacete in the same year, before winning the dry race that followed. It had also rained a lot the previous year, but I won the combined race at Brands Hatch and also had a second and third, even though I still hated it. And in my last ever wet meetings I had good results: I was second and fourth in Austria in 1999 and would have won in Phillip Island the following year had Anthony Gobert not guessed correctly and chosen different tyres to everyone else. That was probably one of my best rides in those conditions, given that I was on the wrong intermediate tyres when the track stayed damp and full wets turned out to be the best bet.

Other riders were prepared to take more of a chance in the wet because they were not in contention for the world championship and saw it as their chance to steal some glory. Pier-Francesco Chili was always one of the fastest, but he could just as easily crash. The same went for Jamie Whitham. John Kocinski was also pretty quick but didn't seem to crash anywhere near as often. Others, like Aaron Slight and Colin Edwards, were a bit hit and miss – quick on some occasions, beatable on others.

My style never suited wet weather riding. The bigger riders tended to be the ones better suited to those conditions. Ruben Xaus, for instance, is one of the taller riders, and I've seen him with his knee on the floor going into a corner on the second lap when the tyres are still cool. Getting your knee down almost acted as a guide – the point at which you felt you could hold the bike upright – but I always struggled to do that. My style of hanging off and leaning the bike over did not allow me to do it in the same way. The only time I can remember my knee consistently touching the floor was when I was chasing Kocinski at Brands Hatch in 1997. And once I had actually reached that limit, I rode really well.

Qualifying in the wet was also a problem area for me. Knowing there were no prizes for a good performance, and never really being all that confident, I would hold back knowing that come race day I could always try to make myself go faster. And there was always a chance that it might dry up by the following day, so there was not much point risking everything in those conditions.

Edwards was always very fast during wet qualifying and he made you think he was going to win the race by a mile, although it didn't always work out that way. He seemed to get to the limit very quickly, whereas I would need loads and loads of practice – at least a full weekend – before I got there. I guess, again, that was just a case of building confidence. It was a similar situation in the races because I would leave myself with a lot of work to do by taking it easy early on, especially during that first race at Albacete in 1998. I didn't realize how much grip there actually was out there until it was too late.

The focus for set-up was to have the bike coming out of corners without too many revs and with a nice, smooth drive, so we would often try to soften up the suspension at the rear and alter the gearing so that the bike would not be so aggressive as to spin the wheel. I seemed to have this problem more than anyone else. Maybe that was because I was a bit lighter than the other riders. Whatever the reason, I found it really frustrating.

Michelin had three different rear tyres for wet weather – we always used 17in wheel size, 3.5in wide at the front and 5.75in wide at the back — and would sometimes try to get me on one of their hard compounds. But I hated that. When I used it at a wet Donington in 1994 it was like riding on marbles. I went from third on the first lap to 14th and I was being passed on every lap. I hadn't thought that having a hard tyre would have made much difference. Ever since then, the softer the rear tyre the better as far as I was concerned, but Michelin would always be worried that it would rip up and destroy itself if the rain eased off a little. And on the most abrasive circuits they didn't like using it at all, even if there wasn't much chance of the rain stopping.

It was snowing during practice at Donington in 1998, prompting me to find a novel way of warming my hands.

Some circuits suited me more than others. The Nurburgring, for instance, was not a favourite. I struggled there in the wet in 1998, yet won one race and set a new lap record in 1999 in the dry. As I have already said, I had back problems and a sore foot in 1998, and when you are hurting you are likely to notice it more in the wet because you aren't riding as aggressively. At other circuits like Misano or Donington, I haven't struggled as much, although there haven't been wet races there for a while.

For somebody who was very fast through chicanes in the dry, I lost a lot of time through the same chicanes in the wet because I couldn't throw the bike through them hard enough. When I see pictures of myself I look horrendous because the bike is upright and I am still hanging right off. It looked like I was frightened and rigid. I never relaxed and let things flow; I always seemed concerned about making any quick movements. It was just the opposite of how I rode in the dry, where my reactions were very quick and I threw myself off the bike a lot. It's not often that I'm critical of myself, but I did always accept that I had several short-comings when it came to racing in the rain.

One of my most enjoyable races in the wet was with Jamie Whitham in 1997 at Monza. We both led the race early on, but John Kocinski and Frankie Chili came past and were starting to get away through the chicanes because I didn't have their confidence. So I just decided to have a dice with Jamie and flicked a few friendly 'V's at him whenever I got the better of him.

The worst wet conditions I've experienced were at Misano that same year. It's not too bad when it's just the surface of the track that's wet, and the weather is dry, but on this occasion it was lashing down throughout the race. The track was like an ice rink and you couldn't even so much as touch the brakes. And touching the painted lines was fatal. The first part of the track was quite grippy, but from the chicane onwards it was terrible. Jamie Whitham crashed in front of me and I could see him sliding along out of the corner of my eye as I turned the corner. I fell off at the same place during winter testing the following year. Davide Tardozzi had said to me, 'Go out in the wet, you need to build a bit of confidence.' Sure enough I was getting quicker and quicker until I just touched the brakes at that part of the circuit and down I went, sliding on my arse.

Some tracks seemed to have more grip than others, like Assen, where the flowing style of the circuit was also not as bad for me as the tight and twisty chicanes of other circuits like Albacete. In the wet I did not have the confidence to lean over through all those corners that come back on themselves. I also went pretty well at Malaysia, where it is still 30 degrees C even when it is raining and the tyres stay warm and continue to work.

Another problem to overcome when the rain is actually falling is how to keep the visor clear. When I raced 250ccs I would take one hand off the bar coming into a corner and lift the visor up a little bit to stop it misting over. I remember one of my early sponsors, Dave Orton, watching me at Gerrards, a really fast corner at Mallory Park, and saying, 'I couldn't believe it. You were leading the race and we thought you were going to fall when you took your hand off on every lap. We couldn't watch you.'

I have tried a number of different methods to solve the problem over the years. One was to tape the visor up, across the top and down the sides, to stop the rain from seeping into the helmet when I was in the tuck position going down the straights. Another trick was to slightly open the visor by about 5mm, and then tape around the rest of it. That meant there was at least a bit of air circulating. But you had to be prepared for your eyes to be sore that night because the wind would be able to get into them. Nowadays there are special strips called Fog City, which you can tape onto the inside of your visor. But if you don't get them sitting perfectly you can still have problems. If there are bits of strip not stuck down properly then either air or water can travel up them and mist over the visor. Shark also produce a visor that has a special coating which, if you breathe on it, will not mist up. There is also a rubber aid that sits inside the helmet and stops warm air from the nostrils getting back into the helmet, and I guess that must work.

Sometimes the rain will stay on the visor, and there have been many times when I have used my finger to wipe away the water on the outside while travelling down a straight. More often than not this would make things worse and I would then have to keep doing it regularly throughout the race. I don't think there has ever been a race in the wet when I have not been messing around with my visor in one way or another.

A clear view has always been essential for me. Even when I go trial riding or motocrossing I am forever getting the rags out to ensure my goggles are

> ## FOGGY FACTOR
>
> 'We would often try and soften the suspension up at the rear and alter the gearing so that the bike would not be so aggressive as to spin the wheel.'

spotless. Everyone else seems happy to continue with mud all over them. It's the same when I'm skiing. The second time I went I got really frustrated because I wasn't finding it as easy. I just didn't seem to have any control. Then, on the third occasion, everything clicked into place again. Michaela reckoned it was because for the first and third times the sun was out and I could see the snow more clearly.

The problems really start when it is wet *and* windy. Your hands get cold and the race seems to go on for a couple of hours rather than the usual 40 minutes. I remember one endurance race at Phillip Island in 1992 when it was cold and rainy for the whole six hours. Race marshals had to be taken to hospital with hypothermia, so imagine what it was like for the riders. When I got off the bike I was so cold I couldn't even take my helmet off.

Wind on its own is not really a problem as it is the same for every rider, but it is never stronger anywhere than in Australia. In the first round of the world championship in 1998, I remember getting off the bike and saying, 'That's the hardest race I have ever had in my life. I was just trying to stay upright for 25 laps.'

I look rigid in the wet but I'm using every inch of the road at Brands to stay ahead of John Kocinski.

The wind was unbelievable, made worse because it was a hot and humid day. There were bits of paper blowing everywhere, and the last thing you want is a bit of paper distracting you for a split second as you're coming into a bend. At the first corner, the wind was so strong that I couldn't even get up the inside; I had to run right round the outside and I lost a couple of places. I was almost blown off the track. Going down the straight where I had my big crash, I almost had to push the bike into the side-on wind to keep it upright. At least after the first few laps I was prepared for it, and at one point I found myself pulling away. I couldn't believe it. I was convinced my lap times were slow, that I must be holding everyone up. But I won the race, and afterwards my face was bright red through exertion. My arms were killing me too because I had been pulling the bike into the wind so much.

Arm pain became a bit of a problem in my later years, especially in the elbow crease. Earlier on in my career the tenderness used to occur in the soft part of the arm just below the elbow. The tracks on which you had to throw the bike around, like Assen, were the worst for aggravating these injuries. The faster you try to change direction, the harder it is on your arms. Some people have real trouble with muscle pump. Neil Hodgson had to have an operation on his right forearm to create some space for the muscles to grow because they were being used so much during a race. I have had injections and used pain-relieving cream, but it has never got to the point of surgery with me.

Occasionally you had to change the gearing between races because of the weather. Again, this could be an issue at Phillip Island, where the wind can so quickly change direction. The gearing could be spot-on for going down the straight with the wind in your face, but then, for the next race, it was suddenly behind you. So the gearing had to be altered slightly so that it wasn't causing you to over-rev.

The heat and humidity of the Far East was another set of conditions which had to be overcome. It was always worst in Malaysia and Indonesia. Even before getting on a bike you felt as though you had been in a sauna. Then you had to climb into a set of leathers and throw a bike around in the heat. That is physically very hard on a rider. A couple of times I have sweated so much that it rolled off my forehead and into my eyes, which stings like hell. The Sentul circuit in Indonesia, however, was not all that demanding, a bit like Monza in that it is very flat with few chicanes. But Laguna Seca can also be stiflingly hot, and although the humidity is not as high there, that race can be very physically tough because the circuit is very demanding.

Conditions have never been as tough, though, as they were at Suzuka for the eight-hour race in 1996. There was about 80 per cent humidity that day and the temperatures were in their mid-30s. Even a walk to the paddock brought you out in a sweat. It really got to me. I was leading the race but Noriyuki Haga was catching me. I was determined to be in the lead when we changed over, but I was so hot and uncomfortable that my concentration suddenly went and, coming into the hairpin, I just fell off. I didn't have the strength to pick the bike up and the marshals had to help me out. I had never felt that bad before. Maybe it was because I hadn't slept well the previous night, or perhaps I was just totally drained because I wasn't fit enough. But, when I looked round, everyone else was also dying. Colin Edwards had two glucose drips in each arm, beating my one. We also had to slip into an ice tub to reduce our body temperatures. It was not a race I enjoyed!

Constant sweat can also cause problems with blisters on your hands. This could happen in the best of conditions, but it was obviously worse the hotter it was. Normally, after a morning race, they would be okay by the afternoon, but on a few occasions, and sometimes if the blisters had been really bad during qualifying, I would go into the *clinica mobile* on the morning of a race and get them to tape my fingers up. They could also cut holes on a big plaster to slide over your fingers. But it never got to a stage where you would lose grip.

RACING TECHNIQUES

8: Beyond the Limit

All falls hurt to some degree, but some hurt your pride more than your body. One of my most embarrassing falls was on New Year's Eve in 1981 when I was riding through a busy junction called Brownhill roundabout, not far from where I lived. There was a line of punters waiting to get into a pub when I came along on a Honda MB50, which looked like a race bike because it had a fairing nose-piece with a sticker of a nude bird on the front. But far from looking cool in front of all these people, I hit some black ice while trying to outbrake a couple of mates who were riding with me. Down I went, sliding right across the roundabout. Had a car been coming at that moment I would have died. As it was, I escaped with just a scratched elbow, ripped jeans and a broken indicator. My mates were laughing, which doubled the embarrassment.

I was always a bit daft on the roads. Another stupid game we played was 'chicken' at a crossroads, where we would ride straight across without looking and pray that nothing was coming in the other direction. We would never pick the busiest junctions, for obvious reasons. It seemed like a good laugh at the time; but you don't realise how crazy these things are until you grow up. I suppose we were a bit of a nuisance at times, hanging around outside people's houses with three or four bikes, or riding up and down outside the chippy, pulling wheelies on the pavement. It's not until you start racing that you begin to treat the motorbike with a bit more respect.

There are basically four causes of a crash: a high-side, losing the front end, mechanical failure or being knocked off. Losing the front end is a lot better than losing the rear end, that's for sure. It usually happens when you go into a corner on the brakes and the front of the bike has been chattering. Often you're aware that this is happening but perhaps not paying enough attention. It can also happen if you are pushing too hard and perhaps lean too far over in a corner. It can happen at any type of corner, although slow corners like chicanes or hairpins tend to see more accidents because you tend to push harder there. I think riders treat the faster corners with a bit more respect and those corners are also harder to pass on, so there is not as much race action there. But these slower falls just tip you onto your side rather than throw you up in the air, and nine-and-a-half times out of ten you can just get up and dust yourself off – unless you lose the front end at a very high speed, in which case the bike might start somersaulting around you.

The other way losing the front end can really hurt is if the bike falls over onto your leg and pushes your toes into the track. All my toes now show the wear and tear of many years' racing, and I have shaved the ends off them a few times. At Brands Hatch in 1990 I made a right mess of my foot when I lost the front end and the bike stayed on top of me. The track came through the boot, then the sock, and planed the skin off the end of my toes. That stings like mad, I can tell you. Troy Bayliss had some problems the year after I retired, doing the same thing to his toes in a pretty minor fall during practice at Phillip Island. Because he did not feel comfortable in some new boots that had better titanium toesliders, he had taken them out and suffered the consequences. He made a right mess of his foot and didn't need much persuasion to wear the toesliders in future.

At the British Grand Prix in 1992 I lost the front end after hitting John Kocinski's oil and sliding out. Again the bike pushed my leg into the ground and I could actually smell burning flesh, which is not pleasant at the best of times, but even worse when you realize it's your own meat that's being cooked! I was frantically trying to kick the bike off my leg with my free foot as I slid along.

The other way this kind of fall can do a lot of damage is if another rider takes the front end away from you when you're trying to come up the inside. That can throw you down, rather than just tip you over, in a bit of a low-side. I cannot ever remember that happening to me, although I have been clipped a few times and wobbled off into the gravel before just falling over. That kind of crash has never caused me any injury, although you see it a lot, especially down the field. It nearly happened in 1997 when I tried to run John Kocinski off the track in Austria. That impact took my front end away and I fell over, although there wasn't a mark on me on that occasion.

The Honda RC30 in 1990 was the worst bike I ever had for front end problems. Right through their range of bikes, Hondas always seem to be fast but not very good in terms of handling. If the track was perfectly smooth there was not much of a problem, but if it was just a little bit bumpy, or if you ran wide onto a slightly dirtier line, it set the front end off chattering like mad. The faster you went, the worse the roll would be. You would just hit a bump, tuck straight under and fall down. Out of ten tracks, the bike would probably be a nightmare to ride on six of them. Although I had a lot of success on that bike, it definitely held me back. I would have won so many more times, especially in England, had I been on a bike that handled better.

Maybe riding that bike had a big impact on the style I developed. If you went into a corner from wide you would go over every time you hit a bump, so I tended to come in from a tighter line and get my knee onto the floor through the corner. When I was riding the RC30 I developed a style where, if I felt I was going to lose the front end mid-corner, I could catch the bike with my knee and push back up again. My team-mate Jamie Whitham had exactly the same problems, but he would actually fall more than I did because he hadn't developed this style of riding round the problems. Before then I didn't really have any handling problems like this, because all my other bikes had been 250ccs. They also probably had a big effect on my style of

*My first superbike race at Donington in 1992 comes to a dramatic end
after I leaned too far over and slid off.*

carrying high corner speeds because 250cc riding is all about
pushing the bike quickly though mid-corner as it is not very fast
down the straight.

You crash every bike you ever ride. I cannot think of a rider
who has not crashed in a full year of racing, although in 1999 I
managed to finish every single race. I did fall, losing the front end
at the Nurburgring after losing a bit of concentration, but I
managed to get back on and finish the race.

It is usually the freak crashes that can seriously injure a rider,
or even kill him. Wayne Rainey was a case in point. His was a
high-side which threw him into some gravel at Misano; the fall
must have twisted his body badly because he ended up paralysed.
Then again, a rider can be lucky. Steve Hislop had a similar fall
at Brands Hatch in 2000. It looked pretty bad at the time and he
was lucky to get away with it and carry on racing the following
season. Another guy who was really lucky was the Japanese rider
that I hit in 1998. I actually ran over his head. He got up and was
fine and completed both races, although I have to say it freaked
me out a bit.

The man to ask about freak crashes is Barry Sheene. Both his
major crashes were the result of incidents which he had no
control over. The first, at Daytona in 1975, happened when a tyre
blew at top speed; he broke a femur, four vertebrae, three ribs, his
forearm and a collarbone, and ruptured a kidney. Then, at
Silverstone in 1982, he piled blindly into the wreckage of an
earlier accident at 170mph and almost severed both legs; his

The engine was still running so I was hopeful of rejoining the race – until I noticed the footrest had been knocked off.

other injuries included two wrist fractures, a host of broken vertebrae, collarbones and fingers. A total of 27 bolts were needed to hold four leg plates in place, and similar metalwork was needed to pin his wrists back into shape. Hats off to him for coming back and racing after that.

It just goes to show that it doesn't take a spectacular list of injuries like that to put an end to a career. My career-ending crash was also one of those freak things, and the damage to my shoulder was fairly extensive. But it annoys me a little bit that people don't realize just how much damage was done. If I had broken my neck, nobody would ever have suggested my getting back on a bike. But now, because I can ride things like motocross or enduro bikes, some people cannot get their heads round the fact that I will never race again because there is not enough strength in my left arm to throw a superbike around a track for 25 laps. There is also not enough movement in the joint for me to get into the proper tuck position for riding down straights.

If you can see a crash coming, you have a split second to minimize the damage. During that 1999 race at the Nurburgring, a race I knew I had to win because of the tragic death of a friend's daughter at our house the previous week, I was coming underneath a back marker at one of the corners. He came across me and I collected him but, knowing that we were going to hit each other, I kind of leaned over with the whole of my body so that it would be our bodies that made the impact and not the bikes. Even with the slightest clash you can always damage something like a gear lever. He went spinning off into the gravel while I carried on, so I guess it looked like I had barged him off the track. Although he was spewing, he didn't blame me but went straight over to one of the marshals and bollocked him instead for not letting him know that I was about to lap him.

Back markers can often cause problems and I was lucky in my final year of racing when a guy almost killed me at Kyalami just out of sheer stupidity. It happened in the final session of qualifying and was probably another of the many warnings at the start of that year that I shouldn't be racing any more. We came out of the last chicane, just at the entrance to the pit-lane. I went up his inside ready to pass him on the brakes at the next corner at the other end of the start–finish straight but suddenly, without any warning, he just cut straight across me to go into the pit-lane. Luckily, I was aware that he didn't really know what he was doing and I was ready for something stupid. I braked like mad and just managed to miss hitting him. *That's all I need, some wanker like that knocking me off at this stage of the season*, I thought to myself, while letting him have some tried and tested hand signals.

In the very next round, I *was* knocked off by a back marker, although it has to be said that my crash at Phillip Island was in no way down to Robert Ulm. There is a point to be made, though. The slower riders tend to think slower than the faster riders, and whenever a dangerous situation is developing they tend to freeze and panic instead of using their instincts or common sense to avoid the trouble.

The two worst countries I have been to that have involved problems with back markers are two that have produced some of the best riders in the world, Japan and Australia. I don't really know why that is, but it seems in Australia they are happy to let anyone into the race. Two or three guys might just as well have got their bikes out of their garages in the middle of the outback near Alice Springs. Then they blow all the dust off with a compressor, ride it down to Phillip Island and manage to qualify by half a second, which means they are only eight seconds a lap slower than the fastest riders, not the usual nine! They then ride round, totally oblivious that there's a race for the world championship happening. If you're going round the track 20mph faster than they are in certain places, this can be very dangerous. When you're trying to win a race and to get away from the guy behind you, you have also got to think what the idiot in front is going to do – the one not paying attention to blue flags and wandering all over the road. In Britain it's fine, because all the wild cards are good riders and deserve to be there for a one-off chance. And in other countries, like America, you used to get some really fast wild cards like Ben Bostrom and his brother Eric, who had a chance of winning the race, as well as some fast but capable guys making up the numbers. In Japan, though, there would be about 15 local riders. The top six or seven would be very handy, but some of the others were totally hopeless. At the end of the 1999 season Frankie Chili and I asked the organisers to reduce the qualifying gap down to about seven seconds so that these jokers wouldn't be able to compete. At the time I said, 'They'll probably wait until some-body gets killed or badly hurt because of it, and then decide to do something about it.'

It's obviously important that every precaution is taken to ensure that the races are as safe as possible. On road circuits, though, there is no question that you are going to get hurt if you come off because you will hit something solid. That is the risk you take with that kind of racing, a risk that Joey Dunlop took for many years before he died in Estonia in July 2000 after coming off the circuit and hitting a tree. I rode round the Isle of Man TT circuit for eight years, from 1985 to 1992, and never once fell off, which is pretty incredible. I knew that if I did crash just that once, it could well be the last time.

I have crashed on road circuits, though. On a 250cc at the North West 200, which is not as dangerous as the Isle of Man TT, I had three or four crashes. I was photographed in the middle of one high-side at a corner which I think is called Church Bend, two weeks before the TT in 1987. I was thrown over the top and looked like Superman flying through the air while the bike carried on upright and veered off down a side street before crash-ing into a metal road sign. The bike was smashed to pieces. Because it was the first crash I'd suffered since breaking my leg

the previous year, I gingerly tested my leg afterwards to see if anything had broken again. My knee swelled up like a balloon, but
luckily there were no more fractures.

So you have to have some luck as well. For a man who has
crashed at nearly every big road racing circuit, Jamie Whitham
has been very fortunate. The only one where he suffered any
serious damage was his crash at the Ulster Grand Prix in 1989 –
a race I won – when he smashed his ankle up pretty badly.
Jamie also crashed earlier that year at the TT; and another guy
came round, clipped his bike and was killed. His team-mate,
Phil Mellor, was also killed that year, and that was too much for
Jamie to take. After that day he vowed never to ride on a road
circuit again.

On a short circuit you are more likely to hit an air-fence or a
tyre wall, or slide off into the grass or gravel, so it's not usually
the crashes that just involve your own bike which result in the
serious injuries in short circuit racing. But the ones that can be
serious are the high-sides. These are caused by giving the bike too
much power in the corner and asking too much of the machine.
The tyre breaks traction and begins to slide round. Years ago they
used to slide round as if you were in a speedway crash and dump
you into the gravel, but the new tyres seem to have changed all
that. Now, when you are on full lean and trying to put as much
power as you can through the back tyre – and there is a lot of
power on a superbike – the bike moves round and slides out from
under you. Obviously, when that happens you close off the gas
instinctively, but nowadays the tyres grip and whip the bike back
in the opposite direction with a massive force that more often
than not throws you high up into the air. Sometimes you manage
to hang on, but those moments don't half give you a scare and
there's not much chance of you repeating it at that spot for the
rest of the race.

The biggest high-side I ever had was that notorious and
dramatic one at Sugo in 1995. I was doing a guest appearance on
a television soccer chat show recently and they kept showing it
again and again. At one point the bike had slid round so much
that I thought it was going to slide right out and not flick me
back. I must have been thrown 12 feet in the air and landed in a

right heap. Luckily there were no serious injuries, just a couple of chipped bones, and I got up and went on to win the second race.

I haven't had too many high-sides, thankfully. In fact, I cannot remember having one at all throughout 1999, either in the races or during qualifying, which is absolutely amazing. And I only had one during the whole of 1998, at the Nurburgring during practice. It was another big one that probably caused the back trouble I suffer from now. I thought I had come out of the corner, a fast uphill esses. I went into the first part on the left and got on the gas to squirt it on through the next bit and it suddenly came round on me as I picked the bike up to throw it over onto the right-hand side. I was probably lucky to get up and walk away from that one.

I also had a couple of really big high-sides on the Honda in 1996. Two came right at the start of the year, which kind of knocked my confidence a bit. The first was at Misano during qualifying, and it was captured by the television cameras. It was early on in the session at a right-hand turn, so that side of the tyre was probably not properly warmed, as Misano is all left-hand corners. I came out of the silly, shitty chicane, where you go hard on the gas for a bit of a dog-leg right. I nailed it flat before the bike let go, threw me off and gave me a bit of concussion. I followed that up with one at Hockenheim, this time on the left-hand side because that track is all right-hand turns. I threw it into the first chicane on the right-hand side, then over onto the left, hit the gas and *Wooof!!* off I went. It was a cold day and the pain almost doubles in those conditions. I thought I had broken my wrist. There was no fracture, but I was really low at that point of the season.

That wasn't the only high-side I've had at that circuit. In 1994 I did break my wrist after coming off right in front of where Michaela was standing, watching the race. We will never know whether there was some oil leaking from the bike, although pictures of the crash show some smoke coming out of the back, just as my hand got caught. In hindsight, it didn't hurt my chances and I went on to win the world title that year.

I have never been a crasher, but whenever I did crash it tended to be at important times during a year, and people remember those incidents. In my first year as a factory rider in 1993, I had a few crashes, including one in Japan and another at the Craner Curves at Donington. The older you get, though, the wiser you become. When you crash as a younger rider, you don't particularly think about it or analyse it. You just accept it as an inevitable part of riding and have a bit of a laugh about it. The older I became, however, the more annoyed I was at crashing.

At my second last meeting, at Kyalami in South Africa, I was furious with myself. I'd changed the front tyre for the second race and set the new lap record while recovering from a bad start, but I was getting plenty of warnings that the front tyre, with a narrower rim, wasn't right as I kept losing it on the bumpy sections.

> ### FOGGY FACTOR
>
> 'When I was riding the RC30 I developed a style where, if I felt that I was going to lose the front end mid-corner, I could catch the bike with my knee and push back up again.'

It tucked under on me twice on the two laps before the crash, but instead of knocking it back and trying to settle for a third or fourth, I was hell-bent on winning the race. And, of course, I went into a bumpy corner again and down I went. Now that was not like me in my last five years of racing. During that time I had got more and more of a feel for the bike, instinctively knowing how far I could go without losing it.

There used to be many more crashes in the 500cc Grand Prix races than there were in superbikes. In the mid-nineties those bikes were a lot harder to ride than they are now. The power delivery from low down was very aggressive – a bit like an on-off switch in that there were no half measures. There was no smooth delivery of power up through the rev range, just an explosion very low down. In 1997, and for a while in 1998, the Ducati was a little bit like that. When you shut off the throttle it really closed the gas, and when you opened it again it would snap back into action and upset the bike. But the 500ccs have also improved with rule changes, the move to unleaded fuel and the like. It's like any other form of racing, though. You don't just take hold of a bike and have it perfect for the rider, you have to work hard at getting it how a rider wants it.

My knee is touching the kerb at Quarter Bridge on my way to winning the Formula One TT on the Isle of Man in 1990.

Trying my best to stay away from the wall during the 1999 Isle of Man TT.

I share a whispered joke with Jamie Whitham on the podium for the Macau Grand Prix in 1992. It was probably something to do with one of the girls!

Slick is on hand as I prepare to go out for qualifying in Austria in 1993.

Celebrating my double win at Brands in 1995 – one of my best days in racing.

I chose the wrong compound for this wet race at Donington in 1994. I never again rode on such a hard compound in wet conditions.

There's no way that No. 4 Colin Edwards is going to get up my inside at this corner in 1995.

My leathers have taken another pounding after an encounter with the gravel.

Fighting with the Honda in 1996 as I enter the back straight at Brands.

I examine the damage after breaking my wrist at Hockenheim in 1994. Michaela was stood watching at the very point where I fell.

Battling with Michael Rutter in the wet second race at Brands in 1997.

It was a good weekend for the Brits at Hockenheim in 1997 when I won the second race and Jamie Whitham was third, with Japan's Akira Yanagawa in between.

It was at this meeting that a bluebottle splattered into my visor, costing me victory at Assen. Here I am leading Aaron Slight, with John Kocinski in the distance.

Foggy Fever hits Assen. There were plenty of Brits there in 1997 but an estimated 60,000 in 1999. That figure resulted in the 'More fans than Manchester United' comment.

Brands Hatch in 1997 was the best ride I ever had in the wet. My style looks a lot more comfortable than normal, which is probably why I won the race on aggregate.

A rider takes a lot of care with his helmet, in looking after it and with the design.

It wasn't difficult to spot a Cross of St George flag to celebrate victory at Assen in 1997.

I'm either just going down into or coming up out of the tuck position. Either way, I don't look too comfortable.

The only time I can remember being knocked off was in one of my first ever international races, in 1986, when I think I was leading the race. I had a really good start but Niall Mackenzie, the British champion and favourite to win, hit me going into a really tight hairpin. The impact knocked me off, although I wasn't hurt and he came round to apologise straight away – after I had been threatening to round up a few mates and sort him out! But he was the big star at that time and I was just the kid starting out, so I was more gutted than anything else and accepted his apology. If it had been a few years later, my reaction might have been a bit different.

The other way a rider can fall, apart from freak accidents, is if the engine blows. That has only once happened to me, during testing at Laguna Seca in 1997, down what I call the back straight there, going up the hill before the Corkscrew. The back wheel locked up completely and threw me right over the front, and I landed smack on my head. If I remember rightly, it was an old engine and the conrod had been sticking out. The two-strokes are well known for it, and it can happen anywhere on the track. I had a lot of these moments when I was riding 250ccs. But if you could get your hand on the clutch there wasn't a problem. You could often feel the back wheel tightening up so you pulled the clutch in and freewheeled off into the grass. That was the only time that has ever happened to me on a Ducati, but at the end of the day you are riding a machine and it can break. And when it does, the chances are that it's going to throw you off.

There have been other times when the bike has been a bit of a mess, but that was down to me. After a fall, you often know straight away that there is no point even trying to fix the bike and get it back in the race. But at Suzuka in 1989, when I was riding with Steve Hislop, Slick and the mechanics knew they had a bit more time because it was an endurance race. We had qualified down in something like 16th place, but I got off to a flyer and was up to seventh a couple of laps before I was due to hand over to Steve. But then the front end tucked under and what was once a racing bike quickly became a twisted heap of metal with bits hanging off everywhere and water spewing out all over the place. Still, we somehow managed to ride it back to the pits. The look on Slick's face was classic – *do I really have to try to get this back on the track*? After pulling bits off and sticking bits back on, the last thing Slick tried to do was clean a bit of shit off the radiator, but as soon as he dislodged it water started squirting everywhere. We didn't have a spare radiator so the only thing Slick could think of was to try to plug the hole with Araldite. So there we all were, as the race continued outside the garage, staring at the radiator for five minutes waiting for the Araldite to set. Steve eventually set off again with a new fairing on which we had stuck our number; he even had to kick an engine bolt back into place at one point. All this time I didn't know where to put myself for crashing in the first place. We finished 33rd but celebrated as if we had won the race.

It's not just road and short circuit racing that can cause problems. Motocross can be just as dangerous if you don't get everything right. I have heard of quite a few people who have had serious injuries while riding motocross. Leon Haslam, the son of Ron Haslam who became the youngest ever rider in GPs at the age of 17, twice broke his leg badly at the age of about 13. And Neil Hodgson, my team-mate in 1997, once split his kneecap right down the middle when he landed badly on a motocross bike, although he was fit to race two weeks later at Laguna Seca. There was another time when he was riding with a party on the Isle of Man on his birthday when one of the riders got a jump all wrong, broke his neck and died. It just goes to show that it is not just speed that kills.

In my last few years of racing I tried to do as much motocross as I could, for training purposes. It seemed like a fairly safe way of keeping myself in trim. The way I saw it, the only way I was going to get seriously injured riding motocross was on the jumps. If you fall off through losing the front end in the corners, it's usually a soft fall, but if you come off jumps and get your landing all wrong, you can be in a lot of trouble.

I had a big crash on a motocross bike just before I won the world championship in 1999 – which, looking back, doesn't seem like the brightest thing I have ever done. I went to Preston Docks on a lovely sunny Wednesday afternoon, the day before I flew out to Assen for the Dutch round of the championship. That was the last time anyone saw Carl Fogarty race properly, but it could all have been so different. All I wanted was a day's exertion to get myself in the mood, and a couple of mates, Garth Woods and Austin Clews, came down with me. In the summer the track is nice and dusty, with lots of jumps. If I'm being honest, I have to say that I don't enjoy the jumps. Quite often I just come down too heavy and hit the deck with a right thud, and on this occasion I got one all wrong. As I was about to land, the bike crossed up and my wrists were tucked under when the bike landed. I also banged my head as I hit the deck. I remember thinking, *I can't believe what I'm doing here. I've got one of the most important races of my life in four days' time. Please, please don't be broken. Please don't swell up*, as I moved it round to check there was no obvious fracture. Austin came running over to see if I was all right, then suggested it might be wise to call it a day. *You silly bastard*, I said to myself. *Just put the bike in the back of the van and get back home where you can't do yourself any harm.* If I had broken anything I would have had to lie to Ducati and say that I had fallen down the stairs. They would have gone absolutely ballistic – and rightly so.

You can also have some big falls in enduro riding. In some ways it's a bit like the TT because you never really know what's around the next corner. When I look back at some of the scrapes I've had on an enduro bike I think I must have been crazy to ever have got involved. There was one time when my goggles had either got misted up or were full of shit. The rest had gone ahead onto a country lane near Coniston Lake, but I couldn't stand not being able to see properly any longer, so I stopped, thinking I would soon be able to catch them up. I fired the bike back up, set off and approached a bend thinking it would be fine to take it in fourth gear, shut the throttle off and just roll round. But it tightened into a right-hand turn and there was suddenly no way I was going to get round. I banged down the gears and the back wheel locked up, producing a big skid mark which I dragged everyone back to have a look at. Somehow I managed to stay upright despite climbing onto the grass verge, still scrubbing off speed, and hitting the dry stone wall. That situation might have been dangerous enough in itself for someone unused to handling bikes, but that wasn't half the problem. If a car had been coming the other way I would not have stood a chance. The driver would not have had enough time to see me as I skidded from one side of the road to the other. It was another case of me thinking to myself, *What the hell are you doing here?*

Most enduro crashes are just silly ones, though. You could be going up a hill, the wheel starts spinning and you can't get your feet back on the ground. There is only one outcome when this happens: you'll come clattering down in a heap. Or you could be going happily along through a field until *bang!* you suddenly hit a bog and get thrown right over the top of the bars.

Everyone thinks my last crash was at Phillip Island, but I've had a few tumbles since then – in motocross, enduro and supermoto riding. I've had a lot of fun recently riding the supermoto bikes at the Three Sisters track not far from my home. While my injuries prevent me from racing a superbike, I'm still able to ride one of these smaller machines. I've only been riding them for a few months though, so I still don't know what their limit is. There is a lot of feeling in the rear, but because the front is so high up I kept feeling the front tuck in on one occasion. I had a full wet tyre on at the front and just blamed it on that at first, but what made it worse was the fact that the British supermoto champion, Warren Steele, was also riding there that day. So, of course, it was game on.

It was a bit silly because I felt like I was racing again and had a point to prove. From having fun one minute, I suddenly became deadly serious the next and wanted to see if I could keep up with Warren. When we were both out on the track it turned out that I was two seconds a lap quicker; I caught him up without any problems and then pulled away by about two or three seconds. I was getting into a rhythm and really enjoying myself, although I could still feel the front chattering away. The next thing I knew I had run just a little bit wide, the front had tucked under and I was lying in the grass and gravel.

I was really annoyed with myself, but not half as annoyed as Michaela was with me. She rode up to me on a little 125cc road-bike she was riding in order to get used to bikes before going onto the roads. She had seen me going past really quickly and had heard all the comments about how fast I had been going.

'I don't need all this shit any more!' she shouted.

'I wasn't going too fast,' I pretended.

'I was watching you. You were riding like an idiot. I'm not nursing you if you get an injury like you did last time.'

'Oh, don't worry about me, I can look after myself.'

'I could see what was happening. It was just because the British supermoto guy was here and you wanted to race him. You were getting too serious. It's not on, Carl!'

She was furious with me – but I never listen!

RACING
TECHNIQUES

9: Celebrations

I've never been one for big showy celebrations after my victories. If I had been the type, I would have wanted to come up with a new one every time, and that would not have been easy with 59 World Superbike race wins! For me, it was always just a raw show of emotion, especially after I had clinched a world title. I saved all my tricks for race time and would rather just punch the

air or bang the tank. I was so excited at having won a race and usually so exhausted that I really couldn't be bothered to go through the motions of all the celebratory tricks. I just wanted to get back to the garage and share the moment with Michaela and the team. But the crowds love to see a different side to a rider's skills when the races are over, so I would pull the occasional wheelie for them, or

An average wheelie from an average rider after a World Superbike win in 1999!

stand on the pegs without using my hands. After my win in Hockenheim in 1997 I did a stand-up wheelie down the back straight and a lot of people commented that they had never seen me do anything like that before.

It was a bit different in England, because then I felt I had more of a duty to let the fans join in with my success. I would always try to find an English flag and ride round the track as slowly as possible, while the guys who had finished behind me were doing their burnouts and stoppies. To me, a punch in the air or a show of my 'number one' finger said so much more than a trick or two. When I hadn't won the race, I didn't feel I should be doing anything to celebrate. I felt the crowd would be thinking, *What's he doing a burnout for? He didn't even win anything.* Nobody probably actually felt like that, but that was just my way of looking at it.

I suppose one of the first times I ever played up to the crowds was during my Formula One TT days at Vila Real in Portugal in 1990. I was so far ahead of the rest of the riders that every time I came down the start–finish straight I pulled a hundred-yard wheelie in front of the grandstand. The crowd went crazy at that, but my dad didn't like all that kind of stuff. 'You shouldn't bother with tricks like that until you've actually won the race,' he would say. 'You never know what can go wrong.'

FOGGY FACTOR

'A punch of the air or a show of my 'number one' finger says so much more than a trick or two.'

Even after I had won the race and the crowd had invaded the pit area, I came up the back straight, which was slightly uphill so it made a wheelie that bit easier, and did another one. I could see my dad waving at me, shouting, 'Put it down, put it down! You might flip it over and crash!'

Pulling a wheelie is not too difficult on a superbike because they've got so much power. I'm crap at doing wheelies on any other kind of bike. All my mates who I go enduro riding with are great at doing wheelies on their bikes, but I'm just not used to riding bikes with that little power. In a superbike race, the whole idea is to keep the front wheel down on the track. If you come out of first-gear corners like you would out of a chicane, such as

Goddards or Melbourne Loop at Donington, then it's all too easy to pull a wheelie during the race, but if you want to do a deliberate one, all you have to do is relax, sit back a bit, open the throttle, gently pull the bike back and slowly change up a couple of gears so the revs are kept quite high.

But I have seen them go badly wrong. I remember James Haydon, now riding in the British Superbike Championship, flipping a 500cc at the Spanish Grand Prix in 1995. I was there talking to Kenny Roberts about a possible ride in GPs for the following year. Luckily, the bike didn't land on James and he was okay, but it caught fire and was burnt to a cinder. James Toseland, Neil Hodgson's team-mate in 2001 with the GSE Racing team in World Superbikes, also flipped a 600cc at Brands Hatch in his first year of racing. He had just come on the scene and had been given a contract by Honda. Having done well in the race, he was brought down to earth by landing on his arse. I also remember Roger Marshall doing the same thing at Cadwell Park.

There have been a couple of times I have had my heart in my mouth when I have just approached the point of no return. One of those occasions was at Aintree when I was just starting out in my career and didn't know any better, and the other time was on the RC45, messing around at Cadwell. I had it almost completely vertical, and I remember thinking, *Perhaps this is going a bit too far!* I also remember seeing Max Biaggi, the Italian 500cc star, do the biggest one of all time. He had just won a race in Czechoslovakia and had it right at the limit for what seemed like ages. You could tell he was not in full control, but eventually, and after a lot of wobbling, the bike came down the right way. He was so lucky. Nobody will ever get any closer to flipping the bike over than he did on that day. You don't see that happening too often though, because these people have a lot of talent and tend to be able to control the bike without too many problems.

A burnout is also pretty easy to pull off. You stop the bike, put it into gear and put two fingers on the front brake before letting the clutch out and giving it plenty of revs. All the weight goes onto the front of the bike which sets the back wheel spinning away. Some people take this one step further with a 'doughnut'. This is when the rider keeps one foot on the floor, acting as a pivot, and he pulls the bike round in a circle while he is doing the burnout. Troy Bayliss is quite good at this. I have never tried to do a doughnut, so I don't know how easy or difficult it is. I think the best way to learn would be by doing it on a supermotard bike, but about the best I can do is to let go of the front brake a little bit and move slightly forward while doing a burnout. Some riders can actually do it with their feet up off the floor on a motocross or enduro bike, but how they do this I have no idea, although it is a lot more practical on that type of bike than on a superbike.

The most famous burnout I have ever done was when I beat Frankie Chili at Assen in 1998. He felt I had caused him to fall with a couple of corners to go, but it was all his fault, and he probably admitted that later. After the race, though, he came storming over towards me while I was celebrating, so I did a burnout in his face, and in front of the TV cameras, before taking my hand off the clutch to give him the finger.

The other favourite celebration is a stoppie, which is basically just slamming the front brake on. Jamie Whitham is really good at these and will do them at every opportunity, even if he has just

Having smoked Aaron Slight for so many years in races, I do it again at the Honda press day at Cadwell Park in 1996.

finished a practice session. I could never really be bothered with them, but I did try one during 1996 when I was riding the Honda and we were messing around at Cadwell. Somebody said, 'Let's do some stoppies' but I just thought, *Here we go, somebody call for an ambulance.* I have been practising them recently on my supermotard, although I'm a little bit wary of going over the top and landing on my arm, so I tend to get it up and then it goes straight back down again. I'm getting too old now to be bothered with all that kind of thing. But the aim is to sit the back end up and balance for as long as possible by closing the throttle off and pulling the clutch in. If you come in too fast you can let go of the brakes a little bit and run on a touch on the front tyre. Otherwise, if you keep the brakes on, there's a chance you will go right over the top.

Most of the riders can do some trick or another, but you tend to find that the more experienced riders do them less and less. Troy Corser is pretty good at tricks, particularly standing up on the pegs, taking one foot off and putting it over the other side round the back. That's pretty cool. Stephane Chambon is probably the best, though. And he loves to do them. Even on a slowing-down lap you expect him to put his bike sideways into a corner, sliding it speedway style to leave a big tyre mark. It's probably no coincidence that he comes from a supermoto type of background, where riders fool around on their bikes a lot more. With a superbike you should have a little bit more respect though. They can be dangerous machines, so the riders do tend not to mess about with them as much.

I suppose the most famous picture of me celebrating is when I pulled a wheelie after my 40th race win at Donington, when I also took one hand off the bars. Another famous photo was taken at Assen in 1995 after some of the crowd had invaded the track, as usual. While it creates a bit of atmosphere, it is never all that advisable at a race meeting because, obviously, there is more chance of someone getting injured than at a football match, for instance. This year a bloke carrying a flag came up to my bike, so I gestured to him to tie the flag round my neck. He thought I meant climb on the back of the bike, so on he jumped. He stayed on all the way round to the pits. Nobody knew who he was, but he was congratulated

More wheelie fun, this time after my win at Misano in 1999.

like he was one of the team when I reached the garage. Officials being what they are, I got my knuckles rapped for that. Apparently, I wasn't properly insured for passengers.

The other obvious way to celebrate a race victory is to go out and have a few beers, especially on a Sunday night. If I'd not come first, the last thing I wanted to do was go and celebrate with the winner or a load of people who had nothing really to celebrate. I guess it's one of the things I enjoy more now that I'm retired. And I'm still involved with the riders because of my work with Ruben Xaus.

After the 2001 race at Monza the roles were reversed and it was Ruben who had to help us out. Jamie Whitham's band, the Po Boys, was playing at a club called the Rolling Stone in the centre of Milan. Ruben is one of the riders who certainly does like to go out and let his hair down on a Sunday night. He's quite popular with the girls and always seems to end up drinking disgusting cocktails. A few of the other riders were there too. Colin Edwards was a little bit subdued because he had been beaten by Troy Bayliss in both races, and Mick Doohan was also out.

We moved on from there to another club called Hollywood,

and Ruben was mucking about, overtaking us in his new car. So at the traffic lights I gently ran into the back of him. He was going mental in the front seat, waving his finger and trying to make out that he didn't find it funny. Anyway, we parked up in one of the main squares and spent about an hour in this place, where they have one-way mirrors in the ladies' bogs so that they can see everything that is happening in the gents. When we found out about this, me and a few mates went in and pulled a moony at them.

After about an hour, at around 4am, we left the club and returned to our hire car, only to find it being loaded onto the back of a police truck. Apparently I had left the front poking out over some tramlines and had brought the city's tram system to a halt all the time we were in there! Of course I didn't have my passport or driving licence with me, so the cops were ready to tow it away. Then, out staggered Ruben and started talking to the cops in Italian, one of the five languages he can speak. It could have gone either way, but he persuaded the cops to let me off with a fine – which was paid by one of the girls he was with – and give me the car back. The only problem now was how to get back to Monza!

Section 3

PREPARATION

'I had no idea how much Carl would change when he actually finished racing. I thought that was what he was like, because I've only ever known him as a racer. But now he has retired he is a totally different Carl Fogarty. It's perhaps the one that has been trying to get out all these years.

'Even if he had done well in the previous race, he would be exactly the same in the build-up to the next, although we might have had an easier week in the meantime. If he'd had a bad weekend, he could not wait to race again and put it right. He could not relax and would try to talk to me about it. And I was probably the only person that he could talk to. Carl could not concentrate on menial tasks like cutting the grass or buying dog food, because all he wanted to do was concentrate on the racing. Even if he had won the championship during the summer, he might only relax for a month or two before starting to think about January's testing.

'It was best not to talk to him on a race day; and he would never sleep on a Saturday night. He would toss and turn all night and was then totally focused in the morning. You didn't speak unless you were spoken to. I used to try and treat him how I would on any day — not to bug him or pick a fight, and maybe keep out of his way. If he did snap at me, which he sometimes did, I would snap back, because that is just me being me. I had to just get on with it and wait for Sunday night to arrive. Then, on Sunday night after the race, win or lose, he would still not sleep! It took me a long time to understand it and just let him get on with it. It used to drive me mad and it took me ages to realise that it wasn't personal. From my point of view Sundays were horrendous. So if I had that feeling, I can't think what he used to feel like. But he wasn't a monster — at least not too often!'

Michaela Fogarty

PREPARATION

PHYSICAL PREPARATION

1: Fitness and diet

I am not saying this just to sound clever, and I don't want to set a bad example, but this is one aspect of racing I didn't pay a lot of attention to. In my opinion, all riders know exactly how fit they need to be in order to be in a position to win a race. I never believed my fitness level would affect how fast I could ride a motorcycle. I suppose a high standard of fitness might have allowed me to ride at the same speed for a bit longer, but that was never really an issue over race distance. I might have been knackered after or during a race, but never once did I feel I had lost a race because I wasn't fit enough. My attitude was always to ride through the pain barrier to win a race, so starting to slow up because I was tired did not make sense. Instead, I wanted to finish the race even quicker so that I could have a rest, so I often looked tired after a race while some of the other guys looked fresh. Having said all that, a rider will always do whatever he possibly can to give himself as much of an edge as possible. And I was no different.

But I never trained as hard as some of the other guys. When I look back, I regret that to a small degree. In fact I didn't really know the meaning of the word training until around 1993. To be honest, I did diddly-squat so far as improving my fitness went, which is incredible when you see how committed the 16 and 17-year-old motocross riders of today are. If I had been fitter in those early days, it certainly would not have done me any harm and there's a good chance I would have been a slightly better rider for it.

Though I was never a big beer drinker, we always had a laugh. In fact, I remember a couple of dogs that could drink as much as me at a bar in Blackburn called Oscar's where we used to meet up after races. Gary Dickinson and I used to put a couple of ashtrays on the floor while we were talking to the dogs' owner and kept filling them up with beer. The woman never did figure out why her dogs staggered out of the bar every night. Not all Gary's jokes were that funny, however. I remember him stitching me up before I got married by getting the bird of one of his mates to send me a card with lipstick on the back. Michaela saw it, opened it and went ballistic. I even went over to Gary's to ask him what I should do about it, because she was seriously angry. The bastard didn't own up to it for another five years.

Even when I did start to do a bit more training, around the mid-1990s, I never followed a planned programme. Some days, though, I would start to feel guilty if I hadn't done anything for a while, so I would go for a jog, which I didn't mind doing too much. I have never used gyms regularly, though. I've always found them boring, and I never really knew what I was supposed to be doing with the weights anyway. I was never motivated enough for all that, and besides, I didn't think weights would bring me an advantage anyway. Whenever I got to the gym, I didn't really push myself too hard. I used to work up a bit of sweat, think that was enough to stop me feeling guilty, then head back home.

I knew that 80 per cent of the other riders were into a proper fitness regime. Aaron Slight was always very fit, and the British riders like Jamie Whitham and Neil Hodgson were also in good nick. Neil was almost obsessive about his fitness and diet. That's fine if you can put up with it, and who am I say to that he was stupid for taking it to those lengths if it worked for him? If I had ever felt that I needed to do that much training to be a racer, I probably would never have carried on. 'Going to the gym isn't going to make you able to ride a bike any faster,' I would say to Neil. But he was determined to follow in the footsteps of the likes of Mick Doohan, another rider who was big on fitness, and he enjoyed it. For me to enjoy it, I had to be doing something that interested me, like riding motocross bikes or trail bikes. But it seemed that most of the time the weather wasn't right for that, and when it was I couldn't find anyone to go out with. So, even at my peak around 1997 or 1998, I might only go motocrossing once a week or every two weeks, and if I went on a mountain bike ride one day, I might not do that again for another week or so. Motocrossing was great exercise, really good for building up stamina. My arms were pumped up after two or three laps, it got my lungs working hard and it was also very mentally tiring. Thirty minutes of motocrossing every day and you'd be as fit as a fiddle.

The other factor against a commitment to fitness training was time. When you have a family and a couple of kids, as well as an expanding business to run, it is difficult to fit training in on a regular basis. There were times, though, when I didn't have much of a choice, such as when I was recovering from my knee operation in the winter of 1997 and through into 1998. My physio, Mike Pettigrew, wanted me to do as much mountain bike riding with him as possible to help build the knee back up – the cruciate ligament had been repaired, which is a fairly major operation. I quite enjoyed that because we would go off the roads, ride around the picturesque Gisburn Forest and do about 14 or 15 miles in around 50 minutes. But by the end of 1997, I had also lost a bit of interest in that.

Once the season had started, I didn't see the need to do much exercise between races. I would arrive home on the Monday or Tuesday and would only have a week or so there before setting off the following Wednesday or Thursday. So my attitude was to save all my energy for the next race meeting, rather than use it all up during the short time I was at home.

What I did do all the time, though, was eat the right foods. For me, this was psychologically rewarding as much as anything else; I was convinced I was staying fit, even in the absence of regular physical exercise. During a race meeting I would eat pasta and bananas and drink sports drinks until I was sick of them. On race mornings I always ate two or three bananas just to convince myself that I had prepared properly. If I couldn't get them, I'd start to panic and think, *I haven't had enough bananas. There's no way I'm going to win today!* That was just the way I was on race day.

Mick Doohan was one of fittest guys ever to have raced, all part of his overall preparation.

I have never been a big one for breakfast in any case. Even at home, I usually wait for an hour after my first cup of tea before I eat anything. Chris Herring, the Honda press officer who used to be the superbikes reporter for *Motor Cycle News*, knew that I always liked to have a simple breakfast before a race – maybe two cups of tea followed by a few bananas later on – and that I hated it when people near me ate stuff I couldn't stomach. He was always winding me up about it. At Suzuka in 1996 he spotted me eating alone at the breakfast table before the race, came over and put a glass of orange juice down, asking if he could join me. He then came back with a plate full of cooked eels and other Japanese crap. 'You're not eating that shit here!' I shouted, putting everyone else in the room off their brekkie.

In all honesty, whatever I had for breakfast or lunch was never going to have any effect on whether or not I won the race. I could just as easily have had steak pudding, chips, peas and gravy and still have been able to win races. In fact, at Donington in 1995 I did just that. I was probably showing off a little bit that lunchtime because at the time I was supremely confident, having just won my first world title, and I was feeling really good on the bike (either that or I was sick of eating pasta in the Ducati hospitality tent). But I often wanted to do things differently to everyone else, just to prove that I was winning races through ability and not anything else like diet. I would always make sure I took a lot of fluid, though – especially at the hotter circuits, because you sweat a lot during a 25-lap race – even though that meant I was pissing constantly for the rest of the afternoon until race two.

For lunch I would usually have some pasta with a light tomato sauce and perhaps a piece of chicken to nibble on or a bit of chocolate for energy. Then, after running on low for race one, I felt refuelled and ready to go back out there to ride another 100 miles. For some reason, I would always feel a lot better for race two. It might have been that I was more nervous for the first race of the day – after all, if you mess up in that one, the pressure is on for the second race. For a long time I was convinced that my record, at least in recent years, would show that I did better in the second races, but it actually works out the other way round. What you will find, though, is that my lap times were generally consistently faster in those second races. That's something I struggle to explain.

After the second race I was always starving. I couldn't wait to get away from the circuit and eat a load of junk food. Having eaten pasta and healthy food all weekend, I wanted steak or burgers and chips. Still, at those times, despite the intense feelings of hunger, I tended to fill up a lot more quickly than normal. Maybe, with all the tension of race day, your stomach shrinks a little bit. My eyes were definitely always too big for my belly after race meetings, and that appetite carried on for a couple of days. On the Monday morning I would always want a full breakfast: bacon, sausage, eggs, mushrooms, beans {but no eels}. But soon I would be back into the routine of being careful about what I was eating.

Some riders go to extremes. A friend of mine played golf with Ben Bostrom on the Thursday before his first race as a factory World Superbikes rider, in South Africa in 2001. Ben would stop every few holes to mix isotonic drinks in the shade and once held up the game for about 20 minutes when one of the caddies had to go and fetch a few sandwiches to keep his carbohydrate levels up. Then, having played in hot conditions for four hours, he was straight back to his car to dig out the skipping ropes for a quick session in the golf club car park. Back at the hotel, he ordered the biggest fillet steak on the menu, as part of his high protein regime. I don't have a problem with all that so long as the riders in question believe it will help them perform better, but Ben's performances improved when he moved away from the factory team and started to relax a bit more and let his hair down. All I did when I arrived in South Africa was nip up to the Kyalami circuit on the afternoon we arrived after an overnight flight from Heathrow and run once round the track with a mate, to get the tiredness out of my system.

Ruben Xaus is another who has a very intense fitness regime. He uses little heart monitors to track his performance while he's out running or cross-country skiing. Those are the kinds of activities, like trail biking across a desert, which appealed to me more because they are also a bit of fun. And it obviously works for Ruben because he's very well built and has very good upper body strength. It's just not something I chose to do, and certainly not something the older riders did. I remember speaking to Barry Sheene about training. 'I've never done a day's training in my life,' he said. From the mid-eighties onwards, though, the 500cc bikes became very fast and very hard to ride, and you had to be a lot fitter to cope with one of those brutal things. I rarely rode one, so it's difficult for me to compare; when I did ride in the 500cc GPs I could never get the bike to do what I wanted it to do, so it's difficult to gauge how much extra I had been fighting it. But if I had been riding regularly, I would probably have found it very hard work and had to bow to the inevitable: a training schedule. And then I would have gone out and done whatever was necessary.

There are other riders in present-day racing who share my attitude. Until the year after I retired, Troy Corser didn't seem to do any training. Then, all of a sudden, he turned up for the first round of the 2001 season at Valencia having lost a load of weight, which raised a few eyebrows, although he was still not as fit as a Hodgson, Xaus or Bostrom. After every race he won at the start of that year he thanked his new personal fitness trainer. The bottom line is, though, that he wasn't thanking him when he retired in the second race at Monza later the same year because his bike was vibrating. If that had been me, I would have carried on and risked the bike exploding in the hope that I could ride round the problem and grab a few extra points. I repeat: fitness is all well and good, but it does not win you races. Colin Edwards was another one who didn't pay much attention to exercise. In fact, he said that he had trained hard for the 1999 championship but that I had 'whupped his arse'. So then his attitude was, 'Why should I bother training if it obviously doesn't get results?' Sure enough, he went out the very next year and won the championship. The Japanese rider Noriyuki Haga lost that championship at least partly as a result of worrying too about his weight. He tested positive for the drug ephedrine, an ingredient of a drink he was taking to help him shed a few pounds. If he had stayed at his old weight, he would not have been docked those points and would still have been able to win races, as he had proved in previous years. But every rider has to make up his own mind how fit he has to be in order to be in a position to get what he wants out of racing – either to win or to enjoy the sport. Maybe I was just lucky enough to be naturally fit, or aggressive enough to make it not that relevant a factor.

There are lots of other new approaches as well. I know that Leon Haslam, who did well when he started Grand Prix racing at the age of 17, has had a gym built on his dad's farm. He's stretched a rope ladder across the roof which he uses to strengthen his forearms. He also practises balancing on one foot, lengthways along a bar with weights on the edge. And he uses a punchbag, not so much for fitness as to help him learn how to control his breathing so that when he is faced with a hairy moment at the first corner he doesn't tense up and make the problem worse. To me, that's all bullshit, but again, if it works for him, that's fine. I guess I'm just from the old school where you get on the bike, open the throttle, go fast, brake later than the next guy, go fast round the corner and win the race. It's simple, and it's all in your own head. Why complicate it?

Even so, now I'm not racing I feel a bit guilty whenever I've sat around for a few days without having done anything. I actually have a little gym in one of the rooms of the house, so I might go for a run on the running machine. The only reason I bought it was to try to motivate myself to do some exercise more often, although I'm one of those people who doesn't ever seem to put on weight. But machines bore me. I would much rather go up to the

Lake District trail biking or test the strength of my injured arm by motocrossing in the back field. It does jolt the arm a lot, but I also think it does some good.

I suppose the few occasions when I have concentrated more than usual on my fitness have been when recovering after an injury. When I was starting out on my career and I suffered a couple of nasty leg breaks, the motivation was there to get back out there and start my career again as soon as possible. But I have to admit that I found it very difficult to force myself to go through the pain barrier after the arm injury that finally ended my career. Having said that, I did put myself through a lot of hard work once the arm was strong enough to take the strain of physiotherapy. Just little things like tying a red rubber band to a door handle and trying to pull it horizontal with my good arm was a real chore. It is always so much harder to regain fitness once it has been lost, rather than just keep it at the same level. And when the specialist has already told you that you are aiming for only 75 per cent of your previous fitness, it is doubly difficult.

When I was recovering from my leg fractures, I didn't do half as much work to try to get myself back in shape. It was more a case of just waiting for my leg to heal up and then getting back out on the track. In those days, I didn't really receive any advice as to the best way to go about things. Even my dad didn't really know what to do for the best, so I just ended up going for a bit of physio once a week. Don't forget that this was a time when I wasn't doing any training – which I hated at that time – and probably going out quite a lot. In fact, I have been told that the fact I was drinking beer – smuggled into the hospital for me when I was recovering from my broken femur – might have been the reason why the tibia got infected where the pins were inserted. It was that infection which weakened the bone and caused the second bad break the following year. I often wonder whether I would have more movement in my leg today had things been as professional then as they are now, when the best doctors would have been on my case with regular checks on my progress throughout the winter.

One problem riders suffer from, apart from the obvious brakes and crash injuries, is something called 'muscle pump' in the forearms. When you are gripping the handlebars so tightly for so long, the muscles get so full of blood from the exertion that they feel as if they're fit to burst. I was lucky in that I did not suffer from it too much, unless I was riding a motocross bike. After a couple of laps of motocross, I'm struggling to hold on and my forearms are like Popeye's, absolutely solid. It looks quite good actually. But other riders have had a lot of problems. Neil Hodgson had to have an operation, basically to create a bit more space into which the blood could flow. One trick to lessen the problem a touch is to relax your grip when you're going down a straight, because obviously you don't need to be changing the direction of the bike and it gives your arms a quick breather.

I did, though, have problems with my forearms – shooting pains and pins and needles in the fleshy part of the arm just below the elbow. And they occurred at Assen more than anywhere else. If you spin a wheel on a spindle and then try to turn it, it is more difficult to do when the wheel is spinning quickly. So, because Assen is such a fast track with a lot of turns, there is a lot of work to be done by the arms in order to pull the bike around the track. Strangely enough, when I rode

> **FOGGY FACTOR**
>
> 'On race mornings I would always have two or three bananas, just to convince myself that I had prepared properly.'

the Honda there in 1996 and the Ducati the following year, the pain cropped up a lot further down and was more tender than shooting. The doctors treated me with mesotherapy – a series of injections which seemed only to numb the pain. Once the injections had worn off by the Monday morning I could hardly carry the suitcases to the airport. After that I never experienced these problems again, so perhaps it was just the fact that both bikes were difficult to ride. For me, it was proof of the fact that your physical condition is affected when the bike is not set up just right.

The funny thing is that during the year in which these problems were at their worst, 1996, I probably trained harder than I have done at any other time. And I'm not the only rider to say that the more he trained, the more painful his arms were. Colin Edwards experienced exactly the same thing, as did

Rob McElnea, another fitness fanatic who had to have operations to relieve pressure in that area. It may sound daft, and people may laugh at it, but this connection between pain and training is a fact as far as I'm concerned. It cannot be a coincidence.

Another way of relieving the aches and pains is to have regular massage. Again, this was something I only really got into later on in my career – probably because that was when the aches and pains of a hard career were beginning to take their toll. One of the problem areas for me was around the breaks in my legs, where the scar tissue would stick to the muscle; the masseurs would dig their fingers in there to try to separate them. Boy, did that hurt. But I would also go for a massage on a Friday or Saturday, even if I was just feeling a bit tired. I wouldn't always do it, it just depended on how I felt. Again, it was probably more of a psychological thing than anything else. It also depended on which track I was at and whether I needed to kill half an hour. One thing was for sure, though: the place was always full of Italian riders, who wanted treatment even if all they'd done was broken a toenail. On the other hand, I felt guilty if I went in there with a broken wrist, and would always ignore stuff like colds or the flu, but I guess that's just a British thing, to suffer in silence. It is probably a lot more sensible to take all the right precautions.

In any case, illness never seemed to affect me during race meetings. Just about the only time I was ever ill at a race meeting was at Laguna Seca in 1997. Monterrey, where the track is, is an area of California famous for its seafood, so maybe I had eaten something dodgy. It all kicked off on the Saturday morning; I was shitting out of one end and spewing out of the other. I spent the rest of the weekend on glucose drips just to try and give myself a bit of energy. During the race I was even sick in my helmet, which wasn't pleasant. Yet I achieved the two best results I have ever had there, with two second places. I was so exhausted, though, that I couldn't even walk up onto the podium or attend the press conferences. I just wanted to go and lie down in a dark room.

The other times I was ill were nearly always during testing – maybe your body knows that you've got a job to do during the race season. But then, at the end of a season, I nearly always had trouble with my sinuses, and I often had a bit of a cold for nearly the whole of the winter. It's probably because, when you finish racing, you let all your defences down and leave yourself open to infections.

I remember one testing session in Australia, the year before I retired, when I felt as rough as a dog for the whole of the test. Maybe it was a stomach bug, maybe I had eaten something on the plane, but I had been constipated for a few days, right up until the final press conference during which I couldn't stop farting. I nearly killed Colin Edwards, who was sat next to me! At another test, my first after returning to Ducati in 1997, I felt terrible. Virginio Ferrari, the team manager at the time, said it was because I had eaten too much hot pasta on a freezing cold day. 'It's the cold air hitting your body,' he said. 'I don't care what it is,' I replied. 'I feel like shit and I want to go home!' I replied. The difference with being ill during testing is that you can park the bike up and go and lie down, because in that condition you're not doing either the team or yourself any good at all.

If I did have something seriously wrong, though, like a cracked rib or a broken bone in my hand, just like I had after that big high-side at Sugo, I would always want whatever injections or tablets were going to try to take the pain away. Maybe I took a bit too much that time in Japan, because towards the end of the second race I was starting to feel really drowsy. Then again, during a race pain can be very distracting and can cause you to lose concentration. In my last couple of years of racing I began to suffer a lot from cramp. People would wonder what I was doing, sticking my leg out while going up the straight in the middle of a race.

Another thing I tried in order to cure my back problems, which were in many ways similar to those caused by a slipped disc, was acupuncture. It seemed to work, but I don't think anyone really understood what the problem was until I had some scans in 1999. They were usually done back in Blackburn though, because the back pain was never really an issue when I was riding the bike; things only started to hurt when I was doing other things to keep fit, like playing tennis or football, where I was twisting and turning.

Track 5
Laguna Seca

This is my least favourite track in the whole world. Maybe that has something to do with the fact that I have never won here. The place itself is fine. We stay in Monterey, which is a nice, quiet, touristy sort of fishing village. And there is the added advantage that I can walk down the street there without being bothered. Then again, that's the same pretty much anywhere in the States – even the American riders are very rarely recognized in their own country. Someone like Kenny Roberts Jr wouldn't be hassled there, because World Superbikes probably has a bigger following than the 500cc.

The circuit is unusual in that, like Misano, it's one of the few anti-clockwise tracks, and the start–finish straight isn't really a straight but more of a long, sweeping, uphill left turn. In fact there's not a proper straight on the whole circuit, and there always seems to be a slight curve to the straightest sections.

As you go over the rise, it's then downhill into turn one in fifth gear – although I never used to call it turn one because to me it wasn't really a corner but still part of the start–finish straight. Just after that there are some rubber poles on the inside, which separate the track from the pit-lane exit. The idea is to get as close as possible to them without hitting them, although one year I gave them a right smack with my hand, which is not advisable. It stings like hell.

Then it's hard on the brakes into what is, in my view, the real turn one, in second gear. It's in between first and second, but I always found first too low. Being in second gear and downhill makes it a difficult corner. It comes back on itself and second gear is tall, so there aren't enough revs to hold you into the corner and you feel like you could lose the front. It was never a corner I liked, or was very strong at. In the middle part, I pick the bike up a little bit, get on the gas for a moment, then lean it back over again into the tightest part before getting on the gas right over the inside of the kerb. Again, because I was in second gear, I was a bit sluggish coming out of that part of the turn. Then you have to run wide over to the other side of the track, over the kerb and a bit into the dust. Then it's hard on the accelerator towards what I call turn two, leaving the bike in second gear.

Just as you touch the limiter, it's on the brakes for one of the track's typically flat corners, where I really struggled. I felt I had to physically turn the bars to lean the bike over, because the bike wasn't able to use the camber to almost fall into the corner. I've lost the front end there once or twice, and I know that I'm not alone. Out of that corner it's hard on the gas in third gear for the next right-hander, which some people take in second. It's a fast corner and it opens up as you turn into a kind of straight. Although third gear is tall coming into the corner, once you're on the gas, third gear is buzzing.

I try to keep it in fourth up the slightly uphill straight, although I used to touch the limiter again. When I pass under a bridge, it's quickly down two gears to second, although again, second is a bit low around this left-hander. It just shows how difficult it is to get the correct gearing for this track. The surface is slightly ripply on entering the corner, but it shouldn't pose too many problems. The revs are quite high exiting that corner in second. I try to leave the bike in third gear up the next section before dropping down into a dip, which is also the fifth turn. The track is so up and down it reminds me of Brands Hatch. This is another corner I don't particularly like, but I try to stay in third through the dip before getting back on the gas for the 'back straight'. You actually have to change from one side to another trying to straight-line that section. I stay in fourth gear before reaching the famous Corkscrew, and drop quickly down into second gear.

A lot of people would again drop down into first, but I find that upsets the bike going into the steeply downhill chicane. The only problem with staying in second is that you can't

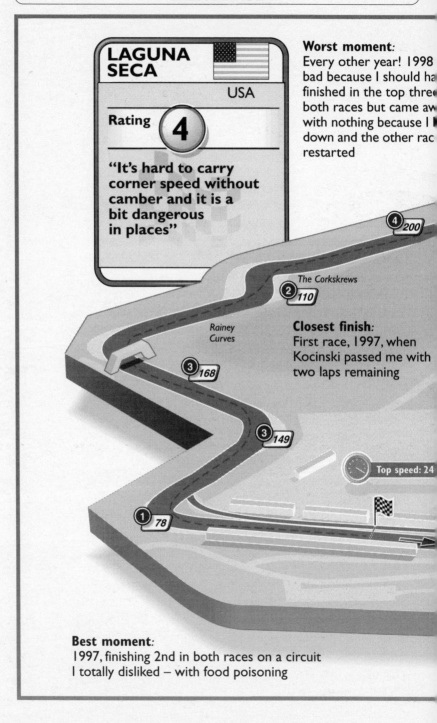

LAGUNA SECA

USA

Rating 4

"It's hard to carry corner speed without camber and it is a bit dangerous in places"

Worst moment:
Every other year! 1998
bad because I should ha
finished in the top three
both races but came aw
with nothing because I
down and the other rac
restarted

④ 200

The Corkskrews
② 110

Rainey Curves

③ 168

Closest finish:
First race, 1997, when
Kocinski passed me with
two laps remaining

③ 149

Top speed: 24

① 78

Best moment:
1997, finishing 2nd in both races on a circuit
I totally disliked – with food poisoning

Worst crash:
When the bike seized up on me
in 1997 during winter testing.
The back wheel locked and
threw me over the top. I was
lucky to escape with concussion

Best other rider:
John Kocinski. He has
won Grand Prix races
as well as Superbike
races here, although
I was close to beating
him in 1997

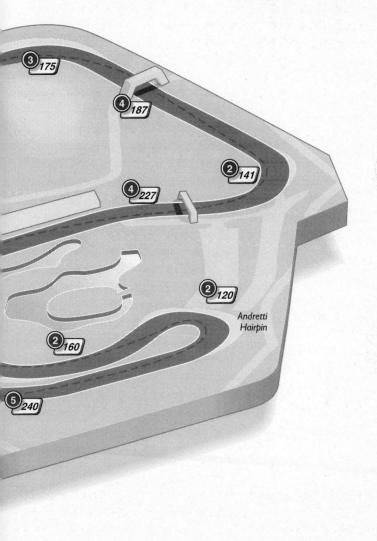

Andretti
Hairpin

brake quite as late because you don't have the engine braking. It's physically very difficult to change direction through this section. As soon as you go in on the left you drop down sharply and you have to change direction immediately, so you tend to pick the front wheel up, making the bike a bit light. Then you flick it over and get on the gas while being careful not to be too aggressive on the power because it's easy for the bike to spit you off.

In the first race of 1998, I had made my way through to fourth place after a bad start when the two Kawasaki riders in front, Akira Yanagawa and Doug Chandler, whose handlebar had broken, had a big crash. As I approached the Corkscrew it was like a scene from *Days of Thunder* – there was just a big cloud of dust. I had to guess where the corner was, and although the bike snaked around a little bit I came through it and found myself in daylight once again – and in second place!

I'm in second when I exit the Corkscrew; it's pretty much all down-hill from there. The bike compresses down while I'm getting hard on the gas and moving up to third gear before the next downhill left-hand corner. I've never been a fan of downhill corners, maybe because I ride quite hard on the front, and as soon as I get into the corner in third gear I get on the gas slightly in order to transfer some of the weight to the back. There is a bump on the exit to that corner, my turn eight, which occasionally upsets the bike.

Then it's down to the penultimate 'bomb-hole' corner, which is similar to the one before, although this one is on the right-hand side. I take it in third, get on the gas and accelerate through the turn up to the last corner, which has probably been my best part of the track over the years, where I can get past other riders. It's where all the action tends to happen, a

FOGGY FACTOR

'A lot of people would drop down into first for the Corkscrew, which upsets the bike going into the steeply down-hill chicane. The only problem with staying in second is that you can't brake quite as late, because you don't have the engine braking.'

typically tight, slow, first-gear corner. As you exit, the aim is to stay on the track because it suddenly narrows as you get on the gas. You can very easily go over the rumble strips and into a bit of gravel. The only thing you have to concentrate on then is keeping the front wheel down as you accelerate hard through start–finish in fifth gear, remembering this time to avoid those little rubber bastards at the side of the track!

In 1996, Honda organized a party for their fans at a hotel near Monterey. I know this is part and parcel of the job, but there were times when you just couldn't be bothered, especially when I hadn't had a great day. So, to have a bit of fun, I made Chris Herring, the Honda press officer, help me stitch the Yanks up. I must have spent about half an hour posing for hundreds of pictures, all taken by Chris with the fans' cameras. The only problem was that he deliberately cut their heads off in all the pictures. They must have been gutted when they got the films processed. Mean, I know, but it was just my own small way of getting my own back on America – never a place where I was made to feel very welcome by the home fans.

PREPARATION

PHYSICAL PREPARATION

2: Kit

A motorcycle racer's kit selection is probably more important than in any other sport I can think of. In most other sports it's all about looking the part and feeling comfortable, but because a rider has so little protection if it all goes wrong it's important that he has every item of his kit working on his side. Luckily, the standards of protective clothing have improved dramatically over the years. If I had been wearing a modern set of leathers when I broke my femur early in 1986 instead of the leathers I was wearing, which were so flimsy they were almost like a set of cotton overalls, I don't think the injury would have been half as bad. I would probably still have broken my leg, but the bone would not have jutted through the skin in the way it did.

Having said that, it is also important for it all to look good as well, because this is one of the key areas where sponsors can promote their names. I have just had the one fashion disaster, but it was a big one. In 1992, when I was a privateer and I won my first-ever World Superbike race at Donington, I wore a set of Fieldshear leathers with pink squiggly worms everywhere. I thought they looked pretty cool at the time, and nobody said anything different, but every time the pictures come out now they have everybody in stitches.

Starting at the bottom of the body, a good set of boots is

essential. Recently, I have been sponsored by Dainese, although I was with Alpinestars for a couple of years. (There are a lot of factors to consider, but the bottom line is that a rider will probably use the manufacturer which is going to pay him the most money.) The best boots contain a gel around the ankle which aims to limit damage should you have a fall. They will also have a toeslider on the outside for those who tend to catch their toes on the floor. I was one of those riders, but in my early days in racing there was hardly any protection for the toes. Things started off with just a bit of cardboard stuck on with bits of duct tape, progressing to a bit of plastic attached with Velcro; and now the best makes of boot have titanium toesliders, which are spectacular when they produce sparks. Troy Bayliss had a lot of problems with his toes the year after I retired. He planed the skin off a couple of them in a crash during qualifying at Phillip Island. He hadn't felt comfortable with the titanium toesliders and had taken them out. He soon had them back in, though!

I had a lot of problems in this area. The restriction of movement caused by my leg fractures meant that I could never properly get my feet out of the way, and I was always catching my toes. Even up to the day I retired, I was scraping boots away. The problem was worse at some circuits than at others. When I did find a pair of boots that were comfortable, I didn't want to change them until the bottom of my foot was killing me. I ride with the ball of my foot hard on the end of the footrest, and that style quickly wore through the sole of the boot. When it got to the big-hole stage, I would be in agony and would have to concede defeat and change to a new pair. That would probably happen about every three or four meetings. Obviously, though, the more you start winning races, the more you can dictate your own needs to the manufacturers. I always insisted on the insertion of a piece of metal under the first layer of rubber so that it would take longer to wear through.

That piece of metal perhaps gave me another race meeting out of the same pair of boots, which was great because I hated wearing in new boots. When you see pictures of me, look at the boots I'm wearing; more often than not they'll appear a bit tatty, because I always preferred to stick with a pair I was comfortable with. Not only would a new pair be too hard and rub my feet, I also had to make a new little indentation in the sole so that the footrest end would fit nicely into it, and that made gear changes just that little bit more difficult. In fact, I never wore a new pair of boots for a race unless I had crashed in the morning race and ruined an older pair. Even when I did use new ones, I tended to find that my lap times were slower at the start of that practice session.

You always know what the best leathers are, because they are what the best riders will be wearing. When I started out, a Japanese make called Kushitani were the best. If you had a set of them, you were regarded as cool. Another good Japanese make was Nankai. By the time I was making a mark on the international circuit, all the manufacturers had improved, and from that point on you wanted the best deal possible before wearing a certain make of leathers, even though some were more comfy than others and the finishing of some makes was better than others.

Some riders like their leathers to be tight-fitting, but I liked to be able to move around in them. I first put a set of Dainese leathers on in 1990 when I did that one-off ride in the British Grand Prix. Then they asked if they could sponsor me the following year. I stayed with them for the rest of my career, although in 1992 there was some kind of fall-out with the UK importers of Dainese, so I had to wear Fieldshear – apart from in the World Endurance Championship when, for some reason, it was okay to wear Dainese again. Obviously, I say that Dainese leathers are the best. Others might be as safe and be four inches thick, but they look crap.

Leathers never used to include anything extra for safety, apart from the leather itself. Now you have extra padding in the hip and shoulder areas, a kind of plastic shell around the elbow, and double padding on the forearm. A couple of years before I retired extra foam protecting each rib was also introduced. There is a back protector to slip inside, protecting your spine if you slide after a crash, and a big foam hump just behind your head to reduce the effects of whiplash (it also helps with the aerodynamics). Finally, the knee protector goes all the way down your shin, so pretty well every bony part of the body has been taken care of.

There are even more developments afoot. At the moment, Dainese are testing leathers that will inflate the instant before you hit the ground, a bit like an airbag on the steering wheel of a car. The riders will soon look like a version of Michelin Man before they come off their bikes. There is real hope that this will help prevent serious injuries. Leathers safety will continue to improve, and it should not mean that a set will look too much different – certainly not like a suit of armour.

The old knee sliders I used to wear were made out of wood, with a bit of leather stuck on the top. Some riders still use this style, but I prefer the Dainese sliders which are made out of hardened plastic. It largely depends on the circuit, but you can make a good mess of a knee-slider during a race, so I usually preferred to start with a new pair so I didn't have to lean that little bit further over to touch the ground with a worn pair. Different circuits would wear different parts of the slider away, depending on the type of corners or the camber of the track, so sometimes I would turn them upside down so that they didn't go to waste, even though I was getting thousands for free!

Normally, underneath my leathers I would just wear only my lucky green T-shirt. But occasionally, if it was freezing cold at somewhere like Donington, I would wear another layer because the suits are vented and it's easy for the cold air to get through, especially in the crotch area. This would have to be a last resort for a race though, and would usually only happen during practice.

My gloves always tended to come with the leathers. They too have changed over the years from being a thin leather covering to having a hardened carbon-fibre shell over the knuckles with a lot more padding around the wrist area to help prevent fractures. Again, they still look stylish, but not at the expense of protection. And I always wanted the best feel I could have through my hands. At one point Dainese added little strips along the middle of the fingers, but I felt they were hindering my grip a bit so I asked for them to be taken off.

My attitude to gloves was the same as to my boots: I could not stand putting a new pair on. Unfortunately, it didn't take long for gloves to wear through at the palms. I used to be covered in blisters, and I still get them when I'm riding bikes for fun. Some racers use inner gloves, but I would go to the mobile clinic to get my hands taped up at tracks where blistering was a real problem, especially for 24-hour endurance races. They also had plasters that slotted down over the fingers, but halfway through a race they would get mangled up and were of no benefit at all. During the superbikes season, my hands usually had a week to recover, so I didn't bother too much about blisters and wouldn't change gloves unless they were a mess after a couple of crashes, or too thin where I was gripping onto the bar. I was never really bothered about how my kit looked, as long as everything was as comfortable as possible.

I always wanted to know where everything was, especially on the morning of a race. At Laguna Seca in 1996, the riders and the rest of the team had to share two cramped motorhomes behind the garage; Aaron Slight had a changing area at the back of one trailer and I was in the one being used for office staff. Just before I was due out for the warm-up, I couldn't find one of my gloves. 'Where's my fucking glove?' I shouted to anyone who was listening. 'Who's moved my fucking glove?' I repeated, when everyone ignored my first question. It was only then, of course, that I could see it on the table, under my nose. I tried to sneak out of the cabin with it, hoping nobody had noticed I'd found it, but the team manager, Neil Tuxworth, who was working on his computer, was sniggering away. The only way I could retrieve the situation and save face was to bend over and fart in his face on my way out to the garage. Pleasant, eh?

FOGGY FACTOR

'I would never wear a new pair of boots for a race unless I had crashed in the morning session and ruined an older pair.'

Last, but certainly not least, is the old skid lid – the helmet. In terms of basic appearance these have not changed too much down the years, although there is probably more venting in the modern versions. If you put an air line onto the outside of the vent, you can feel air coming through the other side, so I guess they must work to some extent. I have been Shark's main rider for a long time, and I probably helped put the company on the map. I have always been happy with the people there, as well as their helmet. Whenever a new model came out at the start of the year there would always be a bit of work to do to make sure it fitted well – it might have been too loose in some areas or too flat against the face in others – but these things are very easy to change, by pulling out foam pads or making them a bit fatter. When I'm riding a bike on the roads, I don't like my helmet to be quite as tight as I had it when I was racing.

A lot of photos of me taken in and around the garage, especially just after a race or qualifying session, show a big red mark across my forehead where the helmet has been a bit tight. That didn't really affect me, though. I just think it was because I marked quite easily. It's much better to have it a bit too tight than too loose anyway, because there is nothing worse than a badly fitting helmet that lets the wind in. Normally I would ask someone from Shark to come to one of the tests before the season started with about three or four helmets so that everything was in order for the first race.

I was always responsible for putting on my own tear-offs. That way, if it was done badly, I could blame only myself. It was supposed to be enough to clip the tear-offs on and then tighten them with a couple of little screws at either side of the visor, but that wasn't enough for me. I always put two bits of Sellotape across the top and one on the side. Then I added some duct tape to that to make it thicker so that it was easier to pull off in one go and I wasn't fiddling around with the thing. Nine times out of ten I would have only one on, and I would wait until I was in danger of losing time and concentration as a result of struggling with visibility before pulling it off. However, if I hit a big fly early on in the race, I'd be forced to get rid of it sooner. For most circuits in the middle of the summer, however, flies are not usually a big problem. The one occasion when this did affect me was at Assen in 1997. A massive bluebottle splattered on my visor just when I was trying to pass John Kocinski and, because I had already used my tear-off, I couldn't see a thing. It cost me the race. The reason was embarrassing at the time, so I only told Slick. Many times, though, I'd forget even to tear it off and only realize that the original tear-off was still in place when I started preparations for the next race.

The other thing that has changed is helmet design. Every rider has their own distinctive design and mine is cool – I know that for a fact. I carried my dad's basic design from 1984 to 1992. This was a white helmet, with red flashes and a red rose for Lancashire at the front. For the first race of 1993, at Brands, I had one of these helmets with a crap number 4 on it. I only ever used it for that first race of the year but, of course, that's when all the photographers stock up with their pictures for the year. So, for the rest of the season, even though my proper design was launched at the next round, nearly all the pictures were of me wearing that hideous thing.

Shark had tried to keep the same basic design but with two sharks down the side, and it did not look right. So I went down to a guy called Miles Carter, who is a helmet designer in Stoke but mainly for motocross riders. I told him roughly what I wanted, including keeping the Lancashire rose, but he must not have listened to a word that I said.

So, before the second round in 1993 at Hockenheim, I opened up my new helmet and it was awesome, but nothing like anything that had been seen before for road racing. It had a shark on the back, looking really aggressive and wearing a cool pair of Ray Ban-style shades. Everyone seemed to like it and Shark made a replica that sold well. I used this same design up until 1996, when a new shape of helmet came out. So then Shark wanted a new design, although I was a bit reluctant because I was quite attached to the old one. I was persuaded to go along with them, so it was changed for 1997 and 1998. It was based on the old one but the colours had changed a bit, with the blue changing from the more fluorescent blue to a more normal blue. It had calmed down a bit.

From then on, we were in the cycle of changing the design almost every year, obviously to sell more replicas like football teams do when they change their strip. If I had ever been slightly unhappy with the old design, the one for 1999 made up for it. It was absolutely gorgeous. They could not have done any better, apart from the white bits at the front which were meant to look like teeth but which I was not too sure about. I couldn't wait to race, just so that I could put it on.

Even though I am no longer racing, Shark brought a new design out for the year after I retired. The teeth have been taken off and the shape has changed, even to the point that the visor is clipped on and off rather than using the old system of screws. It is so nice that it even got me thinking that I wanted to race again, if only just to wear the new helmet!

3: Teamwork

Behind every great rider is a great team. While it's obviously down to the guy on the bike once the green light goes, he has no chance if the preparation hasn't been done in the first place. But also behind every great rider, more often than not, is a great woman. And I would say that, over the whole of my career, Michaela has been the most important member of my team.

A successful rider needs the whole package to be right, and while a wife or girlfriend obviously does not have a direct input in terms of the actual racing, their mere presence can be every bit as important – and not just for the obvious reasons! Such relationships take time to develop, though. In the earlier years, it didn't really matter to me whether Michaela was there or not, but towards the end of my career our partnership had developed to the extent where I didn't want her to miss any of the rounds. She was at all the races in 1998 and 1999. Race meetings can be lonely places and you really need your wife to be there at your side, either as someone to celebrate with or as a shoulder to cry on.

It was so important to me to have Michaela around after my bad crash in Australia, and much harder on her than it was on me. My memory of the whole episode is very vague, and remained so for a few months after the crash because of the bang on my head, but I cannot begin to think what it must have been like for Michaela to see my body laid out motionless on the gravel while she was in the garage at the other side of the track. For a few horrible moments she must have thought I was dead, and she was pretty annoyed when the *Sun* newspaper quoted her as saying so because she had asked them not to print her thoughts in case the girls read about them.

It's always worse watching than it is riding. When you're out there you're in control, but in the garage there is no way you can influence anything. I found it difficult when I first started trying to help Ruben Xaus. I had tried to motivate him before the first race of 2001 at Monza and he was going really well, lying in third with a couple of laps remaining. Suddenly he slid off, and I immediately jumped up and kicked over a chair in the garage.

Michaela liked to have quite a hands-on role in and around the garage. At first she got in the way a bit, but when she realized how the rest of the team worked and when not to interfere, there were lots of little jobs she could do that also helped her control her nerves. She became a constant figure on the pitwall, helping out by noting down lap times, and was soon quite famous in her own right. Now she is working as an ambassador for Blackburn bike manufacturers CCM, so it's good that she is now going out and earning some money instead of sponging off me all the time. In fact, she probably earns more than me now!

The other key personnel in any team are the manager, chief mechanic and your team-mate. Managers and team-mates tend to come and go, although Davide Tardozzi has been a big influence on me in the last couple of years because he got me to think a lot more about what I was doing, rather than simply going out and riding the bike. But the one guy who more than anyone else has sacrificed his own career to help me out was my trusted mechanic, Slick.

Before him all my mechanics really did was clean the bike and change the gearing while another guy, Tony Scott in my case in the Formula One TT days, tuned my engines. Maybe I missed out in those early years by not having someone who really wanted to become involved in getting me to the top by suggesting ways of improving things. It was more a case of, if the bike seized up, there were a few lads knocking around who would fix it. Even my dad was not a technical guy – he was another who just got on the bike and rode it. Maybe if I'd come from a different background, working more on bikes from an early age rather than just riding them, it might have made me better at setting the bikes up. But I still think a lot of riders come into the garage and say, 'Alter that and alter this', go out again and say that it has made an improvement when it hasn't really.

Slick is a strong-minded guy who, when he thought he knew what was best for me, would find it difficult to accept being overruled. But he was always there for me. Having said that, he was sometimes his own worst enemy. He didn't enjoy towing the party line and found it difficult to accept team discipline, especially when I moved to Honda in 1996. That resulted in him being replaced by his own mate, Nick Goodison, who had worked with him in the late eighties. He was probably the exact opposite to Slick, a guy who would think things through before acting, whereas Slick would often act on impulse.

Sparks did occasionally fly when Slick was working with the Italians for Ducati. There was one argument between him and an engineer at Monza in 1998 over some brake problems I was having. I had gone out on new brake pads to run them in, and when I came back into the garage the Brembo engineer immediately took them out and cleaned them. Slick went berserk, shouting, 'Don't you ever touch Carl's brake pads after he has run them in! If you have to, you ask me first. You might have responsibility for brakes within the team, but I've got overall responsibility.' As usual he got a bollocking from Davide for losing his temper, but then I went out for the race and had brake problems. I had to run them in again, because after they heat up through the first couple of corners they don't recover and the pads melt onto the discs. Sometimes things were a bit harsh on Slick. He knew he always had to back down in order to defuse a situation so that I could concentrate on my racing, yet he had to take the responsibility if things went wrong, even if it hadn't been his fault.

> **FOGGY FACTOR**
>
> 'I preferred the type of manager who played an active part in the team and always wanted to know what was happening with their riders and bikes.'

If I ever lost my temper with him it was more through frustration at not being able to get the right set-up. There was an incident at Donington in 1998 which typified this. The fuel cap fell off because the mechanics had not put it on properly, and fuel started spilling all over me and burning my bollocks. When I returned to the garage I went mad. Slick stood up and said, 'Sorry Carl, that was my fault.' He knew all along that he'd had nothing to do with it but he also knew it would be easier to calm me down in that way rather than let it all blow up into a big issue. He thought I would get even more wound up if I couldn't bollock someone, and it was never easy to get angry with the Italians. In any case, I would never have known who to bollock, because I never knew who did what within the team. I might find out on the Sunday night what had really happened, and by then the only response would be something like, 'Well, just make sure he doesn't do it again.' Harsh words were only ever uttered in the heat of the moment and didn't really bother anyone all that much.

Another time, at Misano in 1994, one of our mechanics Gary Dickinson and a guy called Luigi left the back axle loose. Seeing as one spoke Blackburnian and the other Bolognese, it wasn't a great surprise that neither understood a word of what the other was saying. They were doing a gear change and each thought the other had done up the pitch bolt on the axle. Neither had, so when I went out on the bike, whenever I stuck the throttle on, the back end shot up. When I braked, it dropped right down. Apparently you could see what was happening from a mile off. Slick asked, 'Which of you two nuggets forgot to do that?' That prompted a Blackburn versus Bologna screaming contest, with Slick in the middle pulling his hair out.

Once, at Donington, Slick asked a guy called Roberto to check if the generator was working okay on the Thursday because, for some reason, as soon as anyone put the tyre warmers on, the fuse was blowing. When that happens, you have to run off the generator. Roberto had gone away for a few hours and didn't say anything when he came back, so Slick assumed that the job had been done. Just before my first practice session, the warmers were put on as usual. Halfway through the session, the tyres were still cold. Slick freaked out and shouted at Roberto to turn the generator on.

'Oh, it is broken,' he said.

'But I told you to fix that yesterday! I'll bloody well have to do it myself, as usual.'

Slick dashed outside, threw himself on his back and dragged himself along under the truck, following the generator lead. Apparently, all it needed was a bit of tape and the thing was working straight away. Yet again, Slick was reported to Virginio Ferrari and was asked to sit down and apologize to Roberto.

Mind you, it wasn't all one-way traffic. If Slick sometimes didn't want to do a job, he would have a few tricks up his sleeve. Someone might hand him a jerry can and point to the truck for him to go and fetch some fuel. Then he might play on his lack of Italian and say, 'I'm sorry, I don't understand what you are trying to say.' Then the mechanic would give up, swear to himself in Italian, and go and get the fuel himself. Slick used to wind them up something chronic at times.

He once convinced a French mechanic that the word for 'spanner' was 'arsehole'.

'This is a 10mm arsehole,' Slick carefully explained. 'Could you please try and find me another one.' So this guy was wandering up and down the pit-lane asking everyone, 'Do you know where I can find an arsehole this big?' They got their own back on him, though. Raymond Roche was teaching him a few words once and convinced Slick that a traditional French greeting was 'Le saucisson dans le cul est tres bon!' Slick was quite pleased with himself when he mastered this sentence. The only problem was that he was going up to all the new French men and women that he met saying, 'It's great to stick a sausage up your bum', while Raymond and his mates fell about with laughter.

Slick was disgusted another year when Davide Tardozzi told him that we had got a new sponsor called Nut Twist. 'What? We're being sponsored by a fucking Cadbury's chocolate bar?' But Davide had been trying to tell him that we had signed up with NatWest!

It wasn't all down to the language barrier or a clash of cultures, though, because Slick and I could also get our wires crossed. There was one time after a practice session at Donington in 1997; everyone was trying to interview me when I was trying to talk to Slick.

I share a joke with my mechanic Slick during 1995, not an unusual occurrence.

It looked as if it was going to rain so we decided we would use the second bike if it was a wet race, because there was no point getting the race bike messed up for no reason. But, as it got closer to the race, it started to dry up. Slick couldn't find me for another chat, so he decided we would stick to the same plan and use the second bike, even if it stayed dry. So I went into the (dry) race thinking I was on my favourite bike, and sure enough, Aaron Slight chased me down. I was not pleased. And I made my feelings known!

Slick and Gary Dickinson also had their moments when they didn't see eye to eye. Once, in the garage, Slick tried to pin Gary against the wall, and I remember feeling like banging their heads together. Slick had had to choose either Gary or Luigi to do a particular job, because it was too much to do on his own. Slick thought Luigi had a bit more confidence with the bike because it was Gary's first year and he had been thrown in at the deep end. He had been working in a dead-end job in Blackburn, I knew he was pretty handy with bikes, so I had asked Ducati if he could come and join the team. It was a great opportunity for him, but obviously there were going to be a few problems.

When Gary found out he had been overlooked by Slick, he said, 'Well, if I can't work on the motorcycle anymore, I'm of no use to anyone.'

'Gary, don't be daft,' Slick replied. 'You're the third mechanic and very important to the team.'

Later in the day, in the middle of practice, Slick was trying to change a wheel as quickly as he could. He shouted over, 'Gary, just come over here and give me a hand!'

'Oh, I can work with the bike now, can I?' came the reply.

'Gary, just fucking well help me change this wheel!'

"It wasn't so very long ago that I wasn't good enough to work on the bike.'

It was at that point that Slick snapped and went for his throat. I also snapped. 'Will someone change that fucking wheel, please!'

Those kinds of flashpoints usually happened before 1995, when the team was a lot smaller and people were working very closely together. There was more chance of friction then than in the bigger teams of today, where everyone knows his precise role and sticks to it. Things also got a lot more serious, a bit more like Formula One, when more sponsorship money came into the sport.

Slick could be his own worst enemy, though; he never really knew where to draw the line. There was the time when he was playing with our little chihuahua at our house. All he was doing was throwing a stick for the dog to chase. He didn't appreciate that the small dog was getting more and more tired, and eventually when it chased the stick one time too many, the cruciate ligament in one of its legs snapped and it needed a major operation at the vets – and a major cheque to pay for it! That wasn't the only time we had to take Arai to the vets. He had this embarrassing habit of trying to shag the back leg of our other dog, a Great Dane called Bridget. One time he got totally carried away and all of its bits and pieces came out. The dog looked as though it was in agony, wheezing away. The incident really freaked Michaela, who was in on her own; she called the vet, wrapped the dog up in a blanket and rushed it to the surgery. Of course, by the time she had arrived, everything was back in its proper place and the vet looked at her as if she was stupid.

So there was never a dull moment, either at home or with the team at race meetings. Some of the best laughs were with Raymond Roche. He always had a trick up his sleeve. Once he brought his golf clubs into the garage. Just as everyone had finished clearing up after the race he smashed an apple with his driver and it went everywhere. Then he aimed a shot with a proper golf ball over the grandstand facing the pits as people were still making their way out. And he also thought he could clear the adjacent car park. Unfortunately, this shot was not a clean strike and the ball clipped the top of the fence and went flying into the car park, ricocheting off a number of cars while the owners dived for cover. Another time, Fabrizio Pirovano brought a massive catapult into the pit-lane and started to fire water balloons 200 metres into a full stand where people were quietly sitting, minding their own business before the second race. Nobody could understand where the missiles were coming from.

Pirovano was a real character, but I didn't really go out of my way to make friends with the other riders. Sometimes, though, I just couldn't help it. One of the English national newspapers asked me to do a preview of the 1994 season and in it I called one of the privateers, Aldeo Presciutti, a 'bald, fat, lazy Italian who wants to go racing because he has some money'. He had seen the article but couldn't really understand it, and instead of being furious he was made up! He came over to me, saying, 'I even get my name in the English newspapers!' He was actually a really nice bloke.

Things weren't always that friendly, though, and one meeting in Salzburg, Austria, in 1995 actually ended up in a massive scrap between the Ducati mechanics and the track marshals. When things kicked off, Slick was in a no-win situation. He had been told to keep his nose clean yet got a load of stick because he didn't get involved and help out the other lads. It all started when Virginio Ferrari approached the marshals telling them to put the oil flags out for a certain part of the track. Some riders were hitting little patches, and others looked like they were going to crash every time they came round. Eventually, the marshal lost his rag with Virginio and elbowed him in the face. That caused Giancarlo Falappa to rush forward whereupon two guys pushed him over. Another two grabbed hold of Virginio's arms, and yet another smacked him on the nose, breaking it. Then Mauro Lucchiari's dad got involved, hitting a bloke over the back with a fire extinguisher, which prompted the marshals to bring out all their best kung-fu kicks.

All this was happening while I was busy riding round, wondering why no one had been putting my board out as usual. It eventually calmed down a bit and Virginio and the Austrians hid in the bushes, hoping they had not been spotted by the race officials.

A successful rider needs the whole package to be right – and that includes the team behind the scenes.

Then five crack Austrian coppers came running over and piled into the garage where Lucchiari's dad was still watching the race on the monitor. In an attempt to arrest him, they pulled his arms so far behind his back that they dislocated his shoulder, causing it all to kick off again. People were kicking the shit out of each other all the way down the pit-lane. It wasn't until we saw the video that we realized, after dislocating Signor Lucchiari's shoulder, the security men had actually picked him up by the bollocks. We decided there and then that we would never return to that track.

That was about as hands-on as Virginio ever got. But I preferred the type of manager, like Davide Tardozzi or even Raymond Roche, who played an active part in the team and always wanted to know what was happening with his riders and bikes. Virginio was always more concerned with how the bike looked, and his ideas did not often work well. And Neil Tuxworth, my manager when I was at Honda, was probably more involved with the office work than he ever was with the riders. That might be fine for some riders, but I preferred my managers to be much more involved. Sometimes you can see things more clearly when looking at them from the outside than you can from the inside.

But, as with anything else, it takes time to get everything within the team just as you want it. You never strike up any deal or sign any contract and just walk in there with everything in perfect order. These things need a lot of working on. It is always important to have a stable team around you. If you change personnel when moving teams, like I did in 1996, not to mention changing a bike as well, it is a big task to have instant success. Even when I returned to Ducati in 1997, the personnel had changed, people had different roles and it was almost like joining a new team. I found that out the hard way.

You can tell by the tone of a letter I wrote to Ducati on 2 November 1995, after I had made my decision to leave, that I was not doing it without regrets. The letter read:

Dear Claudio and Gianfranco,

Your support for me over the last three years has been the best and I cannot leave Ducati without thanking you for the faith you showed in me for 1993. You gave me a chance that I was desperate for and I shall always remember this.

You have treated me like part of the family and the Cagiva Group will always hold a special place in my heart. I am sad to leave Ducati but I felt I had to search for a new challenge.

It took me two months to make the decision and it was not easy. I have felt the support of every single person in Cagiva and Ducati and the people of Italy behind me in the last three years and walking away from that was not easy.

I hope you can understand my reasons for leaving and I hope that one day we can be together again to talk about the happy times and memories.

My most sincere thanks to you all.

Best wishes,
Carl Fogarty

I was in trouble with Honda before I even started there. On 14 December, before I had even sat on a bike for them, Neil Tuxworth received a letter from Suguru Kanazawa, director of the Honda Racing Corporation, which explained how unhappy he was with an article that had been published in which I had explained my reasons for leaving Ducati.

But it wasn't too long before I had reason to send a complaint of my own back to Mr Kanazawa. The start to my career with Honda had been terrible. So on 2 May 1996, after Slick had been sacked, I sought help from Garry Taylor, the boss of the Suzuki GP team, who helped me draft a letter to the Honda director.

> Dear Mr Kanazawa,
> I am writing to ask for your assistance and advice.
>
> Obviously I am very proud to ride a Honda machine. I look forward to continuing my success, and to bringing more glory to the Honda name.
>
> Unfortunately, for the moment I do not seem able to give my best and this worries me, and I am sure disappoints Honda.
>
> The immediate problem is learning how to ride the new motorcycle, and potentially changing my style or making machine adjustments to suit.
>
> I am sure you are aware that although we had quite a heavy winter test schedule most of it was ruined by bad weather.
>
> As a result I have very little actual experience on the machine on tracks upon which we race.
>
> I desperately need more track time. I did ask that we stay back after Donington after the race in order to try to isolate the problems while they are still fresh in our minds, this was unfortunately not possible.
>
> I ask if you could consider my request and see if there is any way we could get extra practice days as soon as possible. Aaron Slight's style has shown the machine's true potential, and I am aware of the fact that it can be significantly improved upon with your support.
>
> Please consider my request in a positive manner. I am committed to winning with Honda and, as I say, I need your help.

I am even more worried that the team has decided to part with my mechanic Anthony Bass yesterday. I am sure you can understand that he and I have four successful years behind us, and to lose him as part of my team does nothing for my confidence or peace of mind.

I think it is a pity that I was not consulted about this decision before it was made, for of course, I would have done everything I could to make things work for him.

I do hope we find some solution to this problem.

With kindest regards,
Carl Fogarty

So it was clear from the outset that Honda were a completely different organisation to Ducati. That is probably the one thing I regret in my Superbike career – breaking up the winning team I was part of at the end of 1995 by moving on to Honda. And it's difficult for me to say that I have any regrets because I have had a brilliant career and so much has gone right for me. The main thing is always that I'm still alive. If I had stayed with Ducati I am certain I would have been world champion in 1996 and 1997 as well. And I guess that six-times World Superbike champion sounds better than four-times champion. Hindsight, however, is a wonderful thing.

Even when I rejoined them in 1998, the Ducati team was still like a new set-up to me. It wasn't put together until the last minute, and I had not worked with Davide Tardozzi before. It was also a different set-up in that I was in a team on my own and I didn't feel that I was getting as much help as the other riders. Things just didn't gel properly until the end of that year. The following year, Troy Corser and I made up the only Ducati factory team, so there were never the same problems and we got slightly better treatment.

Most members of the team are just there to do jobs under the chief mechanic, like changing the wheels or taking the fairing off before the main guy comes in to plug in the computer. Generally, I only spoke to one guy when I was riding and for most of the time that was Slick. But as engineers became more and more involved, Slick's position became more and more difficult. Things were changing rapidly, but he didn't seem to be changing with them. In 1999 Luca Gasbarro was made my main man and he became the one I would talk to while Slick listened in to what was being said. The other two guys who would also listen in to what was being discussed, apart from Davide, were Phillipe Louche, the tyre guy from Michelin, and Jon Cornwell, the suspension guy from Ohlins. They came up with ideas for improvements (it was me who more often than not made the final decision) but Slick's ideas were not always accepted, which didn't go down too well with him.

I liked the fact that Davide knew exactly what was going on with both bikes. Occasionally he came up with his own ideas, but not all that often, probably because he knew that nine times out of ten I would have the final say. But our relationship meant I didn't need to be distracted, looking at what the other Ducati riders were doing. In 1995 it might have got to me if someone had done a fast lap in practice, but in my final full year I was at my peak as a thinker as well as a rider.

At first I wasn't happy with what they wanted me to do. At the start of 1999 Davide said to me, 'Because of all the problems we had with tyres last year, you are going to have to do a lot more laps on race tyres during qualifying.' Suddenly, Friday and Saturday became harder than race days. Davide would make me do a race distance on a particular tyre then, if it worked, make me go out and do it again on another in the afternoon. Although I didn't like doing that, I knew that if we were successful in coming up with the right tyre, Sunday was going to be so much easier. Sometimes Troy found a qualifying tyre that worked that I hadn't tried, and vice versa. Troy was always considered one of the best riders at setting a bike up, and he still is, but it was surprising how many times he would go the way I had gone. He must have been surprised that year by how good I was. That was probably down to my honesty; I would always admit it if something I had suggested hadn't worked.

We also took to sitting down as a team on a Saturday night, and by race day we usually came up trumps. The results in 1999 were all the proof that was needed that our team set-up worked perfectly. And Ducati have kept the same policy to this day. When I'm around the Ducati team now I can see that their factory riders, like Troy Bayliss and Ruben Xaus, are doing a lot of laps on the Saturday in order to find the right rear tyre.

PREPARATION

MENTAL PREPARATION

1: Build-up

I was never the nicest person to be around before the start of a new season. I was always a bit more relaxed through the winter, enjoying a family holiday and a bit of time at home to do some work on the house, but I changed when I started to focus on the task in hand.

I always knew before the season started which riders were going to be my main rivals. It didn't matter what was said in the press or what opinions the television pundits held, it was always clear in my own mind that it would be between me and perhaps a couple of other riders. So maybe I would pay a little bit more attention to how they were doing when winter testing started.

Sometimes I was a bit too relaxed for winter testing and it did neither me nor the team any good. It should be the case that you push even harder during testing than you do in the race, because without testing the bike to the limit you can never know how hard you can go in the race. You should be really motivated, but that gets harder and harder the longer you race. I was actually highly motivated for 1999 and tested very well; for 2000 I was not as motivated, but I was also unlucky because I hurt my shoulder during a skiing holiday and then damaged the other shoulder when I crashed during testing in Spain. That disrupted whatever physical preparation I would have been doing before the season started.

In the early days, we used to set off in the motorhome on the Monday or Tuesday with Michaela and the two girls. At the time it was good fun because it was all a bit of an adventure. Some of the trips were a fair distance and at least two days away. Sometimes we would hook up halfway with somebody like James Whitham, or we could be driving down a big motorway and spot another of the rider's motorhomes in a car park (if it was Aaron Slight's, I would carry on going!).

But after a while, these trips became more and more tiring, especially the drive back home after two races, even more so if I had not had a good result. By 1997 I was starting to get a bit fed up with the motorhome and the kids were starting school, so I decided that I would start to fly out to races on the Thursday while someone from the team drove the motorhome to the circuits, then Danielle would miss a day at school and Michaela would fly out on the Friday to join up with us. That was not always the case, though, because a lot of the time Michaela's dad Alan and his wife Pat would move into our house for the weekend and keep everything running smoothly while Michaela travelled with me.

Come 1998 I still had the motorhome, but for the following year I thought I would be fine just hanging around the Ducati hospitality and stopped using it. How wrong can you be? I did not get a moment's peace. I was by now the main character in the championship and a big, big name. Fans were forever leaning into the hospitality area to try to get my autograph or to get me to pose for a picture. Even inside hospitality I was getting pestered for one reason or another. As the season progressed, it started to do my head in.

'It's your own fault for getting rid of that motorhome,' Michaela said. And she was right. So for 2000 I agreed a deal to lease a new motorhome, a really smart one, for the seven or eight European rounds. Of course, I never got the chance to use it!

If people could detect a change in me as the season got closer, they would definitely be able to detect a change in character as a race meeting got nearer. Basically, as soon as I left the house, whether to go to the airport or to set off in the motorhome, I would change as a person. I would go into my shell a little bit and be a bit quieter than usual. I was already starting to think about what lay ahead for the weekend. At times I was a bit snappy and a bit off with people. And it probably got worse as my career progressed. All I wanted to do was get out there to a circuit and start talking to my engineers, checking that everything was okay and discussing what we would do for practice the following day.

One of the first things to do was check what we had done, or not done, the previous year and what we could try differently this time around. Usually my memory was not totally clear, so I would ask Luca to give me a read-out, plotting the gear changes around the circuit the previous year. That would bring it all back to me and I would remember that perhaps second gear was a little bit low in a certain corner. From that moment on, I would be like a jack-in-a-box for the rest of the weekend. Even if I knew there was a footy match on telly or a good film on during the break between sessions on a Saturday afternoon, I could never sit down to watch it because I was too full of nervous energy.

My mood also depended on how things were going on Friday and Saturday. If things were not going well, my mind would be totally focused on the racing, so the last thing I wanted to be bothered with was the press officer asking for quotes for the website, or something like that. I guess the fans suffered as well as a result. There might have been a hundred people waiting for my autograph at the back of the garage after a Saturday qualifying, but if I was still unsure about the tyre we had gone for, I didn't want to be stuck out there for another 30 minutes. I wanted some time for myself, or to go and grab some dinner. I apologized to the fans at the end of that season, because I knew I had not been myself for a few weeks, but I told them that the most important thing for me, and for them in a lot of ways, was for me to go out and win races, win the world championship. Sometimes sacrifices have to be made.

You can imagine how I felt, then, when after one difficult qualifying session in 1997 with Neil Hodgson as my team-mate, the Ducati boss Virginio Ferrari arranged a public relations opportunity with a local dealer straight away. The last thing we wanted to do was stand around chatting to people and have our photos taken. We had gone there straight from the track as well, so we were still dirty and scruffy. I was not in the mood at all, and was even more pissed off when this thing turned into a full-blown dinner.

We were sat on the same table as a posh female Italian TV presenter, but I couldn't be arsed to make polite conversation, so I started doodling on the napkins. Obviously, the pictures weren't for public viewing but at one point Neil leant over, saw one and started pissing himself laughing. Then the TV presenter wanted to know what I had been drawing. At first I tried to laugh it off, but she insisted on seeing it, and when she saw a big knob with spunk coming out she didn't know whether to laugh or cry. Neil was nearly under the table choking.

If that had been a different occasion, it would probably have been Michaela who got it in the neck, because she was obviously the closest to me. But wherever I got to a meeting and the bike had felt good, I was confident we had the right tyre and I had been doing the fastest laps, I would be a little bit more relaxed, especially in my final full year. Tyre choice was just about the only thing that made me feel nervous because I knew that if we had the right tyre I

> **FOGGY FACTOR**
>
> 'The fans had paid their money to come and see me win, not to see me stood there signing autographs.'

would win the race, there was no doubt about it. The only thing that could stop me winning a race that year was if I didn't have enough grip. But you never find a tyre that is fantastic from lap one to lap 25. I would still have a bit of a moan, even if I won the race.

The next big step, after finishing off a hard day's work on the Saturday, was to try to get a good night's sleep. Again, the knowledge that we had the right tyre helped a bit. If there were doubts, it could be a nightmare. At Brands Hatch in 1999 I qualified on pole but knew deep down that we didn't have the right tyre for the hot race conditions. I slept for about three hours that night.

A good night's sleep for me on a Saturday night would be seven hours. If I managed eight it would be a miracle, but on average I probably managed five or six because it was difficult to think calm thoughts when the race was on my mind. That number of hours is obviously not good preparation for races in which you need to be totally wide awake, living on the edge of your wits, and I'm someone who generally speaking does need a lot of sleep. I have never been able to nap during the day because I just can't go to sleep until it's dark. I can't even sleep on planes when we are travelling halfway round the world, which caused big jet-lag problems especially for the Australia trip. Michaela used to get annoyed with me for continually saying things like, 'Oh, it's only tea-time in England' when it was first thing in the morning over there. 'You're just a creature of habit,' she would say.

I always seemed to be the worst affected by lack of sleep, although Frankie Chili also suffered quite a bit. He seemed to be particularly affected when he went to Japan. He rarely rode well in qualifying there and sometimes stopped halfway through a session to go to the medical centre for drips. 'Oooh, Carl. I sleep nothing this night, nothing,' he would whine. I'd be thinking, 'Bloody hell, he must have had as much sleep as I've had.' The riders would always ask each other on the first morning there, 'Did you sleep all right?' I asked too, hoping the others were suffering as much as I was, but more often than not the reply would be, 'Yeah, I slept like a log.' 'You bastard!' was often the reply. That's why Barry Sheene gave me a Valium tablet to take on the Friday and Saturday nights before my final races at Phillip Island, and I slept like a log too. Jet-lag was always worse on the way back, though, because on the way to a race you forced yourself to get into their time patterns as quickly as possible.

On the morning of the races, which started at 12 noon with a warm-up at 9.30 am, I would try to get up at around 8am. I might sit around watching television for half an hour and then show my face at the garage for half an hour. There might have been some things running through my head during the night that I wanted them to think about. If there were, I ran through them before the warm-up session.

But I was always a bag of nerves, and if anything that got worse as my career progressed. You would think that as the years passed and I won all the honours possible, the nerves would disappear. Not so. I felt sick every race morning, and even when I'm at a race meeting now I still feel a bit nervous. But at least I'm not crapping myself now.

I guess the worst feeling I've ever had was on the morning of the race at Brands Hatch in 1999. It's not easy coping with the expectations of 120,000 people and I probably had about three hours' sleep that night. When the mechanics opened the garage doors first thing in the morning, there was a massive roar because loads of fans had positioned themselves directly opposite, just to get an early glimpse of me. That certainly did nothing to ease my nerves. People must have thought I was really rude that weekend. If they wanted photographs or autographs, I was just completely oblivious to it all. People came up to me later in the day and said that I had said something to them in the morning and I couldn't remember a thing about it. Anyone who tried to speak to me that day who wasn't a member of the team was just wasting their time.

I was the only rider who refused to do the pit-walk in 1999. If you are the world champion, you can get away with things some of the other riders aren't able to. In the early days I wouldn't have had a choice, but I would argue that because I had been there, done it and won it, I had earned the right to that choice. The other guys should do it because they hadn't won anything, but I was too busy getting stuff ready for the race, making sure my knee-sliders or my boots were okay and that I had had enough bananas. As far as I was concerned, the fans had paid their money to come and see me win, not to see me stand there signing autographs. At best I would turn up for the last five minutes, just as all the punters were being cleared out of the pit-lane.

I still think it is too much of a hassle for the riders. When I went to Monza in 2001, I nipped round to Neil Hodgson's garage to wish him well for the race. I looked at my watch and it was 11.35. He was not even back at his motorhome and changing into his leathers with just 25 minutes to go before the race. When he did get back into the garage he was muttering, 'Bastard pit walkabout.' I know 90 per cent of the riders feel the same way. They are good for a lot of people but not good for a rider preparing for the race who just wants to get on with his own thing. It just seemed to be a stunt for the organizers to make as much money as possible, with no consideration for the riders. At

The pressure is on at Brands in 1999, as I prepare for the race on the grid.

Monza, too many people are allowed into the paddock. If a rider does want to move quickly from the garage to his motorhome, he has to fight his way through crowds of people. I wasn't racing that year, but I had about a thousand fans trying to dive on me whenever I tried to make my way from Ducati hospitality to the garage.

That kind of thing puts me off the whole weekend. I would like to be able to walk around the paddock to say hello to all the other riders and mechanics, not to have to ride a scooter. I don't know for sure, but I bet it's not the same in the 500cc Grand Prix paddock or at Formula One GPs. I told Davide Tardozzi that I was having problems because I was getting more attention than his other three riders put together, and I still had jobs to do at race meetings, so they tried to keep the balcony at the top of hospitality free for me and my friends. Even then the crowds would gather at a point where they could get a glimpse of me and just stand there gawping.

On race morning, there was never too much to be gained during warm-up because you had a race in a couple of hours' time and there was never any point in pushing yourself too hard.

The last thing you wanted to do was go and crash the number one bike by doing something stupid. The idea was just to have a last-minute check over everything and, if for instance a new engine had been put in overnight, to do a few laps to make sure everything was okay.

In the last couple of years, though, the warm-up started to become a bit of an extra practice session. More often than not I wasn't entirely happy with the tyre. So, especially if the morning was quite warm, we would throw in an old tyre to see if we could still get some good grip from it, to see if we could get down to race lap times on it. But sometimes, of course, that can throw your preparations a bit. What you thought was going to work might not come off as expected. Then you were left with no more practice time in which to make a decision that would probably affect the outcome of the race. It was obviously a gamble. It could also work the other way round, of course: you might find out something in warm-up that you hadn't considered previously and decide to stick with it for the races.

Five or six years ago, you would very rarely have found me near the top of the leaderboard after the warm-up. In later years, though, I was very near the fastest times. I guess that was down to motivation more than anything else. I knew I had to go out and push all the time. If it went well in the warm-up, the chances are it would go well in the race. There was no point just going out there and dawdling only to find something was wrong in the race. So I would try to push at about 90 per cent for most of these 20-minute sessions.

If all had gone to plan, by about 1pm I would be on the podium, celebrating. But that just signalled the start of preparation for the next race. Straight away I would be looking for ways in which we could improve. 'Maybe it might be worth just altering the gearing a little bit,' I might say. You could see the mechanics thinking, 'For fuck's sake! Just leave it, you've won the first race!'

But I knew the other guys would be making improvements in their set-up, that they were going to go quicker in the second race, so I wanted to cover myself. That's the way it always was: there aren't many occasions when people win both races. In fact,

I have done it more times than anyone. You know for sure that some riders will have realized their mistake with the tyre choice in the first race, get it right for the second and go out and win it. I have done that a few times as well. More often than not, though, few changes are made if you have won the first race because there is too much to lose by taking the risk.

After the second race, there was always the usual press stuff to do. If you win a race or finish on the podium, you have to be interviewed by World Superbikes' own television people and then you must fight your way through the crowds to do a press conference in the SBK tent. Even if I didn't have a good weekend I would still try to make time for the press. Apart from anything else, if there were reasons why I hadn't done so well, it was important that people realized what they were. Even after Brands in 1999, when I wanted the ground to open up and swallow me, a few journalists followed me into the Ducati trailer to find out what had gone wrong and I was willing to explain – even if the language I used was a bit choice.

When all the official stuff had finished, the preparations for the next round would start. For instance, we might finish the races at the Nurburgring and, after analysing what had happened during that weekend, start looking forward to the next round at Misano. In 1999 we had optional engines, so I might say, 'I would prefer to start off with the standard gearbox.' Troy might ask for the other one. So preparations for the following round would often start before we'd even left whatever country we'd been in for the previous round. You needed to be covered for everything that might happen.

PREPARATION

MENTAL PREPARATION

2: Danger

Every rider accepts that motorcycle racing career is a dangerous sport. For anyone on the outside, it must seem dangerous to the point of stupidity. But because I've known it all my life, it never seemed dangerous to me. When you're younger, you don't view danger in the same way as an older person.

When I rode the TT as a young man, it never once crossed my mind that what I was doing was putting my life in danger. A couple of years on, after I had won it a couple of times, I realized it was no longer where I wanted to be – not only because of the danger but because I felt as though there was nothing left for me to prove there. On the World Superbike scene it has been a similar story. Until the last couple of years I totally blocked out any thought of danger. I began to get a little anxious in the run-up to races at the more dangerous circuits by 1999, although as soon as I got to the track all such thoughts went out of my mind because I had a lot of work to do on the set-up of the bike in preparation for the races.

There is one thing that makes one short circuit track more dangerous than the next and that is the lack of run-off area. Probably the worst for this is Laguna Seca in the States. And my career was ended because I ran off the track and, apparently, hit a tyre wall. Had that tyre wall not been there, and had there been an open field instead, I wouldn't have had a problem.

Deaths on the race track have also been pretty easy for me to deal with for the simple reason that they don't linger in my mind. I have never thought at a race meeting, *No, I don't want to get killed here today.* I guess the minute you start thinking thoughts like that you're finished as a competitive racer. The only time death was ever in the back of my mind was at the TT, but not when I was flying down Bray Hill setting the lap record on the very last lap I did on the island. However, I might have thought about it for a short while back at the hotel, if news came through that somebody had just been killed.

I was nearly sick in my helmet when I saw Kenny Irons killed at Cadwell Park in 1988. It happened on the warm-up lap when Keith Huewen's bike cut out. Irons ran into the back of him and he slid down the track. Another rider, Mark Phillips, fell off and the seat of his bike hit Irons under the chin, breaking his neck. The race was live on television and you could see me shaking my head in disbelief as I rode away from the scene.

The only time a death ever really freaked me out was when Phil Hogg, a lad I knew through some of my mates who had been staying at his parents' guesthouse, was killed in 1989 at the TT. I had already had to deal with a couple of deaths on the Isle of Man. I had been about a mile down the road when Gene McDonnell hit a stray horse, and my mate Gary Dickinson's dad had also died on the island at the Southern 100. I had even seen my own dad fracture his skull. Yet I had always managed to block these things out of my mind.

For some reason, though, Phil's death really got to me. I pulled out of the race on the Friday night and was about to set off home when Phil's dad told me that his son would have wanted me to race. So I was back on the bike on the Saturday morning and came fourth in the Formula One race. From that day on I have never been one to sit and think about the consequences of death or serious injury. You just have to get on with it, and with a bit of luck such as I have had, you can finish your career roughly in one piece and alive to tell the tale.

In 1999 I remember watching Jamie Whitham crash in Brno while I was on holiday in Ibiza. I saw the race from a beach bar, and when he went down I thought, *Fuck me! Jamie's crashed*

Crashing out on John Kocinski's spilled coolant when lying fifth in the British Grand Prix at Donington in 1992. The smoke is coming from my toes, not the bike!

again. It wasn't until I got home that I learned his injuries were serious, including a fractured pelvis. Sure I felt sorry for him a little bit because no one wants to see another rider suffer serious injury, but there is just no space for sentimentality. And it was certainly not weighing on my mind the next time I climbed on a bike.

The fear of danger has just never really been something I have had to contend with. Even when I ran over a Japanese rider's head in the warm-up to the final race of 1998, when I clinched the title at Sugo, my reaction was nothing to do with what had happened. I think I needed a reason to get emotional that weekend because the pressure was getting to me a little bit. I think the morning's accident was just a convenient excuse to allow my emotions to come flowing out.

Even the fact that you have suffered bad injuries yourself doesn't put you off. If you could remember how much the injuries hurt at the time, you would never get back on a bike, and those people who do remember the pain either don't race again or never raced in the first place. I cannot remember the number of times I have said I'm never going to race again. Jamie is another one who has said it a lot. But as soon as you're laid up in hospital and the pain starts to go away, you think, *I can't wait to start racing again.*

When I broke my femur, it was just a case of waiting until I could get back on a bike. When I broke the leg again the following year, questions like, *Do I want to keep doing this for the rest of my life?* began to creep into my mind. It wasn't that I was scared, it was more that doubts were starting to surface that I might never fulfil my dreams of being a world champion. The following year I clinched the title and those doubts vanished. When

> ### FOGGY FACTOR
>
> 'I have never been one to sit and think about the consequences of death or serious injury. You just have to get on with it.'

I broke my wrist in 1994 my immediate reaction was, *Right, I'm never going to race again.* Two days later, I was asking, 'If we strap my arm up, will I be able to race in two weeks' time?'

Maybe riders are just a different breed. When you compare them to other sportsmen, they don't take anywhere near as long to get back into competition. Ben Bostrom dislocated his shoulder and needed to have blood drained from his knee for two weeks after his crash at Monza in 2001; a fortnight later he was picking up a couple of decent results at Donington. Marco Melandri dislocated his shoulder in qualifying for the French 250cc the following week but finished on the podium for the race.

After my big high-side at Sugo in 1995, I was pumped up to the eyeballs with painkillers. I had chipped a bone in my hand and my ankle and the whole of my left side was badly bruised. My knee had come up like a balloon, and that was more painful than the hand and foot put together, which had been numbed by injections. Yet I still managed to drag myself onto the bike, go out and win the second race. And I certainly paid for it on the way home once the painkillers had wore off.

Footballers, for instance, tend to spend a lot longer on the sidelines as a result of injuries that are much less serious. I could understand it if they'd done something bad to their legs, but there's no reason to have more than a couple of weeks out if they've broken a bone in their arm. Riders seem to ride with broken ribs, wrists, ankles – you name it. Imagine a footballer going back out after half-time with the injuries I've just described from Japan! Maybe footballers are told they cannot play by their physios or managers. In bike racing it's pretty much down to the rider, and the championship doctors will do everything to get you back out on the track once that decision has been made. There's always a way of strapping you up to make it possible, although if you've broken a leg then you're probably out for a couple of months. The doctors do have the power to stop you, however, as they did with Bostrom after that first race in Monza. He was all set to race again but the doctors said his knee was too badly swollen. I guess the bottom line, again, is how much you want success and are prepared to go through barriers to achieve that success. If you're not out there, you're not going to win – and you're not going to get paid!

There's no doubt that the sport holds a kind of ghoulish fascination. That's why the biggest crowds always congregate at the slow corners, where all the action of a race takes place. People rarely sit in the stands down the back straight, if they have a choice. They want to see the odd crash, as long as nobody gets hurt, just as much as a good overtaking manoeuvre. It's human nature. I have brought out two videos featuring crashes called *Foggy's Hell For Leather*, and both sold really well. But these weren't clips of people mangling themselves or getting critically injured – just peculiar and amusing tumbles.

Track
6   *Misano*

This is the place where you would have found me at my most laid back. We nearly always stayed in a resort about 10 minutes' drive from the circuit called Cattolica, in a hotel right on the beach. For my final race there, I had arrived in Italy the previous weekend and Michaela and the kids flew out to spend some time with me just chilling out, mucking around on the beach or next to the pool, or visiting the nearby water park.

It's difficult for me on a public beach, though, because I'm recognized just as much in Italy as I am in England. People would even poke their heads through the hotel fencing to try to get my attention and autograph while we were sunbathing. It's a cool little town, though, with some great restaurants, and the whole feel of the place helped me to relax, which I never found an easy thing to do. As race day approached, I would always find myself being less friendly with people. It was nothing intentional, just my way of focusing on the race ahead.

Although it was Ducati's home circuit, Misano was strangely never one of my favourite tracks – at least until I won both races in 1999, and I didn't get to race there again. Maybe it was because we did so much testing there that we usually messed around with the gears too much, trying to find the right set-up. In 1999 I left the bike alone and just concentrated on doing my own thing, and not worrying about what my team-mate Troy Corser was doing. Sure enough, I was faster than him in practice and even clinched pole position. The first race was quite close because my tyres went off and Troy was catching me all the time. The second race wasn't a contest from the word go.

Again, the heat plays a big part here. If it's cold, as it was in 1996, that's when the lap records will go. John Kocinski's from that year stood until 2000, when Troy Corser beat it. It's fairly unusual for a lap record to stand for that long in this day and age.

Crossing the start–finish line, I'm in fourth gear but I quickly move down to second for turn one. This is the kind of corner I can get stuck into, it really suits me. The surface is a bit chattery all around the track and this is the first evidence of that, but I can get right over the kerb on the inside and hold it in second gear before exiting over the red rumble strips.

Then it's up into third for a funny kind of dog-leg kink corner on the right. As Misano is one of the few anti-clockwise circuits, this is one of the few times when the right side of the tyre might not be properly heated, so you have to be careful early on in a race. A lot of riders probably take the next corner in first gear, but I actually stay in second gear. I've had so much practice on this track and I've learned that if you go into it in first, it's really tight coming out and too aggressive. So I switched to using second gear, and although I always had to be careful not to lose my front end because I didn't have any engine braking, I always made some time up through that corner and ran smoothly out of it.

I have now got only one gear change through the next section – and that's important. Because the track is anti-clockwise, the gear lever is on the inside and there's not much space for your foot to manoeuvre. Like 90 per cent of other riders, I change gears by going one up and five down, so you have to take your foot off and dab it forward to short shift it from second to third. This way I only have to do it once, not twice had I gone into the corner in first. And I like to get my toes on the footrest before I go into the long, left-hand corner. The other 10 per cent of riders change one down and five up, so it's probably even worse for them. My team-mate in 1993, Giancarlo Falappa, once tried a thumb lever quick-shift compressor system for the race and was really fast around that section because he didn't have these problems. There was only one system between us and he was considered the top rider, so I only tried it in practice and didn't kick up a fuss.

This part of the track is the worst place for grip once the tyres have started to go off. Again the gearing has to be spot on, and just on the exit of turn three I change up to fourth and straighten

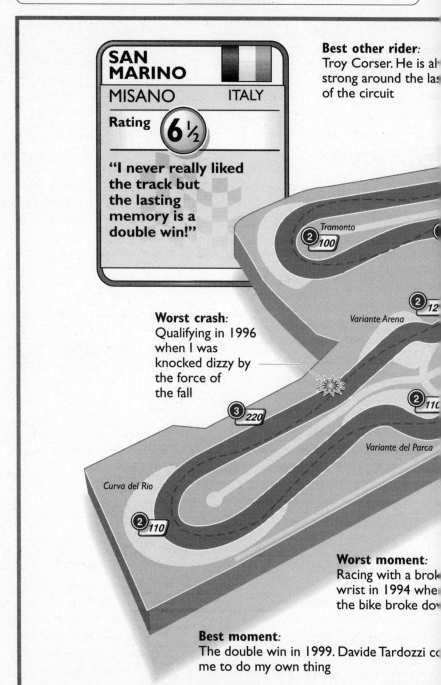

SAN MARINO

MISANO   ITALY

Rating **6½**

"I never really liked the track but the lasting memory is a double win!"

Best other rider: Troy Corser. He is al~ strong around the la~ of the circuit

Worst crash: Qualifying in 1996 when I was knocked dizzy by the force of the fall

Tramonto

2 100

2 12

Variante Arena

3 220

2 11(

Variante del Parca

Curva del Rio

2 110

Worst moment: Racing with a brok~ wrist in 1994 whe~ the bike broke do~

Best moment: The double win in 1999. Davide Tardozzi c~ me to do my own thing

sest finish:

st race of 1999. I managed to hold
by off after my gear changer had
oken and my tyres had gone off

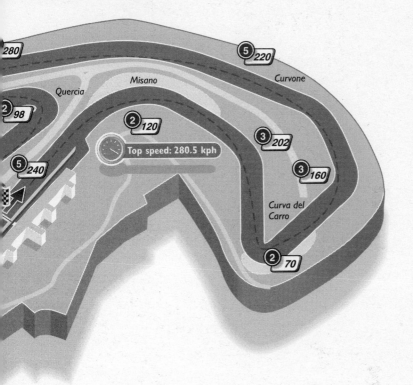

the bike up a little bit before going into the very fast left kink. I stick it in fifth before that Curvone section. It's not as difficult changing gear here because the bike is not on its side, so there's more room for your foot to move around. You're on the gas all the way through this bit, but you can't be flat-out. It's more a case of putting it in fifth, rolling the bike through and then opening the gas again. This is another place where I have been pretty good, and it's an important corner because it determines how much speed you're going to have going down the back straight.

The bike almost reaches 12,000 revs in fifth gear, so there's no need for me to move up into sixth. Just after going under the bridge it's hard on the brakes and down to second gear for a corner called Tramonto. It's a little bit tight going in and tightens up even more once you are inside the turn, so I always like to get the bike in early, get my body over the inside and get everything settled before picking up on the gas, while doing my best to hold a tight line.

Then, trying to move up just one gear into third, I shift everything onto the right-hand side for another dog-leg kink before coming over a bit of a brow and hitting the brakes down to Quercia, only the second proper right-hand bend. There is a bit of an off-camber, but all in all it's a pretty good corner, although I'll be a bit long on the exit in second gear. But then there's a short straight I can get down in second, before reaching the chicane called Variante Arena. I throw the bike in on the right and flick it as fast as I can to the left. The surface on the exit is very bumpy and ripply, almost as though it has melted over the years in the sun. The suspension works overtime there and you sometimes have to adjust your style by keeping your body still to stop the bike from moving around.

For some reason, I have never been all that strong around the last part of the track. Having come through another dog-leg kink to the right in third gear, I try to hold it as far over to the right as I can, because there is the left-hand corner coming up. On the Honda, qualifying in 1996, though, I couldn't even hold the bike upright. I accelerated so hard on the right-hand side that the bike kicked into the dog-leg and came right round on me. It was a massive crash that smacked me down and was caught by the TV cameras. I didn't have concussion but I was a bit dizzy and missed a whole qualifying session laid up in bed in my motorhome.

Then it's down into second and hard on the brakes for the next bend, Curva del Rio, which was only added to the track around 10 years ago. The surface always looks smooth and without grip here – because it is! This is one of those tracks that was all a bit dusty and dirty until race day, by when it had cleaned up. It is a safe kind of track, but the surface has never had that much grip. It tends to improve as the weekend moves on, possibly because there are usually sidecars depositing rubber on the track. Again I try to get in early and carry some corner speed – although it is increasingly difficult once the tyres have gone because the back end starts to move around – before getting on the gas again. Don't use up too much of the road on the right-hand side because then you'll be in the wrong place for the last chicane. Once more the surface is uneven, but it is a straightforward chicane in second gear before driving out and up into fourth...to win the race!

Slick decided he would have his own private race at around 6am after the races here in 1996. He was trying to get back to his hotel with my mechanic at the time, Nick Goodison, who had taken over his job when Slick got the boot from Honda. The Italians use these little three-wheeled van things for carrying stuff around and someone had left one unattended with the keys still in the ignition. Slick jumped in and started tearing off, initially leaving Nick behind. When he got to the hotel he tried to hide it a bit by parking it in an alleyway next to the hotel, but he took the corner too quickly. He managed to park it okay, but it was on its side and all the stuff in the back was strewn everywhere. He pissed off up to his room, leaving Nick to be beaten up by the owner and his broom.

FOGGY FACTOR

'The suspension works overtime at the Variante Arena and you sometimes have to adjust your style by keeping your body still to stop the bike from moving around.'

PREPARATION

MENTAL PREPARATION

3: Aggression

I guess I have always been an aggressive rider, in every sense of the word. I rode the bike aggressively, throwing it from side to side, changing up and down through the gears, and overtaking when it was least expected. But I would not say I was a naturally aggressive person. I can be bad tempered, just like the next man, but I would never go out and pick a fight with anyone. Away from the track I'm quite quiet and reserved, and perhaps a little bit shy, even though on occasion I do like to wind people up. Strangely, now that I've retired, everyone thinks I must feel a need to be on an adrenalin rush all the time. 'What are you going to do now that you are not racing?' people ask, assuming I have a hunger for danger and speed. But I never got kicks out of going down a straight at 190mph. The only buzz I got out of racing was crossing that finishing line in first position.

I have criticised other riders in the past for not having the necessary aggression in the final stages of a race to risk everything for that win. People like Akira Yanagawa, a good rider in his own right, could have a good race but would not have that burning desire to turn a good finish into a win. And it's at the end of a race, when your tyres might be going off, that you really need that desire to tap into. It is all too easy to accept that you have a fault and use that as an excuse for not winning a race. Troy Corser is a rider who tends to drop back through the field when things are not going his way. Sometimes, though, you just have to show the bike who is the master. It might start to move around, but that is the time when you have to grit your teeth. You might be losing time mid-corner, and people might be catching you up as a result, but it's down to you to make the most of what you've got, perhaps by braking later into the corners.

Another way in which a rider's aggression can show itself is the way in which he holds onto a winning position. You would always expect the leader to weave around a bit on the final lap, it's quite normal. I remember Colin Edwards doing it to me from the first lap to the last lap at Monza in 1999, trying to shake me off. I was dizzy by the end of the race, and pissed off, because although you expect it on the last lap, you don't expect it throughout the race. It's okay doing whatever is necessary to win the race, but you mustn't overstep the mark. I don't like it when people do that kind of thing, especially on the straight. If his antics had been visible to everyone, especially the race officials, he might have been disqualified. He was probably just staying within the boundaries, but there's a fine line between dangerous riding and going all out to win a race.

You also always have to show a mean streak when passing another rider. You never make an overtaking manoeuvre when you're relaxed except, perhaps, when you have been in a rider's slipstream and can just pull out and go past. Another trick, which again shows a rider's nasty side, is to come up right alongside another rider and brake really close to him. If you were to leave a bit of a gap it would not throw him off his stride so much, but if you brake right next to him, he will have to back off and give you the right of way. You see that more in other sports like super-cross and motocross to an extent. It's pretty common that a rider will take another out as he is going past. In speedway, if a race is stopped because you have knocked a rider off, you aren't allowed to restart the race. If that kind of thing happened in road racing, it would be considered a lot more dangerous and you would end up with a ban.

That's happened to a few riders in the past. Loris Capirossi knocked another rider off at Mugello in 1999 and was banned

I am much further up the inside of Pier-Francesco Chili into the first corner at Brands at 1997. At the next corner I went up the inside. We touched and we went down.

for the next Grand Prix. That incident followed another occasion when he was dicing with Tetsuya Harada for the lead in the final Grand Prix of the 250cc championship the previous year. Whoever was first over the line would have won the championship. Capirossi came into a corner, did not shut off the gas and whacked straight into Harada. Somehow he managed to stay on in the gravel and went on to win the race. The twist was that they both rode for the same team, Aprilia, so there was all hell to pay, and Capirossi lost his job because of it. Although he was docked his points from the race after Harada appealed against his unsporting behaviour, it didn't matter because Capirossi still had enough to win the world title. And he actually successfully appealed to have the points reinstated two weeks later.

I was once asked whether I would have done the same thing, given the same circumstances. It's a tough one to answer. I certainly would have done almost anything to win that title, but the move Capirossi tried to pull off that day wasn't even subtle. It was pure luck that he stayed on his bike. So I think I would have tried to get one over on my opponent in a less obvious way. Marco Melandri did the same thing in the last 125cc race of 1999. He was weaving all over the place, trying to knock another rider off, which would have given him the title. He didn't succeed, was fined around $10,000 and disqualified from the race. Both Capirossi and Melandri are nice as pie off the track. You wouldn't think they had a nasty streak, but every rider, especially a winner, has to have an aggressive side to him.

Nine times out of ten my aggression has been controlled, but occasionally, in the heat of the moment, I have overstepped the mark. Perhaps the worst example of this was when I tried to knock John Kocinski off his bike in 1997 in Austria. On that occasion I was definitely too aggressive, but I made the fatal mistake of hesitating and when I collided with him I ended up running myself out of the race. I was pushing too hard on a bike that was not as good as his was at the time. Instead of staying in control and finishing second or third, I let my aggression get the better of me and paid the price.

It was not until the next meeting, at Assen, that someone from the Federation International de Motocyclisme (FIM) came round to my motorhome to let me know the official view on the incident. He knocked on the door and asked if he could come in. I kind of knew who he was, but didn't know him to speak to. I was half-undressed at the time and Michaela was getting undressed, so I was not about to invite him inside.

'What do you want?' I asked.

'I am here to let you know that we will be watching you this weekend. We have had one or two complaints about the way you rode at the last race,' he said.

He went on to talk about the round before Austria, at Brands Hatch. I was leading the race when it was stopped, and in the restarted race I crashed while trying to get through to the lead from third place. I took Simon Crafar with me. In race two I passed Chili for the lead and barely touched him, but he still went down and crashed. That incident was a bit fifty-fifty, though. I went very close to him at the top of the hill before the second corner and he should really have given way, but as we both turned in, his bar touched the back of my seat and down he went.

He admitted he had been partly to blame for not backing off, because I had the line. So the FIM guy was trying to lay the blame on me for something that had not really been my fault, and lump it together with the Kocinski incident.

'Oh piss off, get outta here!' I told him and he disappeared with his tail between his legs.

A year on from that incident at Brands, Chili wanted to kill me after the famous last-lap incident at Assen. I suppose your aggression surfaces more at the tracks that mean a lot to you. For me, those tracks were Donington Park, Brands Hatch and, of course, Assen, where tens of thousands of Brits would travel over to watch the races every year. So the pressure might have been one of the factors behind what happened that day.

The tension had been building for that meeting anyway, because there were three Ducati riders all trying to win the world championship. I felt that Chili was getting the best treatment, because his bike was faster than mine and Troy's by 10 kmph. Whether or not that was true, we will never know. Before he became a factory rider we had got on like a house on fire, but as soon as I became a bit of a rival things changed. He had already pipped me on the last lap of the first race by driving straight past me down the straight. I was really annoyed about that because I should have outbraked him at the last corner. I made a mistake with three or four corners to go, so it was my own fault.

There was no way I was going to let it happen again. Every time he took the lead in that second race I had to come straight back past him, because no one seemed to be able to lead a race and pull away at Assen except me. Chili was right behind me for the whole of the last lap and I blocked him off at a few corners. I think this was what eventually pissed him off more than anything else. I knew he would want to pass me down the back straight again, so I shot over to the inside to get him out of my draught. Then he came on my outside so I pulled out, which I had to do anyway because a left-hand corner was coming up.

I weaved a little bit around that corner, which must have put him off, and we went round the corner side by side. I was convinced we were going to hit each other going into the next tight right-hand corner, so I decided to get in there first. I braked and braked, thinking he was going to come banging into my side. When I got that inside line at the corner, I thought the race was mine, but I was terrible around the next few corners – all over the place. I was in the wrong gear at one point, and as I came out of the corner the front wheel lifted up so I had to bang it into third. Chili came up alongside me and went past me, but that wasn't a problem because I knew I had the beating of him going into the last chicane. So I was right there with him for the final two fast lefts.

I came into the inside and, instead of taking the chicane in second as I would normally have done, I banged it down into first and, although the bike was moving around a bit I went up his inside. Then all I had to do was turn in, get on the gas, nail it and go over the line. *Yes! I'd won.* Unbeknown to me, once I had gone up his inside, he had panicked and put the brakes on, immediately let them go and lost the front end. With that fall disappeared any chances he had of winning the world championship.

Chili was spewing mad, and needed someone to accuse. I can't blame him for that, but when everything calmed down, he could only point the finger at himself because I out-braked him fair and square. I didn't even touch him. I had celebrated my win by riding round the track with the Cross of St George flag in my hand before returning to the pit-lane. At that point I had no idea that he had crashed and assumed he had finished second.

He came marching over to me, shouting with a face like thunder, 'Fogarty! Fogarty! What you did round the back was too dangerous! It was dangerous riding, weaving around like that!'

'What are you on about? I just passed you fair and square.'

'No, further back over there!' he shouted before throwing a punch that glanced off the edge of my visor.

A few people jumped on him to calm him down, but by this

FOGGY FACTOR

'You always have to show a mean streak when you are passing another rider. You never make an overtaking manoeuvre while nice and relaxed.'

stage I was furious. So I started to do a burn-out in his face, giving him the finger at the same time.

It probably wasn't the smartest move, and Davide immediately switched my engine off. I'd lost control, and was now shouting, 'Chili! Come on then!'

Davide said, 'Don't do that, you are making things worse. He is to blame and is going to look bad after this. Don't retaliate in any way.'

It didn't end there. At the press conference for the first three riders, Chili came in and parked himself on the front row of the seats set out for journalists. He didn't look like the normal stylish Chili, he looked more like a drowned rat in a tatty old dressing gown. After I explained how I saw things and said that I now felt I could go on to win the championship at the last round in Japan, the guy who was running the press conference asked if there were any other questions.

Chili grabbed the microphone and stood up in front of the audience. 'What this man Fogarty did today was totally out of order. He is a very dangerous man and tried to knock me off the track round the back.'

I immediately stood up, and said, 'I'm not listening to this shit,' and tried to walk off. But he stood in my way. There was a bit of a scuffle before a few people dived in to separate us.

Chili carried on his war of words through the press, saying he was going to knock me off in Japan. I had had enough. There was no way I was going to let his petty grievance ruin my chances of taking the world title, so I wrote a letter to the main man at Ducati, explaining my position. These were the exact words I used:

Dear Claudio,

I think the way P F Chili and Virginio Ferrari behaved at Assen was disgusting and very unprofessional. It's the worst behaviour I've seen in 15 years of racing motorcycles. For Chili to say I tried to run him off the track was absolutely unbelievable because he made a mistake and crashed, then tried to blame me for it all. The other riders and team managers said I did nothing wrong as everyone can see on TV. Right now I want to concentrate on winning the title for myself and Ducati. My family were very hurt by Chili's and Ferrari's

The riders' wives and girlfriends strut their stuff before the 1998 season. From left:
Erica (Scott Russell's girlfriend at the time), Kathryn (Neil Hodgson's bride-to-be),
Megan Slight, Alyssia Edwards, Andrea Whitham, this one looks familiar,
Kim Goddard, Romena Chili and Sam Davies (Troy Corser's girlfriend).

Michaela polishes my helmet, something she's
very good at.

Claudia faces the world's press in 1999. She
looks as interested as I was!

Pier-Francesco Chili tastes the Assen gravel in 1998 before accusing me of dangerous riding.

Noriyuki Haga is on my tail at Donington in 1998. I crossed the line first after the restart but was third in the aggregate race.

I battle it out with Chili at Assen just before he crashed out and handed me the race victory.

My Ducati mechanics mob me after I clinched my third world title at Sugo in 1998.

Perhaps Ducati boss Davide Tardozzi is just about to bollock me for not having enough motivation during 1998.

My frustrations boiled over and I kicked the bike when someone forgot to put the fuel cap back on and petrol splashed onto my groin – not a pleasant sensation.

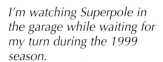

I'm watching Superpole in the garage while waiting for my turn during the 1999 season.

Michaela shares my focus during the build-up to a race in 1998.

I'm already high up on the ladder to success while Neil Hodgson, my team-mate in 1997, was still on the bottom rung!

I lead Aaron Slight on my way to winning my final world title at Hockenheim in 1999.

People have often said that me and Jamie Whitham should be locked up. This was on a trip to Alcatraz before the Laguna Seca races in 1998.

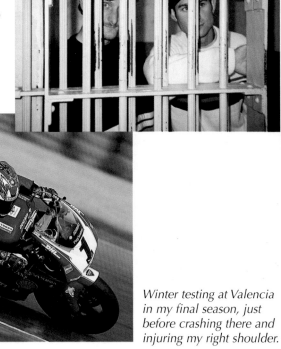

Winter testing at Valencia in my final season, just before crashing there and injuring my right shoulder.

Pulling a wheelie at Donington after winning in 1999.

It's not often that people look down on me at a race meeting but this is an overhead view of me in action at Monza in 1999.

It must be Donnington because I have to warm my hands on the exhaust fumes.

Ruben Xaus, the young Spanish rider that Ducati asked me to help, in action at Sugo in 2001.

Neil Hodgson, who was competing in the British championship at the time, on his way to winning one of the races at Brands Hatch in 2000.

Maximum lean for Troy Corser, who was my team-mate at Ducati in 1998 and 1999.

At home with a few of my trophies, the bike on which I won the 1998 championship, and some other memorabilia.

comments. I myself have lost a lot of respect for them both. For next year I would like to stay with Ducati and I hope to have everything sorted out before I leave for Japan.

Best wishes,
Carl

It all calmed down before Japan, Chili retracting his comments about getting revenge, but we still didn't speak to each other for a long time. The following year, at Donington Park, he approached me and said, 'This is no good like this. What has happened has happened, so let us forget about it all.' We shook hands there and then and there hasn't been a word said about it since. Having said that, we're still not as friendly as we used to be, which is a bit of shame because I do actually like the bloke. The same thing cannot be said for other people in Ducati, because Davide Tardozzi still absolutely hates him. I don't know the reason for this, but I guess it's because Davide reads the Italian press every day and picks up on any comments Chili makes which do not make it back to the rest of the superbike world.

Another time when you must have your natural aggression, or at least your competitive urges, under control is when you push the bike that little bit too hard. But this is about taking notice of warnings as much as trying to control your aggression. It happened to me in my final year at Kyalami when I had a terrible start in the second race. I had changed the front tyre and, although it was better for changing direction, I was losing it on the bumps going into corners. Even so, I had set the fastest lap and was catching the leaders, but the fact that I had a bad shoulder was probably forcing me to try to win that bit harder than normal, so that I could show everyone I didn't need to be 100 per cent fit to beat them. So, again, that aggressive instinct had perhaps taken over, but instead of settling for third or fourth, I pushed too hard and lost the front end. Hindsight is a wonderful thing but it was a stupid mistake for a world champion with so much experience to make. And I am the first to criticize myself for it, because I didn't fall that often. Michael Doohan was the same as me in that he hardly ever crashed. When I did, I was always mad with myself; other riders just shrug their shoulders because they aren't as bothered.

There's one place, however, where you simply don't ride too aggressively and live to tell the tale. People have said that I was an aggressive rider around the Isle of Man TT circuit, but I totally disagree. I might have been aggressive for the occasional lap – in 1992, for instance, when I tried to claw back a nine-second gap and managed to get back four seconds – but never throughout a race. In some ways, I'm lucky to be here after that performance because I was climbing onto the pavements and lost the rear end a couple of times. I got away with it on that occasion.

The best riders the TT has seen, like Joey Dunlop, have been fast but smooth. It's a different style of riding to short circuit racing, where a rider has to be aggressive to a certain extent. But I was a short circuit rider who happened to be going fast around the TT circuit. In those circumstances, too much aggression can be a negative thing.

Unusually for me, I wasn't nearly aggressive enough when I was riding motocross as a boy – maybe only for spurts during a race, perhaps at a specific corner. My riding style was the exact opposite of that in which I made my name later on in my career. It was obviously because at the time I thought I wasn't ever going to be good enough at it, that my heart was not set on it. I'm a lot more aggressive now when I'm riding a motocross or enduro bike. That's really strange, and I regret it in some ways. I should have been better than I was as a schoolboy; maybe I should have been kicked up the backside a bit more. I still wanted to win, but I didn't show the sort of necessary aggression until I began road racing at the age of 20.

4: Opposition

I have never been one to mince my words. I have always believed in being honest, and at times that has got me into trouble. It has also meant that I've wound up a few rivals along the way. But at the end of the day, whichever 30 riders lined up on the grid, I was convinced I could beat them. So what was wrong with my telling everybody that?

At certain times in my career there have been specific riders I knew I had to beat. It has always been the same, from my motocross days to racing on road circuits. At the TT I knew I had to beat Steve Hislop; and I guess my three main rivals during my superbike years were the Americans Scott Russell, John Kocinski and Colin Edwards.

Russell was unusual compared to most Americans in that he didn't have a background in dirt track racing. Instead he had been brought up on enduro riding. When he beat me to the title in 1993 riding for Kawasaki – making him the only rider to win the championship on an across-the-frame four-cylinder bike despite the fact that I had won 11 races to his four – you could tell that he wanted it almost as badly as I did. There was always an intense rivalry between the two of us that occasionally boiled over into a war of words.

Most of the time I was just taking the piss out of him. I didn't want to be his best mate. There was no point my going out for a beer with him, as I would do with somebody like Jamie Whitham, when in a few days' time I would feel like stuffing him up the inside and knocking him off the track. But I actually now get on with the guy, and Slick, my former mechanic, went out to work for him in the American Motorcyclist Association (AMA) before he had a bad crash at the start of the 2001 season. I could never understand, though, why Russell gave in during that final race of 1994 at Phillip Island, when he almost waved me through to my first world title. By that time we seemed to have both grown up a bit and had more respect for each other.

Kocinski was an oddball. He had won the 250cc GP world title and four 500cc GPs before arriving on the World Superbike scene. I was far from the only person to find him hard work to deal with. He had run-ins with his team, his team-mates and the press, especially when he replaced me at Ducati in 1996 as Neil Hodgson's team-mate. At one stage that year, Virginio Ferrari almost implied that I should beat him – while I was riding for Honda! Slick and I used to have a laugh, thinking about how we would have wound him up if he had been on our team. He was, for instance, obsessive about tidiness and his eating habits. For example, if he had put a bar of chocolate down in a certain place in the garage, he would go mental if it was moved. Somehow, I don't think it would have been a wise move to put us in the same team.

Edwards is another guy who I have grown to have a lot of time for since I finished racing. He's pretty laid back, but he's not afraid to speak his mind. His first year in World Superbikes was 1995 – he had won the AMA 250cc championship in 1992 – and it could not have gone much worse for him. His team pulled out towards the end of the season when team-mate Yasutomo Nagai was killed at Assen, but then he won the Suzuka 8-hours the following year before his fortunes dipped again when he suffered a bad crash in qualifying at Monza. He improved a lot as Aaron Slight's team-mate during 1998, and in 1999 he must have thought he had a chance of the world title. Unfortunately for him, I was pretty unbeatable that year. And I am convinced I would have won the championship again in 2000 had I not had

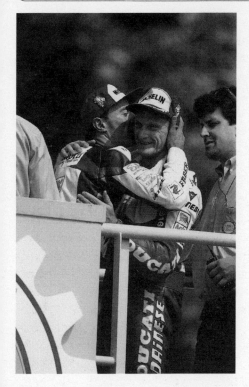

Frankie Chili celebrates his first World Superbike win at Monza in 1995, when my engine packed up on the last lap and I had to settle for second.

the crash at Phillip Island. With me out of the way, he seemed to lose focus a bit and made heavy weather of clinching the world title. But he is still on the young side for a rider and could still do big things. After all, he's now as old as I was when I got my first full factory ride.

Aaron Slight was another rider I found it difficult to get on with. We had been pretty good mates in 1993, but in 1994 he had become a rival for the title. He had said something in Albacete that year to which I reacted badly – it was only something petty, he refused to acknowledge the fact that I had won both races when I was recovering from a broken wrist – and it all went downhill from there. I probably didn't take to him because he was whinging all the time. Whenever I said things about him or his bike, it gave me a boost and helped me make sure that he didn't beat me. That was probably my peak of nastiness.

All these slanging matches were great for the punters, joualists and television crews. Suddenly it was more like a boxing match than a motorcycle race. I would come out with stuff like, 'It's time to put the Yank back in his place' which I said when I came back from my broken wrist in Albacete in 1994. Then Russell would respond with, 'Foggy's back. So what?' And it had to be the top riders. There was no point hating someone you never saw on the grid. People tell me now that things aren't the same without me and all the aggro I caused. The recent viewing figures for BBC coverage have been really good, so imagine how many would have been watching had I still been racing. Riders now seem to keep their mouths shut and let their riding do all the talking. Boring!

The press played their part, though. Some reporter might come up and say, 'Colin Edwards has said this or that about you,' stirring it up. And I loved it when that happened because it gave me an excuse to say something back. They really tried to start a war between me and Colin in 1999, but I actually liked his company too much to get involved in all that stuff again at that stage of my career. Sure, I wanted to beat him just as badly, but that side of things suddenly seemed like too much hassle. So it was never a hatred thing with him like it was with Russell, Slight and Kocinski in the mid-nineties. I had been down the hype road before, saying stuff like, 'His bike is better than he is.' Later on in my career, though, I didn't need to put myself under any more pressure than I was already under.

It all got a bit dull, to tell the truth. In 1999, if Honda made the excuse that the Ducati was better, I would limit myself to saying something like, 'So why is your bike faster through the speed trap?' But that kind of banter is just typical of sport in general. If you beat somebody, they will make excuses. If they turn round and say, 'Yep, you beat me fair and square,' then they'll lose their job at the end of the year. At the end of the meeting, all the riders still tended to get together for a beer in the paddock, despite what had been said in the build-up. When I say all the riders, I mean the English, Aussies and Americans – and Aaron Slight – got together while the Italians maybe went out for a meal with a nice glass of wine. I never did find out what the Germans did.

The hatred thing started in 1990 when Steve Hislop was getting all the press attention before the Isle of Man TT because he had won everything the previous year with three titles and a new lap record. He was all set to be the next big star. But I knew I was going to beat him and was not afraid to say it. 'Just watch me,' I said to anyone who would listen. 'I'm going to win this year.'

I had won the production TT the year before, but when I received the trophy it was about half the size of the main ones.

The three contenders for the 1998 championship, Troy Corser, Aaron Slight and yours truly, line up before the last race at Sugo.

'Is this all I get? Where are those big statue trophies?' I asked.

'Oh, you only get those things for winning the senior or the Formula One race,' I was told. So I wanted the real thing. Jamie Whitham was my team-mate at Honda that year but wasn't riding in the TT because he had given up on road circuits. He soon realized there was no way I could lose, because I had told too many people otherwise.

I didn't speak to Hislop for the whole of the two weeks. I thought that would help me dislike him even more. I just felt as though I needed to put him down, hoping it would put him off. There's no doubt I was not a nice person during that fortnight. In the end my behaviour provoked him into saying similar stuff about me. He made a couple of excuses and pulled in for both races. I won both main races that year and he didn't win a thing, so something must have worked. Although I was mentally aggressive off the track, I stayed fast and smooth on it.

The next year, everything was back to normal. We even stayed in a rented cottage next door to his girlfriend. I was no longer hungry for the success, having done so well the previous year, and

I wanted to be his best mate. And that year, when I was sharing a bike with Joey Dunlop and only taking part in one race because of other commitments, he beat me. So there must be a lesson there, although I hadn't been riding well in the run-up to that race. It didn't help when the bike kept cutting out every other lap, but for one of the few times in my career I was not too bothered. I think I had lost the ambition and determination following the previous year's success.

> ## FOGGY FACTOR
>
> 'There was no point my going out for a beer with someone when in a few days' time I would almost want to stuff him up the inside and knock him off the track.'

At the end of those races I stated that I didn't think I would be returning, but then Honda gave me the opportunity to ride the hand-built factory RVF, straight from Japan, which was too good to turn down. I didn't enjoy riding it, though. It was faster than the bike I rode the following year, but I preferred the 1992 bike, a Yamaha 750. As I have always said, I will do better on a bike that is right for me whether or not it's the fastest thing out there. I'll make up the difference around the corners.

PREPARATION

MENTAL PREPARATION

5: Negotiations and the Media

No rider, no matter how much he loves racing or the thrill of winning, is going to risk life and limb without good financial rewards. Right at the start of my career, I made a conscious decision that I wasn't going to use an agent. I didn't see the point of giving someone 15 per cent of my money when I could talk to the team bosses and sort things out myself. Sure, I might have made some mistakes along the way, but at least I made them myself.

Things have changed, though, and the business side of things expanded so rapidly when I finished racing. It got to the point where Michaela and I simply could not cope, and we weren't getting any time to ourselves. So now we use someone to look after a lot of our deals.

In the early years of my career, I was grateful for whatever bits of sponsorship I could lay our hands on. My dad's company supported my racing, but there wasn't a lot of cash floating around. One guy who helped a lot was Dave Orton, who spotted my potential early on. Then, after deals were sealed from tyre manufacturers, bike manufacturers started to take notice.

After a year as a privateer in 1992, I got my first factory ride with Ducati under Raymond Roche. I was well chuffed with the deal. This is my first ever contract:

This Agreement is entered into on this 25th day of January, 1993, by and between DUCATI MOTORCYCLES SPA, Via Ducati 3, 40132 Bologna (Italy), in person of its legal representative, Mr Claudio Castiglioni – hereinafter referred to as DUCATI

And

CARL FOGARTY, Bolton Road, Blackburn, Lancashire BB1 3PX, England, rider.

WHEREAS DUCATI is willing to participate in the 1993 Superbike World Championship Series with its own racing motorcycles and spare parts, (hereinafter referred to as 'materials'). The materials will be entrusted with a Team where CARL FOGARTY will provide his exclusive services as a rider.

WHEREAS CARL FOGARTY is desirous of participating in the 1993 Superbike World Championship Series, riding exclusively DUCATI materials, providing his exclusive services as rider to DUCATI within the Team as appointed by DUCATI

NOW, THEREFORE, for in consideration of the promises and mutual agreements herein contained, the parties agree as follows.

A) CARL FOGARTY AGREES THAT HE WILL:

1. Not reveal any technical information or matters of secrecy concerning the materials or tests made on the materials to any third party, except to DUCATI mechanics or other persons authorised by DUCATI either during or after the validity of this Agreement.
2. Make a positive contribution to development, promotion and publicity for DUCATI.
3. For an unlimited period, including after the termination (or expiry) of this agreement irrespective of how it shall have been terminated, DUCATI shall have the right (for itself, its sponsors and/or suppliers) to use and to exploit for publicity and promotional purposes, the name, voice, photographs, transparencies, films and

other visual, audio visual or sound recordings of CARL FOGARTY, as well as all titles, victories, records or other, all the above relating to CARL FOGARTY's activity while performing his obligations hereunder. During his visits to DUCATI or at one of the Cagiva Group's Companies, CARL FOGARTY will make himself available for promotional photo services of the products of DUCATI or of other Companies of the Group and by any of DUCATI's suppliers and/or sponsors.

4. To support in good faith, and to guarantee to support DUCATI and not to commit any act in public or make any statement in the press detrimental to DUCATI, the Team, their staff, sponsors or suppliers. CARL FOGARTY shall not perform or be associated with any pr motional activity which could be in conflict or in competition with the names, trademarks or images of DUCATI, its sponsors and/or suppliers.

5. Make himself available to make all necessary tests to fix the materials and to compete in 1993 Superbike World Championship Series.

CARL FOGARTY will furthermore make himself available to take part in the following other races, which either DUCATI or the Motorcycle Division of Cagiva Group may decide to enter:

—English Superbike Championship
—Bol d'Or
—500 GP race at Donington (if within Cagiva Road Racing Department's schedule)

6. Be responsible for his expenses during the fulfilment of this Agreement.

7. Respect the original identification colour and design on the motorcycles as prepared by DUCATI.

8. Guarantee that he will abide by all laws and regulations relating to the racing of Superbike motorcycles as contemplated by this Agreement.

9. During any test performed at the request of DUCATI, during any race or practice in which CARL FOGARTY has been entered by DUCATI and/or the Team and/or the Motorcycle Division of the Cagiva Group and generally during any activity to be carried out

hereunder, CARL FOGARTY shall be covered by an insurance policy taken out by DUCATI in favour of CARL FOGARTY in case of accident and/or death and issued by a primary international insurance company, of which CARL FOGARTY will receive copy. CARL FOGARTY hereby agrees with the terms and conditions and with the amount insured of such insurance policy and confirms that it is fully satisfactory to him. CARL FOGARTY hereby for himself and for his heirs relieves DUCATI from any and every claim exceeding the sums insured by DUCATI. In consideration both for the taking out of such policy by DUCATI at its expenses, and for all other consideration provided herein, DUCATI, the Team, the Motorcycle Division of Cagiva Group, their respective officers, employees, suppliers and/or sponsors shall be exonerated from any liability whatsoever toward CARL FOGARTY.

10. CARL FOGARTY hereby expressly agrees that al preparation and tests for the motorcycles as well as all races and practices and all other activities performed hereunder are at CARL FOGARTY's sole and exclusive risk.

DUCATI and/or any member of the Cagiva Group, their respective representatives, employees and officers shall not be liable to CARL FOGARTY and/or his heirs for any direct or indirect damages and/or financial consequences arising as a result of any accident occurring during theexecution by CARL FOGARTY of his duties under this Agreement. It is mutually agreed that the rendition of the services by CARL FOGARTY constitutes a highly dangerous undertaking in which the risks to life and limb are great. In this connection, CARL FOGARTY agrees to defend and indemnify DUCATI, the Motorcycle Division of the Cagiva Group and any of their agents, representatives, officers and employees against any claim by reason of any injury or damage or losses sustained by CARL FOGARTY, including death, as a result of the performance of duties hereunder. CARL FOGARTY for himself, assigns and legal representatives, does hereby forever release and discharge DUCATI, the Motorcycle Division of the Cagiva Group, and their directors, officers, employees, agents and representatives from any and all demands, claims, causes of damage, obligations or liabilities whatsoever for property damage or personal injuries, including death, which CARL

FOGARTY may sustain or incur by reason of CARL FOGARTY's use and operation of any motorcycle during the term of the Agreement or while said motorcycle is in CARL FOGARTY's or the Team's possession or control.

11. Be available to DUCATI, on an exclusive basis, for any technical or promotional activities that he may be required to perform by or in favour of DUCATI, its sponsors or suppliers for the entire duration of this agreement.

12. The direct or indirect infringement by CARL FOGARTY of the clauses number one and five of paragraph A of this Agreement will cause the immediate cancellation of the Agreement for non fulfilment of CARL FOGARTY with immediate suspension of all and every obligations, even of economic nature, of DUCATI. DUCATI reserves the right to apply for any further major damage arising from above infringement.

B) DUCATI AGREES:

1. To provide CARL FOGARTY through the Team with Ducati Superbike racing motorcycles of the latest model manufactured and available for exclusive racing usage, and to prepare the materials and make them available in a competitive condition for the races scheduled under the terms of this Agreement.

2. To pay CARL FOGARTY an agreed sum – to be paid in three (3) instalments.

Payments will be carried out upon receipt of regular invoice.

Furthermore DUCATI will pay CARL FOGARTY bonuses for 1st place in the following:

1993 Superbike World Championship Series Final Classification
1993 Superbike World Championship Races (each heat, for 1st, 2nd, and 3rd places):
Bonuses will be paid upon receipt of regular invoice at the end of the 1993 World Championship Series.

3. To reimburse CARL FOGARTY for the out-of-pocket expenses incurred by CARL FOGARTY in connection with his providing any

public relations, photographic, advertising, promotional, testing, or trade appearances requested by DUCATI.

4. To support in good faith, and to guarantee to support the good name of CARL FOGARTY, and not to commit any act in public or make any statement in the press detrimental to CARL FOGARTY.

5. The colour and design of CARL FOGARTY's overall and helmet will be mutually agreed upon taking into consideration DUCATI's and CARL FOGARTY's sponsors' and suppliers' requirements. CARL FOGARTY shall affix on such overall and helmet, on all clothing items and accessories badges and patches as supplied by DUCATI. The position of such badges and patches shall be mutually agreed upon by the parties. CARL FOGARTY will be entitled to display the badges of his personal sponsors (maximum three) on his leathers, such sponsors to be previously submitted to DUCATI's approval, which will not be unreasonably withheld.

C) DUCATI AND CARL FOGARTY MUTUALLY AGREE:

1. This Agreement shall take effect on the date of its execution and shall be valid until December 31st, 1993. CARL FOGARTY shall commence the performance of his duties under this Agreement on January 10, 1994.

2. If CARL FOGARTY is or may become, for any reason whatsoever, unable to perform any of his obligations under this Agreement or if his ability as a top racer shall be impaired, DUCATI shall have the right to terminate this Agreement forthwith as of right at any time upon written notice, and/or to substitute CARL FOGARTY with another rider, at its own discretion. Such termination will immediately cause the suspension of any obligation by DUCATI, including those of economic nature, except for those sums already paid up to that moment.

3. The infringement of any of the clauses relating to the obligations of the parties will give right to the non-defaulting party to ask for the immediate resolution of the contract with all consequences as specified by law.

4. This Agreement shall be governed and construed in accordance with the laws of Italy.

5. All disputes arising in connection with this Agreement shall be

finally settled under the rules of the Court of Bologna, whose judgment the parties agree will be final and binding upon them. IN WITNESS whereof the duly authorized representatives of the parties hereto have here unto set their signatures on the date first above written:

CARL FOGARTY

DUCATI MOTORCYCLES SPA
Claudio Castiglioni
President

Obviously, after winning the world title in 1994 I had a lot more negotiating power. For the 1995 deal I was able to build in bonuses for coming first, second or third in the world championship, for first or second places in each race and for winning the Bol d'Or. This was before World Superbikes had grown into what it is today, and the money is completely different now.

A rider very rarely gets anything more than a one-year deal out of a factory, so the same old rumours and press stories started to circulate at the same time every season, around the time of the Laguna meeting usually. It was obviously good if you had a few people interested in trying to sign you because you could then play one off against the other to get the best possible deal.

The year when there were more twists and turns for me than any other was 1996. I had about six offers on the table and genuinely didn't know which way to turn. I wanted to try my hand on the 500cc Grand Prix circuit, but I was being messed about a bit by Kenny Roberts' team. All this time, Ducati were getting a bit hot under the collar. And Yamaha, Kawasaki, Suzuki and Honda were all interested.

On 6 October, I received a letter, from one of the main men at Ducati, Gianfranco Castiglioni, thanking me for my continuous support and cooperation with Ducati and saying that he considered our relationship to be over given that we had not sat down together to discuss the future.

I sent an immediate reply:

Dear Gianfranco,

I thank you for your fax of today.

I would like to explain to you that I have indeed spoken to Virginio Ferrari and fully explained to him the situation that I am in at the moment and that I would very much like to ride a 500 in the GPs if the offer was there.

I have also tried to contact Paola [the interpreter] on numerous occasions only to be told that she is unwell and will not be in work. As she is the only person I can communicate with through to yourself this has obviously been very difficult.

If I do stay in Superbikes next year I would like to stay with Ducati, but it is my dream to ride in the 500cc GPs as I am sure you can understand.

I will be flying out to Spain tomorrow morning for the GP and I hope to know something positive by the time I return on Monday.

I appreciate the effort and contributions that everybody at Ducati and Cagiva have given to me and at no time have I wished to jeopardize that relationship in any way.

I remain sincerely yours,
Carl Fogarty

As things turned out, I didn't go to GPs and I didn't return to Ducati. Instead, I took the offer from Honda and spent a pretty average year with them before agreeing to go back to Ducati the following year. But Honda were desperate to keep hold of me, even though I had signed a letter of intent with Ducati. Neil Tuxworth, their team boss, pulled Michaela to one side in Albacete and said, 'Is there no way you can get him to change his mind? We will give him £750,000.'

That sounded good but it was not about money at that time. I wanted to start winning regularly again and I signed for Ducati for slightly less than that amount. Then, at the end of 1997, the whole thing started up again. There was some interest from Suzuki and I sent them a draft proposal. Then, on 9 September, I received a revised proposal from team manager Lester Harris, which was addressed to Carl Forgety(!), in which Suzuki proposed a much more performance-orientated deal but with a reduction in the original contract fee. This was not what I was hoping for, so I sent back a revised draft including what I considered to be an acceptable basic fee. Within a couple of days, I received a response letter in which Suzuki suggested convening a meeting to discuss all possible permutations, but that they were in no position to match what I had wanted as an initial contract fee.

When I told them that I had made my mind up to stay with Ducati, Suzuki made one final offer of £1 million, but that didn't stop the same cycle of rumours and stories circulating in the press every year. And when it came to these types of stories, I wasn't beyond using the media for my own purposes. A reporter might come up to me and ask, 'Have you sorted out what you're going to do for next year yet?' and I might say, 'Well, I've got one or two offers on the table.' That was enough to get them thinking, then they might throw a few manufacturers at me. If, for instance, they said, 'Is it Suzuki?' all I needed to do was laugh and walk away and there would be headlines next day in the paper such as 'FOGGY IN £3 MILLION SUZUKI OFFER'. Then Ducati would hopefully take the fact that other teams were interested in me more seriously and try to sort out an improved deal as quickly as possible. Those were the kind of games I would play, and the manufacturers played along too. Francis and Patricia Batta, who owned the Suzuki team, didn't deny such stories which just added fuel to the fire. They would then come up to me and say, 'What's all this in the press? We haven't even spoken to you about next year. But would you come and race for us next year?'

> **FOGGY FACTOR**
>
> 'I could take any criticism in the world when I was out on the track and could answer my critics in the best possible way.'

That's not the only way in which I used the media, though. If I hadn't won a race I wanted everybody to know the reasons why, so I always tried to find time for the press after a race. The press conferences were usually pretty boring and not much was said in them, but a few journalists would then try and find me for a more in-depth word. I never admitted that a rider had been better than me on the day. Once a rider starts doing that, he might as well tear up any hope he has of getting a new contract the following year. That happened to Troy Corser in 1999 when, after Assen, he admitted I was unbeatable around that circuit. By the end of the year, Ducati had decided not to keep him on, despite the fact that he had come third in the world championship, pipped by Colin Edwards into second place in the final race of the year.

Here is a selection of my post-race quotes for every race in 1999 – you should be able to tell that whenever I hadn't won the race for some reason it was never my fault!

Kyalami (1st, 1st): 'I won't be celebrating this double victory or my 50th win because of the death of Brett MacLeod in the Supersport race. I made the right choice to use 17in tyres for the races.'

Phillip Island (2nd, 2nd): 'I'm not happy with two second places because I love winning races. Two bad starts meant I had to ride more aggressively to make up positions, but by then Troy had got away. I managed to get into the lead by lap 16 of the second race but Troy was still with me and passed me on the last lap on his home circuit.'

Donington (1st, 2nd): 'I had to struggle a bit to finish race one because I had a problem with the electronic gearshift which meant I had to take my hand off the gas every time I changed gear. After a fight with Chili I took the lead in the second race, setting my own pace and looking after the tyres and the engine. But the tyre was too hard and I had to settle for second place.'

Albacete (3rd, 3rd): 'It's a hard circuit to ride on because there aren't many places to pass and there is a lot of changing of direction. I also had a few problems with the gear ratios as well as a bit of cramp in my right leg. So the best part of this weekend was winning my first Superpole.'

Monza (1st,1st): 'I'm glad they changed the start–finish line, that's all I can say. But it just goes to show: never give in, never. Even if things don't go right in qualifying or you aren't as fast as some of the other bikes out there, just never give in.'

Nurburgring (1st, 15th): 'I wanted to win this race for Hannah, my friend's little girl who lost her life last weekend. This was the most important race of my life and I wanted to win at all costs. The second race felt strange and I guess I crashed because I had other things on my mind and lost concentration.'

Misano (1st, 1st): 'I didn't think my Superpole lap was all that fast, and I know I made a few errors so I wasn't expecting to be on pole. I chose too soft a shock absorber for the first race and it wore out the rear tyre. So I changed the shock for the second race but kept the same tyre. I've never won at Misano before so this is a brilliant moment.'

Laguna (5th, 4th): 'I didn't want to lose too many points at a track I hate. I changed the bike but kept the same tyres for race two and it seemed easier to ride. But, even with that second bike, I still had a few problems changing direction.'

Brands Hatch (19th, 4th): 'Why did this have to happen here? I don't understand it. There are circuits where we aren't favourites but we win, while on others, like this, where we should have won easily, we didn't. I had no grip all weekend and that meant I couldn't get the power down. And that's vital for racing here. In front of all these fans, this result is demoralizing. I have disappointed them and that really hurts me.'

A1 Ring (2nd, 4th): 'The last lap of the first race seemed as if it was never going to end. I was using low gears to slow down in the wet, not touching the brakes and using the whole of my body so that I didn't have to lean over as far. I was concentrating as hard as I could and trying not to make any errors in those conditions.'

Assen (1st, 1st): 'I had to put up with a lot of pain in my right arm, which just goes to show how difficult it is to ride at this track. I tried not to put too much stress on the tyres coming out of the corners. But it's still too early to think about the title. There are still two rounds left and I know what I have to do.'

Hockenheim (1st, 2nd): 'I wanted this fourth world title so badly. I knew that to win it I would have to go all out to win as many races as possible and that's what I've tried to do right from the start. So many people have made this all possible, including all the fans who have followed me at all the circuits. Thank you everyone.'

Sugo (2nd, 5th): 'It wasn't easy on this track because we had a problem with grip, despite choosing the hardest tyres available. Then you have to think about getting past the fast local wild cards. When I managed to get rid of the group in the second half of race two, it was too late to get to the front.'

Celebrating my first World Superbike win, in the second race at Donington in 1992. Michaela and baby Danielle are on the podium, as was Raymond Roche to the left, who finished second and was to become my team manager the following year

Things can work both ways with the press, though. Everybody was behind me during my 1994 world championship campaign, then they all seemed quick to slag me off about one thing or another the following year. It wasn't so much the stories that were written, rather the letters that were published. People were so quick to come up with their own theories about why I had been successful, and I probably hadn't seen a bad word about myself in print before then. That's just typical of the British way, though. They were all behind me before I won a first World Superbike title, then when I was no longer coming second everybody wanted to have a go. Why is it that these people have nothing better to do than to write letters? They have absolutely no idea what goes on at a race track and 90 per cent of what they said was just bollocks. It used to annoy me, but then I started trying to wind people up deliberately. Now, the nastier the letter, the better.

The only story that actually bothered me came out after my injury in 2000, when Neil Hodgson won at Donington. *Motor Cycle News* carried a front-page story headlined 'WHO NEEDS FOGGY?' The actual article was fine – it said there was no need for doom and gloom because there was someone else around who could win a race – and at first I wasn't too fussed, but a lot of other people were really upset by it. So that got me annoyed. And it was probably a good job I was still laid up at home with headaches from the concussion, because I would probably have been even more annoyed had I been fully aware of what was going on. I could take any criticism in the world when I was out on the track and could answer my critics in the best possible way, but they seemed to be kicking a man when he was down. *MCN* must have got a lot of stick about it because the editor wrote me a letter of apology, so it was all soon forgotten.

I have always liked to be controversial, to spice things up a little bit and cause a reaction. I'm still the same, I guess. When I started commentating for the BBC I was a bit scared at first to say anything that might cause too much controversy. I was conscious that this was the BBC, that I wasn't on Sky any more, where you feel more free to speak your mind. But then I was told to be more myself, so I started trying to be a bit more frank and outspoken after a couple of races to encourage the numpties to come out in force, writing their letters to the press.

At least people sit up and take notice of what I say or do now. It wasn't always like that. I was always very disappointed with the level of coverage I received in my early days, especially from the local press around Blackburn. Maybe that was my own fault; perhaps I should have phoned up my local paper, the *Lancashire Evening Telegraph*, a lot more. I expected to be on the front page a lot of the time when I actually only managed a paragraph. They always seemed to be too busy with their football and cricket. The national newspapers probably did more on my early career than the local newspaper. As my popularity grew, so did the coverage but it is when you're starting out that good coverage is most important. But I think what I have achieved has opened doors for other local motorsport guys, because they now seem to get a lot of coverage without having actually won a lot.

Section 4

RACING

'Carl only ever had one strategy: to be tougher and mentally stronger than anyone else. He would never talk about strategy and what he would do in a race. And he never had an actual plan in his mind. The other riders' weaknesses were that they were not as good as he was. He wouldn't say, 'That guy isn't good on the brakes, so I'll brake later than him.' He just knew, even if sometimes it wasn't true, that he was better than everyone else. And he didn't make many mistakes.

'There were days when he had loads of problems, but there was only ever one time when he didn't have self-belief. That was at Sugo in 1998 when he was going for the world championship and it got to him. Others might question their ability and say, 'I only qualified in eighth. I won't be able to do it tomorrow. The best I'll do is fifth.' But Carl would never do that. He would sit there on the grid and think I'll still win because this lot are a bunch of tossers.

'The one incident that sticks out was when he high-sided at Sugo in 1995. He hit the floor so hard that he must have knocked himself about badly and I think he cracked a couple of bones. But after some injections he went out and won. And that's him. Everyone else would be thinking, 'Oh, I'll do well to get some points,' whereas for Carl it would be, I can still win this.

'Carl was a very good starter. To get his nose in front he would often do a semi-dangerous swoop across the field, putting everybody off. That was to stamp his authority on the race straight away. When he was in front, he could follow his own lines and carry his speed mid-corner. Then, generally, he would get away. I don't like to race on my own. But he did. He liked to pull away and do his own thing.

'He didn't achieve his success because he was particularly fit, as he didn't do a lot of training. And it wasn't because he was particularly clever as — while he's a nice fella and I like him a lot — he doesn't put that much thought into things. It was down to his single-mindedness and because he was so bloody good on a bike. It was all natural talent. Riding a bike was not hard work for Carl.'

James Whitham

RACING

TESTING AND STARTING UP

1: Testing and Analysis

Testing was never something I really looked forward to. A session would generally last two or three days, although three would often seem a little bit too long. A third day could often be wasted because a rider was jaded. On my way to a test, I always had a clear idea of what specific things I wanted to try out. More often than not, however, everything changed as soon as I arrived; I might, for instance, have found out that Michelin wanted me to test a load of different tyres. If I was being honest, I don't think I was the best rider at testing. When you've been racing as long as I have, it tended to be a bit of a chore. But once I arrived, I wasn't that bad.

It's hard work trying to combine testing tyres and familiarizing yourself with a new bike before the start of a season. The most radical idea I've ever wanted to test was the double-sided swinging arm which had the media in a flap because it was so new for Ducati. We probably didn't have enough time to test that idea properly, because there is never enough time to test all the things the rider, the team and the tyre manufacturers want to test. On that occasion in the winter of 1999, we did 15 laps with the single arm and 15 with the double-sided swinging arm and the tyre wear was probably the same and the lap times not too much different. It was agreed that it had probably been a waste of time.

Checking out the other riders' times during testing. The smirk would indicate I was fastest!

The hardest thing to do is to test a completely new bike because then everything tends to get mixed up. It's better to concentrate on one particular area and then move onto a new modification. You start with what you know, get up to pace and then experiment with things that have been developed over the winter.

The main thing for a rider is to maintain his concentration. If you're testing a new tyre over 10 laps it's important that you're riding flat out all the time; the results will be pretty meaningless if you're doing some fast laps and making mistakes or taking it easy on others. When you arrive at a track, Michelin will have a pretty clear idea of which tyres should suit the track. If the test results are good, you have to hope that the conditions will be the same when you get back to the circuit for the actual race. That was not always the case though, especially somewhere like Phillip Island. It could be boiling hot there for the test in the middle of their summer, then when you went to race there a few months later, it could be pretty cold. So all your data from the tests would go out the window. There are other factors to take into account as well. The track might have been used by cars in the meantime and the character of the surface might have changed completely. So it can be a frustrating business.

A test does mean, though, that the riders are a little bit more race-fit and that they have more experience of the track. They will also have been able to sort out their gearing, which is always a good thing before arriving for a race meeting. Once the season starts, there is not a lot of time for testing, although Ducati might test a couple of times at Misano, their home track, because it's bad for grip. And in 2001, they set up a special test after the races at Sugo because the Michelin tyres had performed so badly there, so everyone stayed on for a couple of days to try to make some progress before the following year. But that's pretty unusual.

The Japanese actually employ special riders to test specific parts, but the European teams don't tend to do this as much. The Japanese riders actually seem to enjoy it. 'Right Okawa-san, you must ride around for 300 laps.' – 'Okay, boss, no problem,' was their attitude. They would happily ride round and round for ever.

Paolo Casoli, the Ducati Supersport rider, tested some parts for me in 1999 because I was not a fan of testing new things. I preferred somebody else to find out whether it was going to break and throw them down the road before I tried it out. That seems to happen less and less as it's now up to the race riders to see if they can get up to speed with new parts. The only way to test these parts is to push the bike and the new parts to the limit. It's no use getting to the race and finding out that the parts aren't up to the job.

It's as much a motivational task as anything. There is nobody at the circuit so there's no atmosphere, and the track is often like a desert because it hasn't been used for a couple of weeks. And it can be a bit daunting at times. If you're in Malaysia, you don't want to push yourself to the limit, fall off at the far side of the track and have to lie in the grass for too long. It would be a race as to who got to you first: the medical people or the various creatures that live out there.

The main things to examine were the rear tyre, the suspension and the gearing. Then it was down to the telemetry guys to analyse how the engine was performing. This discipline changed a lot down the years.

Various data would be recorded during the race and analysed at a later date, but these kinds of plots would be used more during practice and qualifying on the Friday and Saturday. One would be a map of the circuit, coloured in according to the different gears I was using on the way round. There would also be a figure next to each gear number which stated how much I was using any particular gear throughout a full lap. At one point on the drawing of the circuit there would be a little mark to show the position of the bike in relation to the telemetry graphs on a different printout, which would be represented by a black line from the top to the bottom of the graph. The computer guys can move that black line from left to right and it will move the marker around the track on the coloured drawing, so they always know which results relate to which particular part of the track.

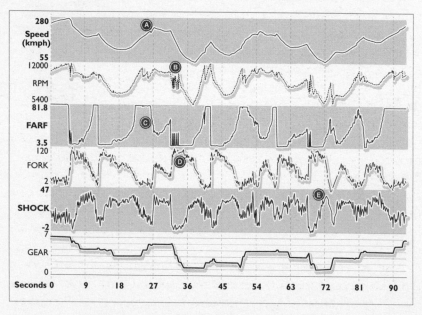

The kind of telemetry graph that the Ducati mechanics used to analyse the bike's performance.

The thing you have to be wary of is that occasionally, when it looks as though you are sometimes momentarily in one gear, it is more likely that the computer has recorded that the gear has not been properly selected for a fraction of a second.

The second readout showed the same map, but at certain key splits – maybe at 16 places around the track. It would tell you the gear I was in, the speed I was going at and the revs per minute. This plot was useful if I was complaining about the bike's performance through a certain section of the track. If that was the case, Luca Gasbarro would divide that section into a few splits so that they could look more closely at what the shock and the fork were doing, as well as the rpm.

> **FOGGY FACTOR**
>
> 'If you're testing a new tyre over 10 laps it's important that you're riding flat out all the time; the results will be pretty meaningless if you are doing some fast laps and making mistakes or taking it easy on others.'

The third was the most detailed telemetry readout (see graph opposite). It could measure several different things, but typically it would include about six different readings from all around the circuit. The first would be speed, and you could detect little things such as when I momentarily lifted the front wheel off the track when accelerating (point A on the example). You can see that my speed was increasing rapidly, and although there is a momentary blip, this was obviously not caused by braking as the overall plot is still upward. Directly below that you can see that the revs have dropped sharply because of that. And further along (point B) you can see where I changed quickly from second to fourth because the revs per minute go up and down. I wouldn't actually have been revving too aggressively at that point because I wouldn't have wanted to upset the flow of the bike as I changed through the gears.

Also under the point where I did the mini-wheelie (point C), on the FARF graph that measures throttle position, there is a very sharp dip. That is because I rolled off the gas as a result of the front wheel lifting off the track, with the aim of getting the power back down again as quickly as possible. The spikes at the bottom

Trying to loosen my leg, the one I broke twice as a young rider, before cramping it up on the bike again.

of the FARF plot indicate when I was quickly downshifting, revving the engine slightly with the throttle to make the gear changes smoother.

Another thing you can notice on my plots, probably character-istic for me, is when I went quickly from a right corner to a left corner. Normally you would see both front and rear shock come up from the stroke which would give you a kind of double 'V' underneath each other (point E). That shows that I was changing direction on the track, and the outlines of the V-shape show just how aggressively I was throwing the bike from one side to the other.

The next plot down is of the fork travel. At point D there is a section where you can see that I almost lifted the back wheel off the track when changing quickly down from fifth to first when entering a corner. Here the fork plot is high while the shock is really low, showing that all the bike weight is on the front end because I was braking hard. Whenever I was braking I didn't want the back wheel to be sliding around, so that the bike was much easier to control. Over the years, we came to use pretty much the same setting for the rear shock and the front fork because the mechanics and engineers knew which settings suited my style of riding.

The bottom plot is another way of telling which gears I was in at any one point on the track. At the right-hand side is the average for each of the parameters throughout the lap.

RACING

2: Adjustments

Luca Gasbarro, my chief engineer in 1999, always said that I was easy to set a bike up for because of my experience. He would sometimes only have to play around with things like gearing. We would often start a race weekend with both bikes almost identical apart

Just check out the leathers I was wearing for my first WSB win at Donington in 1992 – the height of fashion!

240

I always had my handlebars flatter, at five degrees angle (left), compared to anything between eight and twelve for other riders (right).

from one aspect such as the shock or front fork. Then I would go out on one to test it, then the other, and it was basically up to me to say which one felt better and whether we needed any modifications. Those small changes would hopefully take us gradually towards the best set-up. That way we pretty much always reached Saturday evening knowing exactly which setting we wanted to use.

Even things like changing my engine mapping, the kind of thing that is very characteristic of a particular rider, was easy for me towards the end of my career because the team knew exactly what they were looking for and, more importantly, understood exactly what I was looking for. I always wanted the bike to be stable when I was braking, without the rear tyre spinning, so the engine braking could be altered by changing the throttle position without too much difficulty.

It's more important to make changes during a qualifying session than it is between sessions. That way you have an immediate chance to see whether the change has worked. If you wait until the start of a new session, then you might go in the wrong direction and waste most of that session trying to get it right again. But Slick always said that it was difficult to tell whether the changes had had an effect or whether it was just that I was getting better dialled into the track and the bike, and was improving because of that.

The hope is that you get everything right by Superpole, and then you don't really need to do much to the bike before the morning warm-up, when you put on new discs, chain sprockets,

It's not just in the garage where things are changed. Here I am trying to make adjustments to the bike mid-corner, at Donington in 1999. Maybe I needed to adjust the clutch or tighten the brake lever on the sighting lap.

pads and oil filters. When you have run these for a few laps in warm-up you should then be ready for racing. There were loads of times, though, when we changed stuff between warm-up and the first race. And after seeing how everything performed in race conditions, a few changes might need to be made between races. These were normally limited to the rear tyre, though, because the first race would have given you the first chance to see how the tyre worked under race conditions, however much you tried to test it in advance. Conditions can also change so much between qualifying and race day that all preparation goes out of the window. In 1998 at Brands Hatch, it rained so much on the Saturday that the team was working in six inches of water in the garage. The floods caused by the rain washed so much crap onto the track that, come race day, the hard tyre we had wanted to use was far too hard and was chattering everywhere. I was only able to finish in fourth place for the first race because Honda had correctly chosen a softer tyre. I had to wait until the second race to use a softer compound, and came second.

There are also other measurements, such as oil pressure, water temperature and fuel pressure, that are looked at after the first race. Plus there are a series of checks to ensure that the gearbox and gear lever are working properly, and that the fuel injection system is working smoothly.

When you view the full technical specifications, it's easy to see just how many adjustments could be made to make the thing go quicker. This is the full rundown for the Ducati 996 I rode to the world title in 1999. So now you can go out and build your own!

FOGGY FACTOR

'It's more important to make changes during a qualifying session than it is between sessions. That way, you have an immediate chance to see whether the change has worked.'

GENERAL SPECIFICATIONS
Overall length: 2045mm
Overall width: 680mm
Height: 1100mm
Seat height: 800mm
Ground clearance: 130mm
Handlebars height: 830mm
Footrests height: 410mm
Weight (including oil and coolant):
    162kg
Fuel tank capacity: 23.3litres

ENGINE
(4-stroke 'L' twin)
Bore: 98mm
Stroke: 66mm
Displacement: 996cm
Compression ratio: 12 0.2:1
Crankshaft horsepower:
    (95/1/CE) 123.5kW;
    (168CV)@11,500rpm
Crankshaft torque: (95/1/CE) 107Nm;
    (10.9kgm)@9,000rpm

Valvetrain
Desmo DOHC, 4 valve heads, timing
    belts with lightweight alloy pulleys

Lubrication and cooling
Liquid cooling–closed circuit with
    bend radiator
Circuit capacity: 2.5litres

Ignition
Electronic ignition
CPU controlled gearshift cut-off
Wiring harness designed for easy pin-to-
    pin Marelli DAS3 data acquisition fit
Champion QA55V spark plugs

Fuel feeding
α/n electronic injection Marelli
Competizioni MF3S injection/ignition
module
60mm throttle bodies inside the airbox
Fuel pressure 5bar
Triple injector throttle bodies (2
    Marelli IW724 plus 1 Marelli
    Competizioni IWF1)

Exhaust
Complete Termignoni exhaust system,
    with 0.8mm stainless steel pipes,
    57mm outer diameter, carbon fibre
    mufflers

Primary gears
32 teeth crankshaft gear
59 teeth driven gear

Gearbox (transmission ratios)
1st: Teeth 32/16
2nd: Teeth 28/18
3rd: Teeth 27/20
4th: Teeth 25/21
5th: Teeth 24/22
6th: Teeth 23/23

Final drive
15 teeth small sprocket
38 teeth big sprocket
Regina 1350RNV4W chain

CHASSIS
Frame
Open steel tubes trestle stiffened and
closed by engine crankcase
All the fairing, fuel tank, airbox and
intake ducts are made of carbon
fibre
Wheelbase: 1425mm
Adjustable trail 96.6–109.2mm
Adjustable rake 23 degrees 30
minutes–24 degrees 30 minutes
Ohlins steering damper

Front end
Ohlins upside-down fork – adjustable
compression and rebound dampings,
spring and bottom-out spring preload
42mm stanchions
Low 'inverted design' fork bottom
120–125mm adjustable strike

Rear end
Ohlins aluminium body shock
absorber – adjustable compression
and rebound dampings, spring pre-
load
Stroke: 74mm (before bump rubber)
Wheel travel: 120mm

Front brake
Hydraulic system with discs:
Ø320mm
Master cylinder: Brembo (PR19)
Ø19mm
One-piece (p4.32–36) Brembo
callipers, with Ø32–36 pistons

Rear brake
Hydraulic system with Ø200mm and
3.5mm thick lightweight disc
Brembo PS11 Ø11mm foot master
cylinder
Brembo P2105N calliper, with two
Ø24mm pistons

Wheels
5-spoke magnesium light alloy front
rim, MT 3.50in x 17in size
Front tyre: Michelin 12/60
5-spoke magnesium light alloy rear
rim, MT 5.75in x 17in size
Rear tyre: Michelin 18/60 17

Electric system
Voltage system: 12V/12V
Three-phase generator: 12V – 280W
Battery 12V – 4 Ah Yuasa YTR4A-BS

3: Qualifying and Superpole

Sometimes there can be as much cat and mouse during qualifying as there is during the races themselves. Whenever I was going quicker than the rest of the riders during a session, I would suddenly find a number of riders trying to tag along behind. The worst riders for doing this, and you soon got to know who they were, were Yasutomo Nagai and Piergiorgio Bontempi. Bontempi used to muck around right through practice and then just jump on your back for one lap and end up qualifying quite well. If it was the faster guys, someone like Aaron Slight for instance, I would back off and stop him from tagging along. I wouldn't want to show him where I was quicker on the track and nine times out of ten I would just let him through, unless I wanted to get a fast lap in for qualification purposes. You never want to give anything away to anyone until the race itself.

Not that tagging along is a bad thing. I would have done it myself had I thought it would benefit me, but I never seemed to be as good at it as some of the others. They would be able to go quick and stay with me right away, after previously just cruising round. I tended to have to do a few laps before I was up to speed. Maybe that was why I was never that good at Superpole, especially in its first year.

Sometimes you can see riders desperate to exit their garage at the same time as the rider who's setting the pace. It doesn't happen so much on a Friday, but towards the end of the Saturday morning qualifying, when people are jostling for their Superpole positions, it can get a bit more frantic in the pit-lane. People want that extra bite and that little extra tow.

If that happened to me, and I found that someone who wouldn't come through was right up my arse, I just drove round for one lap and straight back into the pits. All the mechanics would be wondering what the hell was going on, assuming there was a problem, but then I would drive straight past the garage and back out onto the track, by which time the other guy would have cleared off. I would only be happy when I could settle down, have a look round to see that no one was behind me and concentrate on putting five or six quick laps together.

In my first few years in World Superbikes, I did what a lot of riders still do and tried to shove in one quick lap halfway through a session, just to unsettle everyone and get them worrying. Troy Corser did this a lot. But, after a while, the other teams got wise to what was happening, especially if Troy suddenly knocked a

Things aren't going too well as Luca Gasbarro, my chief engineer, and Philippe Louche, the Michelin technician, are in my face after a practice session.

second off the best time with a one-off lap. In my final full year I was not in the slightest bit concerned with what the other riders were doing. All I wanted to do was concentrate on finding the right rear tyre, and that meant going out and doing as many laps as possible as near to race speed as possible.

Before then, though, whenever someone stuck a fast lap in, I tended to think, *Shit, I need to go out and beat that.* But there was no need for that because, let's face it, nobody remembers what you did in the first two days of qualifying. Perhaps I was easily distracted, especially in 1998 when Troy Corser was on the same bike. If he suddenly put a really fast lap in, I would think, *How the hell has he done that?* It was only at the end of the year that I found out what he was doing. But I have to say it worked and it buggered people's plans up, mine included, because I would sometimes start to change the set-up of the bike as a result.

Having said that, I was always conscious that I had to get at least one decent lap in, to be around sixth or seventh before Superpole. I was often happier starting Superpole a little bit further back so that I wasn't hanging round and getting cold. Sometimes I've been on pole after qualifying and gone out and claimed pole position from Superpole, when you have one lap to determine grid positions. Other times I've been last out, as the quickest riders go out in reverse order, and messed up.

That happened in my last ever Superpole at Phillip Island. I started last and didn't put a good lap together, mainly because I panicked when a couple of drops of rain fell on my visor. I just wanted to finish the lap before the rain came down. I was all over the place; and it looked as if I was riding with a wasp inside my helmet. That meant I started Sunday's races from the second row of the grid. And, who knows, that could have been another contributory factor in what happened in the second race. If I had done better at Superpole, started on the front row and got a good start in the second race, I might not have had to fight my way through the field as I did – with disastrous consequences. But Superpole has never bothered me because I've always known I could go out and do that fast lap.

If I had enough time at the end of a practice session, I would put a qualifying tyre on and go out and practise the lap. That would be for peace of mind more than anything else. It wasn't a big deal to try to find the right qualifying tyre. Michelin were usually pretty sure which of their qualifying tyres would suit the various circuits. There wasn't a big difference between any of their qualifying tyres, to tell the truth. I would tend not to go for the softer ones, but more often the middle one. I felt that the softest did not suit putting the bike on its side and trying to get on the gas mid-corner, as those tyres moved around too much. I had struggled badly with Superpole in 1998 so I tested that middle qualifier quite a lot during the following winter, and as a result, I was almost the best at it during 1999. If I had qualified fourth and not fifth for the final race of that year, I would have won the prize for the best Superpole performer for 1999 – a prize I didn't even know existed.

It's easy to think that because you've got this very sticky tyre, you'll be able to go out and do a fast lap straight away. But the ones Michelin make aren't all that different from their race tyres – it's probably equivalent to a soft race tyre. It's all in your head. On the soft Michelin race tyres, as long as you had done one lap to warm the thing up, it would be possible to do that one really fast lap during the old style of qualifying. If you had the confidence to do it, nine times out of ten you could pull it off and not crash. And you also knew that you'd probably have three or four chances to put in a really fast lap. But when I knew I only had one lap to have a go at it in Superpole, my way of thinking changed. Whenever I won Superpole I automatically felt that I must have been on a tyre that was unbelievably grippy, but that wasn't necessarily the case.

Until Superpole was invented, it used to be a lot more simple: whoever qualified fastest through the Friday and Saturday started in pole position. And you had to do well on the Friday just in case it rained for qualifying on the Saturday. Now it doesn't really matter where you finish after qualifying on Friday. You know that even if it rains on Saturday, the grid positions will be decided by a wet Superpole during which riders have 12 laps in which to set their fastest time. If a rider accidentally does more than 12 laps their best time is deducted for every lap over the 12, so the key is to make sure you're in the top 16 after the Friday, which was never really an issue for me. There was never a possibility that I was going to miss it.

Probably one of the worst grid positions I have ever had was at Donington in 1998. After qualifying I was 14th and I went out to put in a very fast lap for Superpole that would have put me in the top six, without any doubt. But after my lap it started raining and snowing so they scrapped the whole thing and grid positions went back to the way they were at the end of qualifying. So I was on the fourth row of the grid on my own track, which was not a good feeling to say the least. I don't think I was ever on the fourth row again after that.

I was always happier on the front row. I also knew I was a good starter so I wasn't too upset if I was on the second row of the grid. I often started on the second row and ended up first into the first corner. You can't, however, plan where you want to finish on the grid. If I'd had it my way I would have tried to come fourth so that I could miss all the tedious press conferences that waste an hour. The bottom line is that you ride that Superpole lap as hard as you can. Sometimes it put me on pole, sometimes in sixth or seventh, but you had to take the rough with the smooth. Some riders are better at it than others. Troy Corser was probably the best when I was around, but Neil Hodgson seems to be doing very well at it now. Edwards, Slight and Chili were always a bit like me – hit and miss. Corser was good eight times out of ten.

> **FOGGY FACTOR**
>
> 'In my final full year, I was not in the slightest bit concerned with what the other riders were doing. All I wanted to do was to concentrate on finding the right rear tyre.'

In qualifying, it could have been any number of riders for any number of reasons who were up there at the top. But you shouldn't just look at who has done the fastest lap; the more important thing is to see who is doing consistently fast laps in the lap-by-lap breakdown. That's the important sheet after each session and it's usually a good indication of who has got the right tyres and who is going to be quick during the races. However, it doesn't always work out that way. I was recently at Donington and Hodgson and Edwards were clearly the fastest guys out there, yet Chili won one race and was second in the other and he had done nothing in qualifying. Edwards had a nightmare.

The other thing you find now is that other teams are copying what we did in 1999 and putting in race distance on their tyres on the Saturday. This is the sort of stuff spectators in the grandstands aren't really aware of. All they can judge the riders on is who is at the top of the timings. But there's an awful lot of strategy going on behind the scenes and quite a small proportion of it is geared towards actually getting the best time going into Superpole.

I'm sure I would have been better at Superpole nowadays, with the rule changes. Now if you crash on your Superpole lap, you can only drop down one row of the grid – the riders felt it was too harsh on those guys who had ridden consistently well all weekend, made one mistake on their Superpole lap and suddenly found themselves starting from the fourth row of the grid. There was a worry, though, that someone might make mistakes early in their Superpole lap, realize they had messed up and then just gently tip off later on in the lap, but that would have to be up to the officials to decide. The new rules would have suited me fine because I always had a fear in the back of my mind of falling and starting from the fourth row. From that position it would have been very difficult to get past everyone and win the race. If I had known that the worst place I was going to start was on the second row, then I could have really gone for it. So maybe I was always riding at 80 or 90 per cent. I never looked totally relaxed and smooth. Instead I was snappy and aggressive, a bit twitchy.

Having said all that, I don't think Superpole is anywhere near as exciting as the old qualifying sessions. In the last ten minutes of the final session then, the computer was flicking up and down like you would not believe. The best thing now is when, just before Superpole, there are a few spots of rain and the officials declare it a wet Superpole. Then, all of a sudden, the sun comes out and the riders have 12 laps in 40 minutes in dry conditions. This happened at Brands in 1999 and people still say it's the most exciting qualifying session there has ever been. The crowd knew when it was my last run, my last chance to get from fourth or fifth and into pole position. There were 40,000 there on the Saturday and Fred Clark on the public address was keeping them informed of my splits to add to the atmosphere.

Superpole doesn't mean anything until the last guy goes, when all the final positions are decided. The only tension you feel is as you wait to see whether that last guy gets on pole; if he doesn't, then it feels like a waste of time. It should be 'wet' Superpole format every time. It used to be the case that if you went over the 12 laps you were disqualified. My team would be waving the board furiously to let me know how many left. Still, every now and then there's an impressive ride. I will always remember Neil Hodgson at Brands in 2000, another wet Superpole. He just sat in the garage and didn't go out at all for the first 15 minutes. When he did go out, he did his 12 laps in one go, getting faster and faster and faster. And he ended up with pole position. That was the point when I thought Neil came of age as a rider. That ride was more impressive than what he did in the race and had done in the previous British round at Donington, where circumstances had combined to almost give him the win.

When it was a normal wet weather qualifying, Davide Tardozzi sometimes had to kick me up the arse to get me to go out, especially on the Friday. My attitude was always that things would clear up by the Saturday and Sunday. The team obviously wanted me out there just in case the weather stayed the same, but even when I did go out I would tiptoe round, feeling my way into it, and would be five or six seconds off the fastest lap for a while; then, when I had found my confidence, it was usually too late and the session was over. But that just probably mirrored my attitude to wet weather racing in general. I just did not enjoy riding in wet conditions, especially in my last couple of years.

In dry conditions, though, and especially in 1999, I could do a Superpole lap almost as well as anyone. Probably my best ever was at the Nurburgring that season. I remember Valentino Rossi coming up to me at Misano, where I also got pole, and saying, 'That lap you did in Germany was unbelievable.' I also put a good lap in at Albacete. After I had finished there were still four or five to go but I knew nobody was going to be able to close that gap. My final lap of the wet Superpole session at Brands was also really good. I was almost losing the bike at every corner because I had thrown caution to the wind, knowing that I had already qualified in fourth or fifth. That kind of excitement cannot be repeated under the current format, and I hope the officials have a rethink about Superpole.

Track
7 Monza

I like Monza. And it's not just its lovely smooth surface. Milan is a beautiful city, the setting for the track is in a big, leafy park area, the atmosphere is fantastic and, as the third oldest track in the world after Brooklands and Indianapolis, the place is steeped in history. The fact that it's in Italy, where the fans – the *tifosi* as they are known – are crazy about Ducati and its riders, just adds to the magic of the place.

And I didn't do too badly there, winning four times!

I used to love riding this track when I was out in front as I could go through the chicanes so quickly. Then all I had to do was hope that the bike was quick enough down the straights, which it generally was, although the Hondas were usually a bit quicker. Typically, in the only year I rode for Honda, it wasn't the fastest bike out there. Monza was also a track which was not too physically demanding.

I pass the start–finish line in fifth gear and get up into sixth at the fastest point on the track, just before the first chicane, when you're moving at around 300kmph. You have to keep the revs up and change gears pretty quickly because the bikes don't like pulling sixth gear, especially with a small back sprocket. When choosing the gearing, you also have to take into account that you'll be slipstreaming down that straight. If you were reaching 12,000 revs on your own, you'd be over-revving once you were behind another rider. So, if it was pos- sible, I would slightly undergear the bike and that meant I never got the perfect lap in qualifying because I was usually on my own. To get a good lap time, you would have to try to draught someone down those straights.

Then it's down to first gear for that first chicane, called Prima Variante. It's important to have a definite braking point, but the thing to watch out for as you're coming up to that point behind three guys is that you might be going 10kmph faster than normal. If you brake at the same place, it's a case of 'Whoa! Shit!' It's common to see people outbraking themselves at that point and running up the kerbs. Jamie Whitham once skimmed straight across the gravel here when his front brake disc blew. You could barely see where the bike had made an impact because he was going so fast.

I enter the first part of the chicane in first gear, and coming out of it I hook up into second gear for the second chicane. You have to watch it a bit on the left side because you are flicking it hard onto that side while going over the kerbs. The corner was changed for the 2001 season, making it even worse in a lot of people's opinion. It was at these chicanes the previous year that Troy Bayliss came charging through from fourth place to first without hardly touching the brakes. It was hard to believe that he stayed on the track. The new corner is a slow, first-gear right-hander followed by another slow left-hander. It took all the fun out of it as far as I was concerned. I didn't think the old layout was all that bad.

Out of there I am quickly up to fifth gear just before the Curva Grande, one of the fastest corners we race on. I've always been really quick around the corner, managing to keep the bike very flat and carrying a lot of corner speed. By the time I got to the exit, I was almost touching the limiter in fifth gear. When you bring it up, the revs just drop slightly by a few hundred. There is a massive wall around the outside of the track and at this point you always see a bunch of guys, I think they're Italian, who sit there cheering from Friday until the end of the two races.

Then it's hard on the brakes from fifth to first gear for a very slow flip-flop chicane called the Variante della Roggia, which has seen some frantic last-lap action in the past. Chili went straight on there in 1996 and almost hit me as he came back on; I was in first gear so I was confident of avoiding him. I briefly hit third and dropped straight back down to second before going under the trees for the double right-hander Curva di Lesmo. If it has been raining, you have to take extra care there as it often takes a lot longer for the track to dry out under

Using every inch of the road at Monza, trying to build up as much speed as possible before entering the back straight. You can just see small stones flying up from the road, which indicates that not everyone was using that much track.

the trees. It's a little bit bumpy and ripply going into the first of those corners and I often had problems with the front end chattering, on both the Ducati and Honda.

Coming out of the second right-hander in second gear it's a long drag, slightly downhill under the bridge in fifth gear before going up again to the second-gear chicane called Ascari. It's quite fast and I've always been quite quick through the first part of it but run out of revs later on, while some of the riders, who are slower into the first part of the chicane, switch up to third. But it's very important to get a run coming out of Ascari onto the long back straight, and you use all the road, the rumble strips and even a little bit of the gravel.

From fifth gear I'm down to third gear for the last Parabolica. As you go in, third gear is a bit tall, but I can live with that as long as I go in smoothly. As you get into the corner it becomes faster and faster, so on the exit I'm at the limiter and up into fifth gear for the start–finish – to win the race by five thousandths of a second!

That's what happened in 1999, but only because the line had been moved from the bottom end of that straight to shortly after the exit of the Parabolica. I wanted to win the race so badly because I knew the Honda was a quicker bike, but I was so much faster through the chicanes. It felt as though I almost deserved to win. I had managed to win the first race by a tenth of a second, when I broke away from Edwards on the last lap. I expected him to come past me on the back straight but he didn't and I managed to hold on.

In the second race, Chili was also involved and was in my way until I went past him under the trees when he made a mistake on the last lap. After that I had a gap to pull back on Colin, which I was never going to be able to do on the straight. But I went through Ascari so quickly that suddenly I was right behind him again. Having chased him down the back straight, I entered the Parabolica with a lot of work still to do. Again, I went into the corner so quickly that I was catching him all the way round, but because his bike was quicker I knew I had to get into his slipstream at the perfect time.

Just as we were both exiting the corner I was right up behind him, knowing I would have to pull out to pass him. But I didn't want to change up to fifth because I knew I would lose a thousandth of a second, so I left it in fourth with the revs near the limiter and me in such a tuck that I could hardly see what was happening. As Edwards came out of the corner he pulled to the inside to shake me out of the slipstream. It played perfectly into my hands as it left the way clear for me to move alongside him over the finish line. If the line had not been moved up to that end of the straight he would have pulled away to win the race across the old finish line. Neither of us knew for certain who had clinched it. I was sure I had, but I didn't want to appear over-confident. I looked over to him and all he could do was shrug his shoulders. I tried to ask a marshal and he stuck up two fingers, which could have meant either he thought I was first ('V' for victory) or second. So I carried on round the track thinking, *It was a good race, and I'm sure I've won the bastard!*

MONZA

ITALY

Rating **9**

"The surface is great, I'm great through the chicanes, it's flat, pretty safe, and the atmosphere and weather is good"

Worst moment:
Almost high-siding on the exit of Ascari in 1997 – not a good place to come off

Closest finish:
The second race of 1999, beating Edwards by 5/1000 of a second. They don't con closer than that

Best other rider:
Chili and Edwards are
the two riders who I
have had fun with at
Monza. Chili probably
shades it because
Edwards' bike was always
so quick

Worst crash:
I have never crashed
here. That's why I
love it!

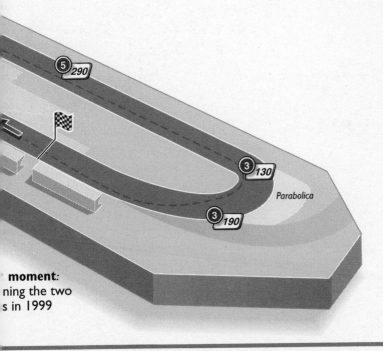

moment:
ning the two
s in 1999

Back in the pits, the computer was adding to the confusion. Colin was put in first place, although no time had come up for me. When it came through, my name quickly jumped up to the top, and by the time I had got round to the pits my mechanics were jumping up and down. *What's going on?* I thought. 'You've won, you've won!' they shouted. That was it. I was up onto the footrests going absolutely mad.

Obviously, there were big celebrations., but we did not get anywhere near as drunk as we had the previous year. The trouble was, nobody realized just how drunk we were getting. We were all in a bar after the races drinking something called Red Beer, which turned out to be nearly as potent as wine. All of a sudden everyone was arguing with each other and it really kicked off. Jamie Whitham had someone from Honda by the throat at one point so we all decided to try to get back to the track, where my motorhome was, or back to the hotels the others were staying in. Slick had brought his van and took a couple of people back, not realizing that he still had his sunglasses on at four in the morning and so could hardly see where he was going. That's probably why he virtually took off at one point and ended up in the middle of a busy dual-carriageway, facing the wrong way. Gary Dickinson was in the back and had smashed his head on the roof, but even that hadn't managed to wake him up from his coma.

FOGGY FACTOR

'It's important to have a definite braking point for the first chicane but the thing to watch out for, as you're coming up to that point behind three guys, is that you might have been going 10kmph faster than normal.'

Our trip home was not much better. We went in another car, but I was furious because I could tell that Andrea, Jamie's wife, didn't know where she was going. So I just demanded that they stop the car and I got out and started walking, not having a clue where I was. By this time Michaela and Andrea were arguing, people were crying, and after an hour of wandering aimlessly, they turned up to persuade me to get back in.

Apart from that night, I love Monza!

RACING

RACE STRATEGY

1: Starting

There is no doubt that I was a good starter. And the plan was simple: try to get to the first corner first and then just clear off. That was the perfect race strategy for me. It didn't really matter whether I was in pole position or fourth on the front row. Until the rules changed in 1998 it made hardly any difference whatsoever because the grid rows started in a line. Even when they were slightly staggered, as they are now, there was still hardly any advantage between first and fourth. It could be argued that the rider on pole was in the best position because he had the inside line into the first corner, but it could also work the other way: a bad start could see the pole position guy trapped up the inside. It was all down to how good a start you had. Even if that was from the second row I could still find myself leading into the first corner.

Again, before Superpole arrived on the scene, I would get to the white marker then roll the bike back a foot. The thinking behind that was that when the lights were still on red and the guy with the flag was making his way off the grid, I would be blipping the throttle and edging slightly forward. When the green light came on my wheel would be bang on the line and I would already have a little bit of forward momentum. You could get away with it in those days because they didn't seem to be as strict on jump starts. Even when they stopped us from doing that, I still got good starts, but the front wheel tended to jump a little bit more. In 1999 at Kyalami they warned us that they would use video evidence, from cameras on each row of the grid, as part of a clampdown on jump starts. It caused me to freeze. I had Corser on one side and Slight on the other and we were all checking to see whether we had crept over the white line. When you are sat on top of the bike it's impossible to see over the top to check where your own front wheel is. Still, I managed to drop the clutch, clear off and win the race. I thought it was the perfect start, but there were complaints afterwards. Slight thought I had rolled, while Corser thought Slight had rolled. It had just provided everyone with a new excuse for a moan.

You have to be careful, though, because your race is effectively over if you are found to have done a jump start. It happened to Ben Bostrom at the start of the 2001 season at Valencia in the second race. He received a ten-second stop-and-go penalty and was so mad about it that he received another ten-second penalty for going too fast in the pit-lane.

Despite the fact that I have always been a good starter, even in my motocross days, I have also always been very nervous – never more so than in the old days when you had to bump start the bike. The engine was switched off, you pulled the clutch in, ran with the bike and jumped on. It was a horrible experience. My mouth was always dry and my legs were like jelly because I was so nervous. Even so, I still did them pretty well.

In the last race of 1985, in the Marlboro Clubman's round, I had to win the race and Darren Dixon had to crash for me to be champion. That was never going to happen, but the race was still live on BBC's *Grandstand* (Murray Walker was commentating; he called me 'George Fogarty' for the first five laps, so there was nothing new there.) I wanted to win the race badly. How the bike started I will never know because I felt physically sick and could hardly stand up. When the lights went to green, my legs folded underneath me but I dropped the clutch and somehow it fired off and I shot off into the lead. But it felt as though I was pushing the bike at about three miles an hour. It was not so nerve-racking for the TT, because it was just you against another guy going out at

*I'm up on the bike and tucked in before the other riders, Chili (7),
Neil Hodgson (7) and Niall Mackenzie (41) at the start of the race at
Brands in 1997.*

the same time, so all I wanted to do was get away before him, and
nine times out of ten I managed to do that. Push starts were soon
phased out, though, and obviously it was never done in superbike
races. You'd have been pushing until you were blue in the face.

The funniest start happened in my first ever road race. I was
riding my dad's Ducati, which was supposed to be a 500cc but
there were vicious rumours that it was 600cc! When the numbers
were drawn out of the hat for grid positions, I was down on the
fifth row. I was pissed off because I wanted to win that race,
despite the fact it was my first and I had no experience. There
was no way that, as a scrawny 17-year-old, I was ever going to
bump start that thing. However, the bike had an electric start, so
the plan was to slyly use that. I started to run with the bike but,
because I was shitting myself, I hit the start button and was
weaving my way through the field before the flag had even
dropped. I had gone from fifth row into the lead while most
people were still running with their bikes! 'You couldn't have
made that any more bloody obvious, you bloody idiot!' my dad

said to me afterwards, totally embarrassed in front of all his
mates. I was, of course, disqualified, and I was nearly in tears. I
can laugh about it now, but I didn't find those things funny at the
time.

The thing to concentrate on, apart from not jumping the start,
is to keep the front wheel down. As long as you can get the clutch
out and keep the front wheel down, you'll be okay most times.
My starting style probably came from my days in motocross,
when I used to lean right over the tank in order to keep the front
wheel down. You are also in a straight line with 30 other guys,
with the catgut stretched across and tied in the middle. When the
button was pressed the catgut flicked
away and you just had to react quickest. I think I flipped it, or did a
massive wheelie in my first ever
motocross start, which is all part of
gaining experience.

FOGGY FACTOR

'The thing to
concentrate on, apart
from jumping the start,
is to keep the front
wheel down. As long
as you could get the
clutch out and keep
the front wheel down,
you'd probably be
okay.'

I think I crouched over the bike a
lot more than the other superbike
riders on the start. And I used to blip
the throttle a lot before slipping the
clutch out. Some guys don't like to
blip the throttle but you're doing it
that quickly it's almost the same as
keeping the revs constant. But if you
let go of the clutch all at once the front wheel will rear up, and you
could go over the back. If the front wheel has come up you have
to go back on the clutch a bit again to settle things down. If I ever
did get a bad start, I would tend to make up for it through the first
corner. I would quickly be able to suss out where to go, even if it
was round the outside, to make sure I came out of that first corner
in the first three or four.

Wet starts are perhaps even more important in that the first
rider into the first corner does not have the same visibility problems caused by the spray from riders in front. The key thing
about starting in the wet was to make sure the back wheel didn't
spin. Again, probably because I wasn't all that confident in the
wet, I used to do this quite a lot. I also think it had something to

do with the fact that I was a little bit lighter than some of the other riders. Maybe it also had to something to do with the bike set-up, or even because I was crouching too far over the front of the bike.

It sounds obvious but a wet start is totally opposite to a dry start: you must do everything less aggressively and more smoothly. It's almost like pulling away from the traffic lights in your car on a sunny day in Blackburn. Then, once you're moving, you open up the gas and, hopefully, the back wheel won't spin or start to slide around. Even if it did, the temptation was always not to back off and to keep the revs at the same level. And you would probably open the gas even more if you could see that everyone else was coming past you. This happened to me in my last ever start, when the conditions were still damp by the start of the second race. When I let go of the clutch on the line, the back wheel started to spin, everyone came past me and I was well down the field by the end of the first lap. Yet again, there's another factor that might have contributed to the events of that day at Phillip Island.

Another little trick to remember is not to put your front wheel on the painted white line, but just a little bit to the side. It's always fatal to touch the painted kerbs during a race. Nine times out of ten, if you touch that white line you are down. It happened to me at Magny Cours in 1991. I was going really well but, into a really fast corner onto the back straight, I just touched the white line and it flicked me off. Valentino Rossi did it in Mugello in 2001 when he crashed on the last lap with second place in the bag. If you do happen to touch them, you have to let go of the throttle straight away and not go anywhere near the brakes. You could even fall off without touching the brakes, they are that lethal. And some paints are more slippery than others. It depends on the type of paint and how long it has been down there, I guess.

It's perhaps even more important not to have your wheels touching the paint when you want maximum drive at the start. I have even seen teams with rags trying to dry the paint and the section of track just in front of the rider. They'll be bringing hairdryers out onto the grid next!

RACING

RACE STRATEGY

2: Strategy

Let's assume that the unlikely happens and I'm not first into that first corner – that's where my aggressive riding style kicks in immediately. I was always one to take risks very early on in a race to make sure I was as far up the field as possible in the early stages.

The more experience I got, the better I became at attacking that first corner. Even if I entered a corner in fourth or fifth, I could still exit it in first. It's strange when you think about it, but I could also beat someone like Troy Corser through the first corner. For a rider who is very good at doing one-off fast laps, you would think he'd be very fast from the start. If you don't get past a lot of riders at that early stage, you end up with a lot of guys on very fast bikes in front of you and it's not easy to get past them. Then, by the time you've worked your way up through the field, you'll have used up a lot of your own energy as well as a lot of the rear tyre of the bike.

It's amazing that in all the years I've been racing, I've never really been involved in any first corner carnage. Even when I watch now, I think, *How on earth are they all going to get round there?* But when you're out there on the bike there seems to be a lot more room than there actually is. You know when riders are getting close to you and you either lift the bike up a touch or drop it out of the way to create that little bit of extra space. Luckily, more often than not I was away with the leading pack. You have more chance of getting caught up in all the crap when you're going into the corner in 19th or 20th position.

Probably the earliest I have ever been knocked off in a race was the third or fourth corner, at Albacete in 1997. I was third, and local guy Gregorio Lavilla came inside me, hit me and went down. He was practically dragging me down with him and I had to pick the bike up, run through the gravel and come back onto the track – in last place.

One of the worst first corners is at Laguna Seca because you've got some speed up going over the brow of the straight before dropping downhill. It's a tricky, slippery corner at the best of times, without having all the other riders around you. But you can make up a lot of time there, so if someone laid odds on which of all the circuits would most likely cause a pile-up, I would expect that to be favourite. Monza might also now have a case for being the worst, now that the track layout has been changed. You can always expect problems at the end of a long straight entering a very tight first-gear corner. Everyone is braking as late as possible and scrubbing off speed, so that the entire pack is dragged together. Donington is probably one of the better ones.

If I was down in third or fourth after the first couple of turns, that was okay, but if I could see the leaders getting away and a couple of people were in my way, I would do everything possible to pass them quickly. I might have to make an aggressive move, even if it meant messing up my next corner – anything as long as I went past them. That's the same for everybody. It's not until you get four of five laps under your belt that you can perhaps settle down a little bit, get into a rhythm and start to assess where you are in the race. But whether you're in second place or in the lead, you've got to get your head down and try to go as fast as you can for the rest of the race. It cannot be any simpler than that.

Some riders talk about saving their rear tyre during the race, but they're talking out of their arses. Very occasionally, on one or two tracks, I might have thought about tyre conservation just a little bit. At Phillip Island, for instance, because we always knew we would have tyre problems there. Misano was another place where we struggled. So I would perhaps try to tuck in behind somebody and use their bike to drag me along. The main thing was to try not to spin the back wheel. That's just common sense. My style of riding didn't suit the bike spinning; I wanted it pushing forward, and if the wheel was spinning I would back off a little and try to short-shift the gears. So I would be trying to save my tyres, but not in the way other riders mean. They might say, 'It took me ages to get to the front and I destroyed my rear tyre, so I couldn't win the race.' That's bullshit. No matter where you are in the race, you don't want your back wheel spinning from lap one to the end of the race.

So, apart from at Phillip Island to a certain extent, at every other track I would be going as fast as I could to win the race. Exactly how do you save a tyre anyway? Stop halfway through the race and give it a breather? If you start trying to save a tyre and the guy in front is going as hard as he can, he's just going to pull away. If that rider isn't pulling away, then you don't have to be as hard on your rear tyre. Under those circumstances, I would delay passing him if I thought it was inevitable I would go through, and as long as there was nobody pushing me from behind. Then it would be a case of picking the right moment, overtaking nice and smoothly and then pushing hard for the next few laps. If I wasn't getting away, I would push even harder until the end of the race. I wouldn't just sit there thinking the race was sewn up. At Phillip Island in 1998 I did have a comfortable lead and, because it was that track, I was conscious of not destroying the rear tyre. I went from leading by six or seven seconds to winning by a second. But it was all under control because I knew that was all I needed to do to win the race. Even so, the tyre was knackered at the end. If I had carried on pushing while I was in the lead, it would have blown and I would have lost the race. So you do have to use some common sense now and again.

But when somebody's catching you, or you're trying to pull away without success, then everything goes out the window and you go as fast as you can. In the second race of 1999 in Australia, I was neck and neck with Troy Corser the whole round. I was sat behind him, caught him up, passed him and tried to pull away. But then I got caught up with some back markers, something which had cost me the first race, and he was back on my arse again. There weren't many laps to go and I knew Corser had the energy and motivation to stay with me and try to win the race. After I lost the lead, the rear tyre was chattering and I was just riding round, knowing that it was going to come down to the last lap. He made a mistake, I passed him and thought I would win the race, but he came through on the line to beat me by five-thousandths of a second. And at no time during those final five laps or so was anyone thinking about conserving their tyres!

I think riders use tyre conservation as an excuse for being beaten, especially Corser. If he said that he had used his tyres up too much early in the race, I would think, *What are you trying to say? That I didn't?*

Another important aspect of race strategy is the use of boards on the pitwall to tell the rider what is happening during a race. I always wanted my board to be kept as simple as possible. There was no need to tell me what position I was in because I already knew that. The only time they might put the position on was during a wet race, whenever the team suspected I couldn't see how many other riders were in front of me. Usually I just wanted to know how many laps remained, but even then they only started to count them down when there were something like 10 to go. The only other information would be either +3, to say that I was three seconds in front of the rider behind me, or −3, to tell me that the rider in front was three seconds ahead.

If I was second, the team would let me know about the more pressing gap. For instance, if there was a danger I could be caught from behind, they would tell me about the guy behind me. If, however, there was more chance of me catching the guy in front, they would concentrate on that gap. Having said that, there was always more of a chance that the information on my board would be about what was happening behind me, because I could

> **FOGGY FACTOR**
>
> 'If I was down in third or fourth after the first couple of turns, there would be no great problem. But if I could see the leaders getting away and a couple of riders were in the way, I would do everything possible to pass them quickly.'

pretty well gauge whether I was catching the bloke in front.

The trend these days is for more information about the times to be added. A lot of teams now use +1.2 or +1.7. I didn't want that. 'Look, let's work in point five of a second,' I would tell the team. 'That's all I need. Point one of a second doesn't mean anything to me and will only confuse me.' And it would always bring a little smile inside my helmet whenever I had been going along at +2, +2, +2 and suddenly the board showed +2.5.

On certain occasions, usually towards the end of a season when I was closing in on the championship, they would let me know who it was behind me. And in some races, all I wanted to know was where my title rivals were. For instance, at Sugo in 1998 I was half a point in the lead going into the final race of the year, so the only thing I wanted to see on my board was how Aaron Slight was doing because I knew that as long as I was in front of him I would win the title. At one stage the board read:

$$
\boxed{
\begin{array}{l}
\textsf{Foggy} \\
\textsf{+2} \\
\textsf{Slight 4}
\end{array}
}
$$

That meant Slight was in fourth place and two seconds behind me, although I was second in the race. On the next lap it was '+3 Slight 5', so I knew things were heading in the right direction.

Many other riders always want to know who is directly behind them, even in the races at the start of the season. Perhaps they think that if they know another rider's style, or how his bike is set up, they can predict when he will make a move to pass. That didn't really bother me. If I was desperate to find out who was behind me I would have a quick look round, which was something I did a lot more than the others. I didn't lose time or concentration by doing it, so it was never an issue – except for my dad in my early career. He was sure I was going to fall off at some time if I carried on doing it, but the very fact that he was telling me not to do it made me do it all the more. I always knew what I was doing and it never cost me any time.

More often than not, in fact, I would have a pretty good idea of who was behind me through pure instinct. If the gap stayed at

+1 for five or six laps on a certain track I would guess, say, that it was Aaron Slight who was being typically difficult to shake off. *I bet it's bloody Slight. He's the only one who won't give up round here* – that's what I'd be thinking before having a quick look round to confirm my suspicions.

From what I can gather, there used to be some right ding-dong arguments between Davide Tardozzi and Slick about what to put on the board. They used to get into a right panic. If I was a team manager, there would be times when I wouldn't let my rider know that he was pulling away from the guy behind, and there might also be times when, if he had finally opened up a bit of a gap, even if it wasn't a full second, I would put +1 on the board to give him a bit of encouragement to push even harder. It all depends on what is happening in any particular race.

I can understand why the team would try to think for me in certain situations. If I had been +2 for a few laps and had pulled out half a second more by the next lap, they might only decide to tell me when I had reached +3. That way it maintained my determination to keep the gap the same, and when I did achieve another full second it would give me the confidence that what I was doing was working.

Boards can, though, cause confusion. In Austria in 1998 I thought I was leading by four seconds at the start of the last lap – then Slight came steaming past me! I must have read some other rider's board. It's easier to do than you might think, because a lot of guys use the same fluorescent orange and yellow colours to try to make their boards stand out.

'Get that bloody board out as far as you can!' I would say to Slick. 'You're a big bloke, just make sure that it's out further than the rest.'

'But Honda are in front of us, so there's nothing I can do.'

'Well, just hit the bastard then. I want to be able to see that board!'

It actually doesn't make it any easier that all the top teams tend to be at the same end of the pit-lane, so all the boards come out at roughly the same time. Especially somewhere like Monza or Hockenheim, where the first few riders are usually bunched together; it can be really difficult to pick out your own board.

And you don't want to have to turn your head slightly from behind the shield in case it alters your slipstreaming down the straight. The most important information at those tracks is the number of laps remaining because you have to make sure that you're in the right position entering that final lap. Pluses and minuses mean nothing there.

At the TT you're signalled at three points around the track. The first used to be at Ballacraine, but it's now at Glen Helen. So, somewhere after Glen Helen and before Ballaugh, someone would jump out with the board, and you were always dying to know whether you were in the lead and by how many seconds because you couldn't see any other riders and had no idea how you were doing. The next timing point is at the Ramsey Hairpin, so the next good place to signal is when you come out of the Gooseneck and head up the mountain. But there isn't much distance between those two points. If, for instance, I was number 1 and dicing for the lead with number 12 Steve Hislop, then you would have to wait for him to come through before working out the lead. And by that time I would almost be at the Gooseneck, so there would be a risk that I wouldn't get the information in time, so the guy with the board might have to move further up the mountain. Of course, the final timing point is through start and finish.

The funniest story regarding boards was when Wayne Gardner was riding for Mal Carter, Alan Carter's father. He was a real character, but he was known for calling a spade a spade. Gardner was riding in one of his first races on his Yamaha at Donington in the days when they used chalk on a blackboard. He was that far behind that Mal drew a picture of a snail on the blackboard and stuck it out for Gardner to see the next time he came past. I can imagine doing something like that – although I'd probably draw a big cock instead!

RACING

RACE STRATEGY

3: Overtaking

There was only ever one place where I was totally happy during a race – in the lead. But there were the odd occasions when it was better not being out in front going into the last lap, at circuits such as Monza and Hockenheim, where the slipstream effect means there is very little you can do to prevent another rider from coming past at certain points on the track. On any track, if it's a close race, there is always some point where you'll need to block a move on the last lap. But at Monza and Hockenheim, where the straights are the longest in the championship, the only way you can block a pass is to weave all over the track, which can be dangerous and illegal. So the last position you want to be in coming into the final lap is first.

At Hockenheim, you actually still want to be in second place when you're coming out of the final chicane. At this stage, there are usually three or four riders still in contention on this circuit. If you're in fourth, you have an awful lot of work to do; if you're in third, you have a chance because you can slipstream the guy in second place, who, in turn, is slipstreaming the rider in first. I have done that, and it has been done to me. Having said all that, although you know where you want to be, it doesn't always work out that way because there are another couple of riders thinking exactly the same thing.

It's pretty much the same at Monza. You ideally want to be exiting the last chicane in second place, before the long run down to the last corner. If you get into that last corner in first place, you've won the race. Having said that, the last time I raced there I still managed to win the race even though I didn't enter the final turn in first place. That was because I was very quick on the exit of the corner and came out right behind Edwards, almost touching his back tyre. He came onto the inside, trying to shake me off, but instead cleared the air pocket for me to come through. I won by four inches.

However, that was after the start–finish line had been moved to the front of that straight. When it was at the bottom of the straight, the opposite applied. You knew that if you were leading going into the final corner, the guy behind would definitely be able to slipstream you over the line. That happened to me in 1997; I didn't have a prayer. The Hondas were quicker than my bike on the straight, so I outbraked them going into the final corner, took the lead and saw the chequered flag. But I also knew what was going to happen. I was crouched down as far as was physically possible behind the visor, just waiting for them to fly past – which they did. I was nearly crying. If the start–finish line had been where it is now, I would have won that race without a doubt.

Even on circuits like Donington, which don't have long straights, strategy still plays a part. If someone is right behind you entering a first-gear hairpin, then they are going to come up the inside of you and have a go. But on any final lap anywhere, it's down to who wants it most, who wants to find that tiny gap to squeeze through. If you're leading, all you can do is take a tight line and weave just enough to upset the other rider.

Before it boils down to the last lap, though, you normally will have had to negotiate the dreaded back markers. As I have already said, Australia and Japan are the worst two places for overtaking back markers. In Australia in 1999, they cost me both races. I was catching Troy in the first race and was badly held up by back markers, losing the two seconds that made all the difference. In the second race I was pulling away from him when one of them got in my way again. I lost the lead and Troy gained a

I lead Neil Hodgson and Pier-Francesco Chili, my two Ducati team-mates, during my 40th career win and my first back on a Ducati in 1997 at Donington Park.

second wind and pipped me on the line by an inch. I was furious at the time, but I had a laugh with him afterwards.

'How much did you pay those two Aussies to get in my way?' I asked him.

'They could see you coming, mate!' he replied.

'You're dead right they could.'

And in Japan, when a wild card sees the blue flag when he's about to be lapped, it seems to mean to him: 'Fast rider coming – must try harder!' There is more chance of them moving into your line than of moving out of the way. They also cost me a race, in 1993 at Sugo, when I had built up a three-second lead over Scott Russell. I tried to get underneath a wild-card idiot who would not get out of the way, I gassed it too hard, and the bike flicked me off. Raymond Roche and a guy called Jacques, who was working on the team, found the rider later and pinned him against the wall at the back of his garage. Jacques was ready to punch his lights out and Raymond had to pull him off, although he also wanted to kill him.

There are basically three ways to overtake: on the inside on the brakes, slipstreaming and round the outside. I would say that around 80 per cent of all overtaking manoeuvres are done on the brakes up the inside of another rider. It's also the easiest way of passing another rider. You get as close as you can to the other rider before pulling out to the inside. You instinctively know how close you have to be; if you are any further back than that, there's no way you're going to attempt to pass. Then, when you have moved to the inside, it's up to you to be later on the brakes than the other rider.

Obviously that makes the bike unstable and will affect your lap times, because you will have scrubbed off a lot of speed by braking so late. You aren't likely to be able to keep as tight a line through the corner as normal, but that's not a problem because you're forcing the other rider out wider as a result. Also, you won't be able to carry as much speed mid-corner as you would normally, and because the bike might be unstable you have to be careful when you get back on the gas. These are all factors to bear in mind when you are overtaking on the inside, although none is important if you're on the last lap and it's your last chance to overtake the leader. For me, and especially at the wider corners like Redgate at Donington, it was fairly easy because my lines into the corner were tighter than most. I was already at an advantage if I wanted to go up the inside, and I didn't have to lose much speed there. The danger is that you go into one of these corners too hot and, even though you've gone up the inside, you have to run too wide on the exit. That leaves you vulnerable to riders coming back up your inside before getting onto the next straight. It doesn't happen too often, but it's still something to be aware of.

FOGGY FACTOR

'The key to slipstreaming is timing and making sure that you're in the right gear. The thing not to do is to run up behind the other rider and then change gear.'

Trying to pass on the outside is much more difficult because all the other rider has to do is move slightly wider by letting go of his brakes, pushing you even wider and maybe off the track. So you don't see this manoeuvre all that often; in fact you could probably go through a lot of races without seeing it at all. Basically, you're going the long way round and that is never a good way of going round a track. If it does happen it is at the faster corners, and it does look really good. Again, because I carried more corner speed, I was probably more likely to pull this off than most.

The key to slipstreaming is timing and making sure that you're in the right gear. The thing not to do is to run up behind the other rider and then change gear. The correct way to overtake by slipstreaming is to run up behind, change the gear so the bike is pulling through the revs nicely, and then pull out. The theory is that the guy in front has punched a wide hole in the air. This allows you to follow at the same pace, even when you pull out from directly behind him, while using less power to maintain your own speed. So, when you do reach top gear just as you pull out of the slipstream, you are going much quicker than the guy who was in front of you.

The thing to be wary of is the bike in front suddenly slowing, and there are a couple of telltale signs to look out for. A puff of blue smoke from the exhaust might mean he is having engine problems and it might be about to blow. Black smoke might mean he has missed a gear. Either way there's a danger of slamming into his back at frightening speed, in a similar way to my career-ending crash in Australia.

Another danger is that you can be dragged along too quickly, because then you can be approaching a bend at the bottom of a straight too quickly. There's many a time when you actually just have to roll the throttle off a bit.

It is a weird feeling, being pulled along so quickly, and the same goes for when someone is slipstreaming you. I could actually feel the bike being sucked back when someone was about to come past, and there is nothing you can do about it.

Track

8   *Phillip Island*

This is a track that has seen possibly the highest and lowest points of my career. Now it will always be remembered as the place where my career was ended, but I prefer to remember winning my first World Superbike title there. Even so far away from home, it was absolutely amazing.

Having won the first race pretty comfortably, all I needed to do for the second race was come fourth if Scott Russell won. I was leading at one point, but I felt nervous and dropped back to third where I could keep an eye on the two Kawasakis of Anthony Gobert, who cleared off, and Russell in second place. I was as happy as Larry just staying put.

Then Russell waved me past and I didn't know what was going on. I thought, *He's going to try to knock me off here.* But he allowed me through and the world championship was mine. I could not pull any wheelies or stand on the pegs for the lap of honour, despite there being quite a few British flags in the crowd. All I could do was sit there with my head in my hands, crying my eyes out. Then, when I eventually got back to the pits, I had to push the television crews and the rest of my team out of the way so that I could hug Michaela.

Generally, I was a lot better around the back part of the circuit than the front half. I would pass the start–finish line on Gardner Straight in fifth gear, and at the fastest part of the track, just before Doohan Corner, I just about touched sixth. It's very hard to spot your braking marker for that downhill fourth-gear corner, a very fast bend. For some reason, they've painted white numbered markers at the side of the track, but to spot these by looking down at the track when you are travelling at nearly 300kmph is nearly impossible and there never used to be any braker boards at the side of the track to help you out. I once complained about this and I think now they've been set up.

It's a classic fast corner where I always struggled to outbrake anyone and get past another rider. It should have been a good place to pass after slipstreaming someone down the straight, but because I braked that little bit earlier than the others, although I was quicker in mid-corner, I was never able actually to overtake them.

The turn gradually levels out and there is a slight uphill slope as you come out in fourth gear, before you drop down to third for the Southern Loop. I go in off the gas and then pick up the throttle a little bit and try to carry some corner speed, while keeping the bike tucked in rather than letting it drift wide. I ran straight off at that point and into the gravel during the Sunday morning warm-up in 1998 when the brakes failed to would properly. The bike fell over into the gravel and I came into the pits really mad. Slick apologized to me for not telling me they had put new pads on the brakes, which would not have worked as well as the old ones at first. Maybe I should have been taking it a bit easier during warm-up in any case, at least for half a lap. He just about got the bike ready in time for the first race, which I went out and won.

Then it's hard on the gas in third gear, up to fourth and then quickly into fifth for one of the fastest corners on any circuit, because you're almost flat out coming to the top of the brow where the bridge is.

This is where it all happened on that fateful date. Even now I'm still not perfectly clear about what happened. On a normal lap, you come off the gas a bit as you come into the corner so that everything is transferred to the front end of the bike. I was trying desperately to get back up with the leaders after a poor start and was sitting on the shoulder of Robert Ulm at 140mph, lining up to pass him at the next slower corner. It would appear that his bike cut out, I hit his back end and the rest is history. As daft as it sounds, though, this is generally a very safe track and it has to be remembered that mine was a freak accident.

Assuming this time that I don't fly into the tyre wall, knock myself out, smash my arm in three places and wake up in a

PHILLIP ISLAND

AUSTRALIA

Rating **7**

"I found this a very difficult track because the weather always plays a big part. It's also the worst track in the world for destroying rear tyres"

Closest finish: Beaten by Troy in the second race by five one thousanths of a second in 1999

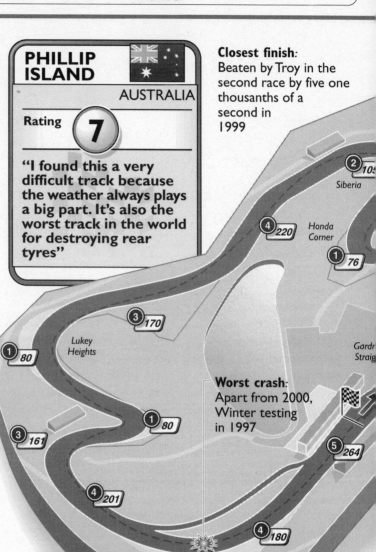

Siberia

Honda Corner

Lukey Heights

Gardr Straig

Worst crash: Apart from 2000, Winter testing in 1997

Best moment: Celebrating my first World Superbike title back in the pit-lane by hugging my wife Michaela

Worst moment:
The crash in 2000 which prematurely
ended my career

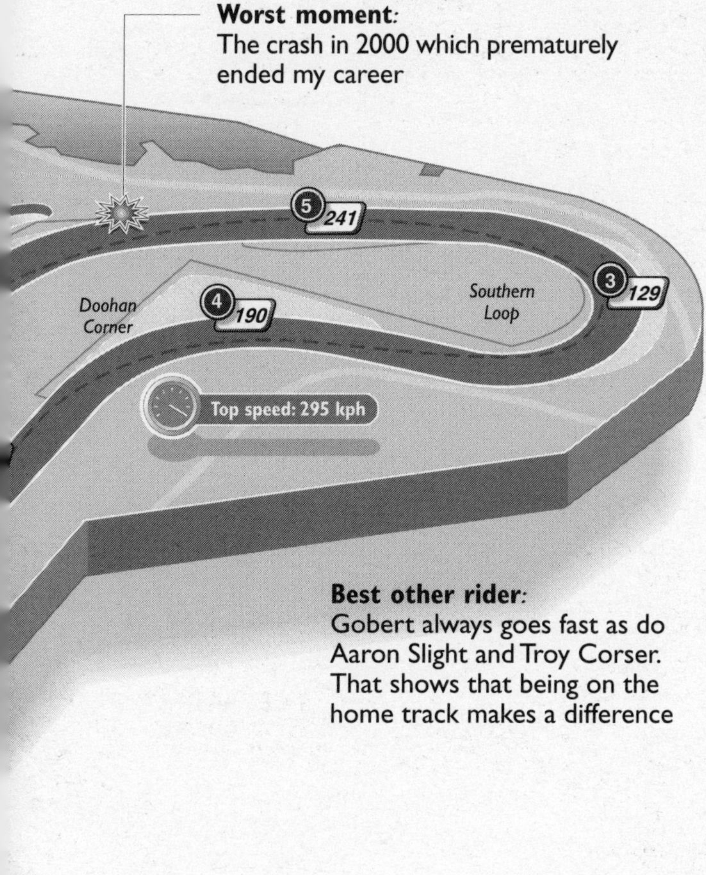

⑤ 241

④ 190

③ 129

Doohan
Corner

Southern
Loop

Top speed: 295 kph

Best other rider:
Gobert always goes fast as do
Aaron Slight and Troy Corser.
That shows that being on the
home track makes a difference

Melbourne hospital bed, I accelerate out of the corner in fifth, before *bang, bang, bang, bang* it's straight down to first for Honda Corner. The main thing to concentrate on here is stopping the bike from snaking around while it's going from a very high speed to a very low speed in such a short space of time. It would largely depend on how the bike was set-up as to how quickly I went down the gears. Some years I had no problem outbraking people after coming down through the gears quickly, but it was always a bit hit and miss.

It's a poxy, bumpy little corner and you have to be careful not to lose the rear end, especially early on in a race because it is the first slow corner on the right-hand side. Out of the corner, I change up to second and leave it there to roll round Siberia, which is a bit like the Southern Loop. This corner seems to hang on for ever and it's a classic point for photos – it can look as though you are riding off into the sea. Again, some years I had a really good set-up on the bike and was able to accelerate all the way round while keeping a good line at other times, especially with the Honda in 1996 and the Ducati in 1997, the bike always wanted to run out wider. I always seemed to run out of time during qualifying when I wanted to try out different ways of keeping the bike tighter in at Siberia and the Southern loop. It seemed I was losing traction by trying to lean the bike even further over in an attempt to keep the tightest possible line.

Coming out of Siberia, I accelerate slightly uphill in third, then up into fourth before a very fast bend – a kind of 'esses'. I really hang over the left-hand side before quickly changing direction to the right-hand side. There used to be a lot of bumps on the entry to that right-hand bend, but the whole circuit has now been resurfaced and it's a lot smoother. Then it's uphill in third to Lukey Heights where, again, I'm holding a bit of throttle all the way round a long fast left where it's possible to pass somebody on the inside, before dropping down to another very slow, first-gear corner.

Then I short-shift up to third to a very difficult part of the track. The back end can really slide around, even when the tyres are fresh. Third gear tends to be a bit tall, but by the time you have wound it on it's better to be in third gear. The final turn is another very important part of the track. In fact, you win races at Phillip Island at the first and last corners, which happen to be my weakest parts of the track.

In 1999, I came out of that final turn in the lead, but Troy Corser came out that little bit quicker, got into my slipstream and won the race by five-thousandths of a second. I used to change to fourth just before the final bend but I've never been happy with that as, again, it's a bit tall. It was too much for third gear – by the time you are exiting the bike is revving its tits off – but it always felt as though there wasn't enough power to hold it together in fourth, that it was just running away with me slightly. You can't alter the distance between third and fourth on a Ducati, like the four-cylinder guys can, so we were at a little bit of a disadvantage. But, then again, the Ducatis usually have a broader span for their gears, so there isn't usually a problem.

In winter testing in 1997, the throttle stuck wide open. It was probably the most frightening crash I have ever had. As I tipped in, the back came round speedway style. If the back end had come round and tipped me off, I would have been seriously hurt. The massive slide seemed to go on for ever before the front end tucked under and I slid off into the grass. Luckily, there wasn't a mark on me. That was my first day back on a Ducati and it really put me off taking that corner the next day. I didn't think anyone would believe me that the throttle had stuck open, but luckily it showed up on the telemetry, which got me off the hook!

One of the main things you have to take into account at Phillip Island is the changeable weather. The wind can

> **FOGGY FACTOR**
>
> 'Assuming you don't fly into the tyre wall, knock yourself out, smash your arm in three places and wake up in a Melbourne hospital bed, you accelerate out of turn eight in fifth, before *bang, bang, bang, bang* it's straight down to first for Honda Corner.'

change direction very quickly, which always seemed to upset both me and the bike, and I always seemed to have problems with the helmet pushing down on my ears and nose going down the straight. They say you can have all four seasons in one day at Phillip Island. When it's hot, it's very hot, but the temperature can suddenly drop by 15 degrees, as it did during the second race in 1998. It made me catch my breath, the change was so sudden.

Another thing you have to look out for are some really big birds – not the women who flock to the island for the weekend's racing, but massive things that look like turkeys. I have no idea what species they actually are. They seem to amble along the track, and before you know it they're walking straight across the track. Sometimes you have to send someone out to do a lap to frighten them off because these things can do some serious damage. I have never hit one but an Aussie rider, Martin Craggill, once pulled out of someone's slipstream to overtake and hit one with his shoulder. The impact almost took his arm straight off; it was badly dislocated behind his back and he was out of racing for almost a year. The only other place where there are similar wildlife worries is Indonesia, where one year a family of baboons made their home inside the circuit and would just sit there and watch at the side of the track as you screamed past them.

Phillip Island has never been a great track for British riders, as I also remember Jamie Whitham and Neil Hodgson struggling there. It was better for me because I was able to carry some corner speed at some points. It has never been great for creating atmosphere either. Australia is probably one of those countries that is still more into Grand Prix racing than superbikes, with around 40,000 the best attendance. But that's possibly because it is in the middle of nowhere. The Aussies do, however, tend to come onto the track at the end of a race and make a lot of noise around the podium.

As I've already explained, this is one of the tracks that's very hard on tyres, but one year it was not the tyres on my bike which were causing all the problems. As usual, I had hired a car to travel to and from the circuit and we used the car to ride round before a test session, trying to dry the track out. Slick was driving, and as we approached the hairpin corner I shouted, 'Slow down! You're not going to make it round!'

'Don't fret, of course I am,' Slick said, by which time we had run out of even more track. He stomped on the brakes and the other mechanics were able to see the smoke from in the pits. The car juddered its way round the corners but the tyres were absolutely ruined, with flat spots all the way round where the tread had been left on the track. When we took the car back to the hire place the tyres were virtually bald. Slick thought this was hilarious, but I didn't see the funny side when I had to cough up AUS$500 to cover the cost of new tyres.

Section 5

OTHER TYPES OF BIKE RACING

'When I've been on rideouts with Carl, I've found that he's just as competitive when he's out having fun as he must have been when he was racing. Whatever bike he's riding, the competitive edge just doesn't seem to go away.

'At one point we were coming up to a sharp left-hander. He was going so fast that I was a bit scared we were going to be collecting him off the wall. But he got his knee down on the knobbly tyres of his enduro bike as though it was second nature and got round without a problem.

'He had no problem through the speed sections all day, it was as if he'd stepped off his road bike and onto his enduro bike. There was just one really steep section filled with boulders where his legs weren't long enough to keep him on the bike, so he came off on a few occasions. I don't think he was best pleased about that, but when everybody else is laughing about it you have to take it in good spirit, and he soon saw the funny side.

'Carl's obviously best suited to road racing, but like a lot of other riders if you have that ability to win you can use it for different types of riding. He chose superbikes and had a marvellous career. But I think that, with his natural ability on a bike, he could just as easily have turned to another bike sport without any problem.'

Dougie Lampkin
World Trials Champion

OTHER TYPES OF BIKE RACING

COMPETITIVE

1: Endurance

There can't be many riders who have competed for just one year in a motorcycling discipline and ended up as world champion, with a record of having won every 24-hour race. But that's what I did in my only season of competing in the World Endurance Championship in 1992. Granted, the opposition was not of the highest calibre. I never thought there was anyone in the championship capable of beating me and my Kawasaki team-mates Terry Rymer and Jean d'Orgeix, so it was more a case of just keeping the bike going. We managed to do that, so we won the championship.

The one thing you need above all else for endurance riding is concentration. Apart from that, it's basically the same as riding in a World Superbike race, apart from backing everything down a notch. You cannot go that fast for 24 hours. The first hour of the race is usually quite mad – like the start of any race really. You're fresh, the bike is fresh and everything should be working spot-on at that stage in the race. But as every hour goes by, the bike starts to move around more and gets dirtier. And when the light begins to fade, that's when the powers of concentration have to be at their peak.

One of the things you have to look out for as night approaches is a slow rider. And there are a lot of them around in the World Endurance Championship. But I was a pretty experienced rider in 1992, and even though I didn't have that much experience of endurance riding, I could still gauge how fast to go at various stages of the race. Having said that, I was never particularly quick during the night. It took me a while to get used to it, but eventually I got into a bit of a rhythm.

The standard of lighting differed from track to track. Some would have a few lights here and there, others would have just little reflective markers on the inside and outside of corners. Then again, by night time you'd been round the track so many times you could shut your eyes and ride round. I guess we were lucky that year because guys are always spilling oil on the track and in the dark you have no way of knowing where it is on the track. We never had any problems like that and didn't break down all season.

Le Mans, where I did my first-ever 24-hour race, was probably the worst place to ride round in the dark because it's a tight, twisty little circuit. The faster circuits like Spa or Bol d'Or were better because you didn't have to hang off the bike half as much. It was at Le Mans that I made the fatal mistake of endurance racing – falling asleep! I just laid down for a few minutes, not expecting to drift off. The next thing I knew there was a bang on the door from one of the Kawasaki France team telling me to get ready because I was out on the track in 10 laps' time. Normally, if I fall asleep that's me out for the count for seven or eight hours. I'd only had enough time for forty winks, so I was totally knackered when I climbed back on the bike. It took me three laps to wake myself up and realize properly where I was.

I learned from that mistake, and I never did it again. The only way to stay awake is to keep on the move, and preferably outside. I drank a lot of coffee for the caffeine and was always nibbling on bits of chocolate or stuffing myself with pasta. I didn't mind how

---

FOGGY FACTOR

'I drank a lot of coffee for the caffeine and was always nibbling on bits of chocolate or stuffing myself with pasta. I didn't mind how much I was eating because it was helping me stay awake.'

much I was eating because it was helping me stay awake, and I knew I would be burning it all off within a few minutes anyway. By seven in the morning I'd be looking forward to my bowl of cornflakes as normal. Whatever you do, though, you must never go into your little room where there's an inviting bed tempting you to close your eyes. I don't know how the small privateer teams managed, because we had everything like food and doctors laid on a plate for us in a mini-village, while they seemed to have nothing.

During that 1992 campaign there were three 24-hour races and three 8-hour races, at Suzuka, Phillip Island and Johor. I was never a fan of the Suzuka race, although it's a massive thing for the Japanese manufacturers as it demonstrates how reliable their bikes are. It was never a big deal for me. I used to think that it interfered with my main goal, the World Superbike Championship. By the time we were back in England it was usually about time for the Brands Hatch round and we were still feeling the effects. Still, I had some good results and some bad results at Suzuka, and again it's all about concentration for your 50-minute stint. Then, when you're not on the bike, you have to have the right back-up to make sure your blisters are treated and that you have replaced all the water lost through sweating so much. The trick is to bandage any area that's starting to feel sore, because after another few hours on the bike it's going to feel a lot worse.

I actually found the 8-hour races more physically demanding than the 24-hour races. That's because an 8-hour race is more of a sprint race and the guys that finish in the top ten of the Suzuka 8 Hours – the top superbikes and Grand Prix riders – don't tend to do the 24-hour races. In the others you were up against the 24-hour specialists, mainly Frenchmen like Herve Moineau, who weren't as fast.

It was while Moineau was being treated in an ambulance at Spa that I had one of the scariest moments ever on a bike. He had hit some oil on the track and I also hit it coming round the Blanchimont corner. There was nothing I could do; I was heading straight for the ambulance with nothing like gravel to slow me down. The bike twitched but I stayed on, missing the ambulance by inches. Had I hit it, I'm sure I would have been killed.

I had no time to react to that incident, but I had much more to plot in the build-up to the penultimate race of the season at Phillip Island, where I was also riding in the World Superbike race. We had done enough in the endurance race to clinch the world title, with one round in Malaysia remaining the following week. Terry Rymer had been my team-mate all the way through the season, so we were on equal points. I started to think that if I was injured in the World Superbike race in Australia I might not be able to race in Johor and Terry would win the title outright, so I took the first chance to pull in during the second race, claiming that the Kawasaki wasn't handling properly.

It was a difficult bike to ride, the fastest out there but a big bulbous thing. It was more like a big Formula One bike than a superbike. And that was the last year prototype bikes were allowed in world endurance, where anything a factory built was allowed to race. It was really difficult to climb over and I had to spread my legs sideways, unlike Terry, who was a lot taller than me. It was particularly difficult to ride in Suzuka, a round that was never going to affect the championship. It kept decking out everywhere and the fairing was catching on the floor. Terry crashed it, and because we were down in ninth or tenth I was willing him to leave it in the gravel. But he picked it up and, although I was ready to change over, rode through before, sure enough, crashing it on the very next lap. This time he was on my wavelength and did not get back on. 'I was pressing the starter but it wouldn't go, so I just left it there,' he said when he returned to the pits. Of course, when the mechanic picked it up he pressed the start button and it fired up straight away. I'm not sure what the team thought about that!

One of the hardest things about endurance racing is recovering afterwards. You were on a high after winning a race, but then you had to face the long journey home. After the first one in Le Mans, we drove to Paris before catching a morning flight, but I was so tired that every time I shut my eyes, I felt as though still I was on the track. Lights were coming towards me until, suddenly, I came to a bend and woke up with a jolt. I guess my body had just become accustomed to going round and round and round the track. I know a lot of other guys had the same problems.

The World Endurance Championship still exists, but it seems to go unnoticed. It was a lot bigger in the seventies and eighties. The British press aren't interested. It's always been more of a French thing, like the TT is a British thing. I think we've had a couple of world champions in the last few years, but I'm afraid to say I wouldn't even be able to remember their names.

OTHER TYPES OF BIKE RACING

COMPETITIVE

2: Enduro or trail riding

Whenever I travel with a group of fellow bike fanatics to the Lake District, our days up there are a mixture of some serious enduro or trail bike riding and some serious fun. A typical CCM 'rideout' day will usually consist of a few hours in the morning before stopping at a pub in the middle of Coniston for lunch. Luckily, the landlady knows us, knows what we're like, and is very broad-minded. It's actually a really nice place (but we always tell her the food is crap!).

Then it's off for the afternoon ride. In the summer, a van follows us around, keeping in radio contact and meeting us at certain points to repair any problems or replace any broken parts like clutch levers. Then it's into Bowness for a meal and a few beers before staying in one of the log cabins at Whitecross Bay. There's always some feeling worse than others when it comes to the next morning, but there's nothing better than fresh air and a good ride for clearing the head.

The trails we follow are rights of way over moorland, which I guess were roads a hundred years ago. I've no idea how the hell people got up some of them with a horse and cart – sometimes I cannot get up there with 600cc underneath me! It's perfectly legal – when there's no foot and mouth crisis – but it will be interesting to see just how long it stays that way because, as always, there are those who want to stop people having a good time. That's one of the downfalls of living in England – everyone seems so jealous. If you go anywhere else in the world, you can almost do anything you want.

Ramblers are a case in point. We actually behave really well towards them. We always slow down, shut gates behind us, say a polite 'good morning' as we pass and the bikes don't leave a mess. In fact, ramblers leave more of a mess behind them than we do with their litter and dog shit. But you can tell from their expressions that they really hate us. They are the types of people I'd hate to have living next door, always complaining if the television's a bit too loud, always moaning until they get their own way. Hopefully, this type of day out will grow bigger and bigger, but somehow I fear that something or somebody will get in the way.

Although we behave well towards other people in the country-side, we don't always behave well to one another! Kev Moore, who I mentioned in the introduction, is just a total idiot and prankster. He has his own company and a nursing home and the other blokes all tend to be successful businessmen. My friend Geoff, who owns a helicopter company, is another regular. They aren't guys who just sit at home counting their money or mowing the lawn, they love to be out on bikes or water skis behaving like idiots. And you have to watch your back.

During one ride on a narrow trail, just about the only time we have been to the Peak District, the bloke in front had a puncture and we all had to stop and lie the bikes on a grass banking. A bloke called Toddy got the wheel out and started to mend the puncture. Kevin got off his bike and walked up from the back of the line, stood behind Toddy and started to piss on his back while he worked on the bloke's puncture. It was streaming down his back, down his leg and filling his boot. It was the funniest thing I've ever seen in my life. 'What's the matter with you?' Toddy asked, then everyone realized why I was howling. He turned round to see what was going on and started wrestling with Kev on the ground. They have been known to piss in each other's helmets, and my gloves were once filled with tomato ketchup. My

Riding an enduro bike in the Bahrain desert while on holiday as the guest of their Crown Prince.

favourite trick is to spray people with mud by dropping the clutch and spinning the back wheel. But I usually come off worse. Whenever we come to a gate into a cow field, it's a fair bet there will be a heap of cow muck on the other side, where the cows have been waiting to be let out. There's always a race to get to the gate to open it and cover everyone behind in crap.

But they also look out for each other. If someone comes off and a part of the bike is damaged, everyone mucks in to sort the problem out. Everyone except me, that is. I'm the one who sits around while the others sort it out because I've always been used to other people doing that kind of thing, so I'm probably not the best person to get involved.

And there is a serious side to it because we have some hideous crashes. On the public days, there's one rider to lead and one bringing up the rear to make sure everyone who has paid their money is okay. The rest of us have to take it at a more leisurely pace but I always want to go as fast as possible. And some of the new boys also push it a bit close to the edge. I remember one guy disappearing over the side of a track where there was a six-foot drop into some massive ferns. He completely vanished from view so I rode round the corner to see if I could see him from there. Still no sight of him; then the ferns started to rustle in a straight line, as though some monster from *Jurassic Park* was about to emerge, and he rode back onto the track a few yards further up. If that had been me, there would have been a pile of rocks at the bottom and my bike would have been a write-off.

Another big danger comes when we're approaching the brow of a hill. It's often deceptive, because you can't see what's over the other side. One time, when I was in front, I thought it was just flat field over the brow and I didn't see the gate until right at the last second. I anchored my brakes just in time and managed to stop – but that wasn't the end of it. The others came charging over the top, and when all the clanging and clunking had stopped there was a pile of about six riders and bikes, amazingly without any injuries. Luckily, it's usually nothing more serious than cuts and bruises and the van is always on hand if anyone has to call it a day.

During winter, though, there are no organized rides and we have to look after ourselves, without any back-up. And that can cause problems. Kevin once led a group straight through a river which was so deep in parts that the water was up to the top of the tank. Sure enough, off Geoff went, up to his neck. The first thing you have to do is pick the bike up as quickly as possible before water enters the airbox. On this occasion he was too late and it took them ages to drag the bike out and get it started again. Geoff was freezing his nuts off for about an hour while they sprayed WD40 on the electrics and dried the bike out. If that happens to someone else it's hilarious, but if it happens to you it's not funny at all.

Not surprisingly, I tend to be great on the fast, flat ground, but get me on a slope, when you need to be delicate on the throttle, then I'm probably the worst. I genuinely think it's because I'm not heavy enough. The big lads seem to be able to get the back wheel down and get a bit of grip. Maybe I'm too aggressive on the throttle, but I always end up spinning the back wheel halfway up hills, especially on slippery, grassy sections. Eventually, someone has to come down and get the bike up for me, which I absolutely hate. And it's usually somebody who's not as good as I was on the other sections, so that makes me feel even more like a failure.

Maybe I attack the flat sections a bit too much sometimes. We were once riding in Wales, several months after my crash in Australia when my arm was only just strong enough to handle a bike again. We were following signs for the sighted practice lap of the Affron Rally, which I was riding in under the name of Alan Pendry, another of my mates who used to do a bit of motocross riding. A couple of the marshals recognised me but didn't make a big deal out of it, although word soon got round. I was slightly worried about the arm, because the muscles were still weak, but I was really enjoying the ride, following the little orange arrows which pointed left or right to warn you of a bend. At first, I over-compensated whenever I saw an arrow, knocking down a gear and almost stopping before realizing that the bends were a lot faster than I had feared. Then I got some speed up in fifth gear on a small hill. The next arrow didn't point directly right, it was at a bit of an angle. I took that to mean there wasn't much of a bend, but it hit me in a flash that it was actually a chicane. I slammed the back brake on, dropped down the gearbox and ended up speedwaying into the corner, sliding the back wheel round. I knew I wasn't going to stop in time so I had to pick the bike up, straighten it and go over the edge – there was no other option. I landed on a rock and stayed on the bike before hitting a tree stump full on. That threw me over the top and I landed flat on my backside, 10 feet below the actual track. There wasn't a mark on me, but I thought, *You idiot, anything could have happened to you there*. A couple of lads had seen what happened and climbed down to pull the bike back onto the road. After that scare, I took it a bit easier for the rest of the day.

But when the results came out, Alan Pendry was in sixth! It was the best position he had ever been in on a bike. I had

FOGGY FACTOR

'My favourite trick is to spray people with mud by dropping the clutch and spinning the back wheel.'

expected to be in the top 20 at best. On the Sunday, I took it more seriously, changed my bike from a 640cc to a 600cc to make it a bit more rideable and tried to have a bit of a go. It had the opposite effect: I went slower rather than faster, probably because I was now trying too hard. I didn't get a finishing position because the chain snapped and I was unclassified. If I had finished that final section, I would probably have been in the top 10 overall for the two days, which I thought was pretty amazing, even though it was only for club-level riders. It's something I might have a go at again because it was great fun.

Steve Berry, from BBC's *Top Gear* programme, was with us a few times at the start of 1999, once after breaking his leg while riding a scooter, of all things. He caught his foot underneath it while pulling it out of a garage and the leg snapped – a right mess. It might not have seemed so bad had he crashed a Ducati 996 at 125mph, but to do it on a scooter must have been a bit embarrassing. He was obviously a bit nervous about his leg while riding with us. On one occasion he pulled up at a gate at the top of a slight slope in front of some other riders who had stopped. He put his foot down to steady himself but, because of the slope, there was no ground there and he toppled over, knocking four other riders down like a pack of dominoes. I managed to stay upright before rolling around with laughter.

You need to be a pretty big guy to ride these things. A lot of the time the sections you're tackling aren't for fast riding, but almost the same as trial riding. And if you're trying to flick your way up them on a big 600cc, it's better to be a big strong lad than someone like me who's all over the place, spinning the back wheel. The best guy we've had at it for a while is Paul Edmondson, who won the world championship a few years back then went off to America and, I think, has suffered a few injuries since. He was very fast and had a background in motocross racing like a lot of the enduro riders.

Track

9   *Sugo*

I wonder if it was after the first race at Sugo in 1995 that the clothing company Airwalk decided to be one of my sponsors. My high-side at the track that year was the biggest I've ever had. The rear end came so far round that I thought, *Well, it's just going to slide out on me now*. But it flicked me off so hard that I seemed to be walking on air, I was that far off the ground. I was very lucky to escape with cuts and bruises and a cracked small bone in my hand and foot. Had that happened during Saturday's qualifying I don't think I would have been fit to race, but because the adrenalin was flowing and the pain didn't really set in until the evening, I managed to pick myself up with the help of a few painkilling injections and win the second race. I've always said that it was at that point that I was at the peak of my riding.

I have probably had more accidents at Sugo than anywhere else, and I would say the same goes for 90 per cent of the other riders. But in general it's a good circuit, although it's hard to learn because the corners all look the same. It's laid out well, although the run-off is not as good as it could be and the grip is not brilliant. That's probably why there always seem to be a lot of crashes. It's down to the asphalt. I have raced there in hot and cold conditions and have always struggled with grip in the rear tyre.

When I first started the races were in August, which is in the Japanese summer and unbearably hot. In the last couple of years of my career the races were held at the end of the season when the temperature was just nice at around 20 degrees maximum. The only problem then, especially in the afternoon, was that the sun could get very low and blind you at a couple of corners.

The start–finish line is midway along the uphill main straight, which can be the quickest part of the track when the wind is from the west. I take the double right-hander first corner in second gear, with a similar braking point to other riders. You go in fast, pick the bike up, and then you're back down straight away before the track straightens out. The grip isn't good; apart from the 1995 crash, I also crashed in 1993. You could say that moment cost me the world championship, and it was certainly my lowest moment at this circuit.

I had beaten Scott Russell in the first race, and for the first time that year I was leading the world championship. That lasted just two hours, even though I should have won the second race as I was a second or two in the lead and again ahead of Russell, my rival for the title. But a backmarker got in the way and I tried to squirt past him, in between turns one and two. I lost the rear end and my title hopes went down with me.

Coming out of that second turn, the track drops down into a horrible, fast, third-gear corner. You're on and off the gas, and as you close off to go into the corner the surface is very bumpy. You see a lot of people lose their front end at the apex. I was one of them when I was riding for Honda in 1996. I actually broke a rib in two places, an injury which wasn't discovered until two weeks later at the Assen meeting. There aren't really enough revs to keep the bike in third gear but, coming out of the corner and using every inch of the rumble strips on the outside, you're soon accelerating away.

The next corner is a poxy, tight, first-gear corner. I've tried to stay in second over the years, but it was no good. Again, it's very easy to lose the rear and I remember Colin Edwards breaking his collarbone after high-siding in front of me in 1996. This is a circuit around which you can never lose concentration in terms of getting the right feel between the throttle and the rear of the bike. If you relax for a split second and give it a handful, the bike will let go so quickly.

Exiting that corner, I change up to second very quickly before the uphill chicane, where they have the first intermediate split time. I always struggled to change direction through this chicane unless we had a perfect set-up. On occasions, my feet and footrest seemed to be catching the surface. We got it right in 1998 by lifting the bike up and I went back to exactly the same set-up in 1999. That's the opposite of what you would expect. The bike usually steers better when you drop the forks through, but it didn't seem to work for us there. It's the only circuit where we would do this, but lifting it up by only as much as 5mm seemed to give me more ground clearance through all the corners, and especially that chicane.

For the next double right-hander, High Point and Rainbow Corners, I stay in second; if I do move up to third, I'm straight back down to second. It's fairly smooth going into the first part, but again a lot of people are caught out losing the rear trying to accelerate between the two apexes. The second corner of the two is another bumpy one where I struggled for ground clearance. I always wanted to lean the bike over to get a good drive down the back straight. I was forever catching my toes on the floor, and I was always conscious of the fact that I didn't get as good a drive out of this corner as the other riders, who kept it a bit tighter while I was on the rumble strips. Maybe the gearing set-up on the Ducati at Sugo didn't quite punch out enough. I could lose about 10 yards at one of the best places to pass.

The back straight, preferably keeping it in fifth, is some-where where you can tuck in right behind another rider, pull out at the last minute and get them on the brakes at the Horse's Back Corner. That's a tight, second-gear right-hand corner, again quite banked and another spot where I some-times caught my boots on the floor. I've often worn my boots through here, and you can easily plane the skin off your toes, especially early on in a race when a full tank of fuel is weigh-ing the bike down. It's probably something to do with the injuries I've had to my knee because this never seemed to happen with my left foot. If you do it once, though, it hurts that much that you won't do it again in a hurry.

Then I quickly change up to third for another double

corner, this time a left-hander called the 'SP In' and 'SP Out'. For the first and maybe second lap of a race I would be a bit cautious there, as the tyres wouldn't be working properly on the left-hand side. Again, I have struggled to find the best gear at this point. Some years I left it in second, but I came up with the best set-up in 1998 when I took the corners in third. The back end can move around coming out of SP Out and the bike can be light at the front because the track rises. It can lift as you accelerate out in third.

You can't see the next corner, Last Corner, until it jumps up on you. It used to be a longer, sweeping corner but I guess it would have been too fast for today's bikes, without enough run-off, so now they've built in a chicane. It is, without doubt, the most hideous, crappy chicane I have ever ridden through. It's so slow it's unbelievable. It's not so bad going into the chicane in first gear, before you flick the bike over to the left, but there's also a crown on the road. If you flick it over too fast, it can bring the front wheel off and the rear wheel round.

But the real struggle is coming out of the chicane. All the riders, except for the Japanese, have problems here. The Japanese are so quick through that section and I have no idea why that is – perhaps it's something to do with

> ### *FOGGY FACTOR*
> ---
> 'You're on and off the gas and, as you close off to go into turn three, the surface is very bumpy. You see a lot of people lose their front end at the apex.'

Dunlop tyres – but I know that I hate it and I can't get on the gas to get some drive up the hill. The rear of the tyre snakes until you can get into second gear, put the bike more upright and change up into third up the slope. If you could come fast out of that section, it would set you up nicely to overtake at the bottom of the main straight at the first corner. Over the years, though, I probably lost half a second around that final third of the circuit while making the time up on the rest of the lap.

I have done quite well at Sugo, though, and for the last couple of years I was probably the fastest of the non-Japanese

SPORTSLAND SUGO

JAPAN

Rating **7**

"Sugo has a good layout and, if it hadn't been for local riders, my results would probably have been better"

Closest finish:
It's usually a close finis in 1999, I held off Yara for second place by a of a second

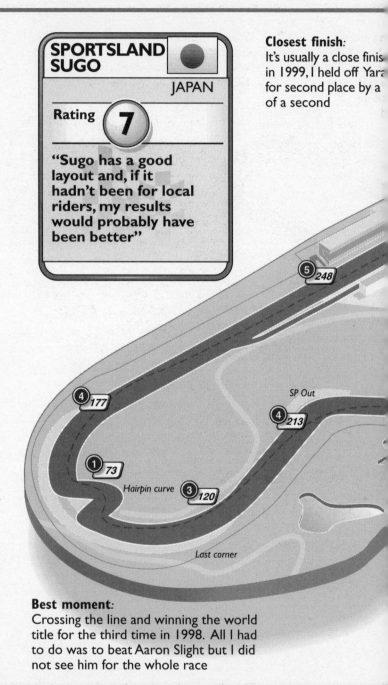

⑤ 248

④ 177

SP Out

④ 213

① 73

Hairpin curve ③ 120

Last corner

Best moment:
Crossing the line and winning the world title for the third time in 1998. All I had to do was to beat Aaron Slight but I did not see him for the whole race

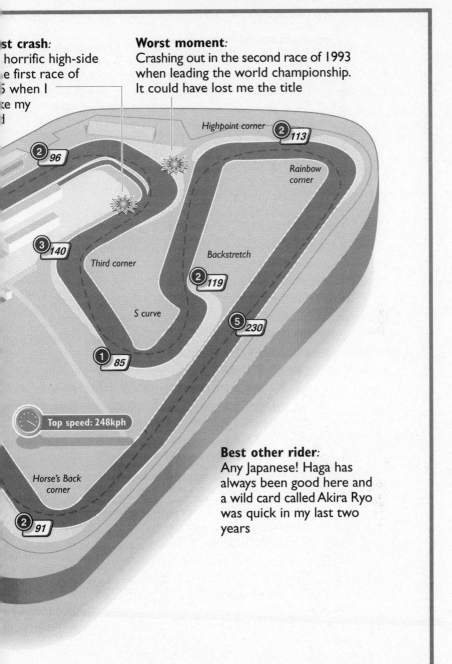

st crash:
horrific high-side
e first race of
when I
e my

Worst moment:
Crashing out in the second race of 1993
when leading the world championship.
It could have lost me the title

Highpoint corner ② 113

Rainbow corner

② 96

③ 140

Third corner

Backstretch

② 119

S curve

⑤ 230

① 85

Top speed: 248kph

Horse's Back corner

② 91

Best other rider:
Any Japanese! Haga has
always been good here and
a wild card called Akira Ryo
was quick in my last two
years

riders at the circuit. But I didn't have to win the race for my most memorable moment. For the final race of 1998 I was leading Aaron Slight by just half a point. All I had to do was finish in front of him. It was a very tactical race, and for the first couple of laps the team was telling me he was only a second behind. I even started to catch the leader, but with 10 laps to go the bike started to vibrate at the back. *Please don't do this to me now*, I thought. I was sure the tyre was falling apart so I slowed down and kept my eye on Slight, who was five or six seconds behind at this stage. Although I lost second and third place, fourth was good enough to win me back that world title. When I returned to the pits, we found that the tyre had spun slightly on the rim. Just as at Phillip Island in 1994, I was overcome with relief and emotion after a real battle for the championship. We tried our best to have a big night out in Sendai, which is not easy because the city shuts at nine o'clock. Jamie Whitham and Neil Hodgson helped us down some beer and champagne in a karaoke bar until five in the morning when we had to go straight to the airport.

The best thing about Japan, apart from a curry house we found near our hotel in Sendai, was taking the piss out of the locals because they couldn't speak a word of English. (Mind you, my Japanese isn't too clever.) They actually seem eager to please in any way possible, but very few of them have a clue what you're on about. My favourite trick was, when ordering food, to point at the menu, pretending to ask about a certain dish but actually saying, 'You suck cock?' Our whole table would be falling around laughing while the waitress carried on nodding, saying 'Hai' – the Japanese for 'okay'. Another trick, while signing people's shoes or T-shirts, was instead of signing my name, to write stuff like 'I'm a dickhead' or 'I munch stump'. It was pretty childish, I know, but you do have to make your own entertainment in Japan.

On one of my first trips there for the Suzuka 8 Hours race, I invited a bloke called Tony Hudson, who didn't really know how to work on the bikes but was just hanging around in those days. He couldn't believe his luck when he got the offer of an all-expenses-paid trip to Japan, and when he got there he was just like a tourist, taking pictures of anything and everything.

They all went out one night and tried to get into one of the members only clubs. The only way they'd got anywhere all week was to point out that I was a famous racer by carrying with them the programme for the race and pointing to my picture. But this time Tony had the programme and he told the girls on the door that he was Steve Hislop, because they did look similar. I guess Westerners must all look the same to the Japanese because they welcomed him with open arms. They were given the best table in the house, on a raised level next to the dance floor. The next thing they knew there was a steady supply of complimentary beer and someone forever on hand to light cigarettes. All of a sudden the music stopped, a bright light shone on our table and the DJ babbled something in Japanese before shouting 'Steve Hiswop!' Tony had to stand up to take all the applause and spent the rest of the night signing autographs.

The truth is that it's easy to get away with stuff with the Japanese. We used to stay at the hotel at the Sugo track, which is a bit like a prison because there's nothing for miles around and not a lot to do. It was so easy to nick stuff from the drinks and ice-cream machines, and you could play tennis for ages but just pretend not to understand what they were on about when they tried to charge you for three hours instead of one. One night we crept into the bar they had in the basement and brought up as many bottles of beer as we could carry, to drink in the foyer upstairs. The barman couldn't understand why we wanted a bottle opener while we were playing cards in our own little casino, because all he sold was canned beer. Slick drank enough of the bottles to leave all his winnings behind when he was dragged off to bed.

OTHER TYPES OF BIKE RACING

COMPETITIVE

3: Motocross

Once I'd eventually got into schoolboy motocross the main aim was to beat my mate Gary Dickinson. We were really competitive with each other and I could usually give him a pretty good race. It's just that he conveniently forgot to tell me he'd been riding for six years before I even started! We perhaps took some stupid risks in the heat of our battles, just hoping for the best going into corners and not really knowing if we would be able to get round. That made us realize just how quick we could go, so it was a way of teaching ourselves. We were soon too good for the junior class, but instead of putting us into the next stage the Amateur Motor Cycle Association (AMCA) officials decided we were good enough for the expert section. And that really pissed me off because I wanted to carry on winning races in the senior section!

But my heart was never in motocross. I knew was never going to be good enough to be a world champion. There was nothing else to do, though, at that age; I wasn't yet old enough to go road racing. I think I lacked a number of things, like aggression, strength and determination. All I wanted to do was go to a race meeting, get it out of the way and stick the bike back in the garage until the next race. Looking back, if I had been pushed harder by my dad and told to practise or eat decent foods, I might

As a seventeen-year-old riding my Yamaha 125cc motocross bike.

have been a lot better. Now, I wish I had started earlier and taken it a lot more seriously.

Having said that, in the local club stuff I was always in the top three or four. I was second in our championship and won the last ever race I took part in at schoolboy level. But our club was never all that competitive. When we met the best riders from other clubs in the national semi-finals, Gary and I were totally blown away. I think I was last, last and last! It wasn't surprising because these 15-year-old lads were almost professional at that age. All our stuff was crammed in the back of a van, while they had proper kit and motorhomes and took it very seriously.

I was better when the track was dusty, dry and without bumps – as much like a road racing track as possible, you might say. There was one time at Carnforth when the track was so dry that you could almost go round with your knee down. But when it was muddy I was terrible because I didn't have the strength and aggression to plough through it. All the qualities I had as a road racer were missing when I raced motocross bikes; as soon as I started road racing at the age of 18, I wanted to win straight away.

When I watch motocross, it seems to be the most relaxed guys who are the quickest. Belgium's Stefan Everts always seems to be conserving energy, while the others have a tense body language. There's a big difference in technique between motocross and supercross. Motocross is a lot faster whereas indoor supercross tracks have a lot more jumps and whoop-di-doos, so it requires a lot more timing to ride those courses. I'm not expert enough to do that, so I've never really had a go. I think I'd struggle like mad, and there is no easy way to learn. You can't do a jump and then do it a little bit faster. It's not like taking Redgate Corner, and then taking it a bit quicker. If you're doing a triple jump, you have to go all out for it. And if you do it wrong, it can be very painful.

I still see motocross as one of the best ways of keeping in shape. There is a shortage of good venues, especially in the region where I live, although in the summer of 1999 I did quite a bit of motocross riding at Preston Docks, about 10 miles from my house. The plan was to really attack motocross at the start of 2000 to get me in peak condition for the season, then to keep it up throughout the summer to maintain that fitness. But that didn't work out, firstly because I injured my shoulder in a fall during my first attempt at skiing in the Italian Alps with Ducati team boss Davide Tardozzi in January, and secondly because a month or so later I injured my other shoulder in a crash at the first test session of the year in Valencia. The docks site was ideal because it was just wasteland and you could make up your own track – until all of a sudden you came across a rider coming the other way on his particular track! Now it has been developed into a professional organization with cafeterias and machines to grade the track. But the drainage, especially in winter, is not too good so I didn't go there when I was recovering from my major injury.

FOGGY FACTOR

'I still see motocross as one of the best ways of keeping in shape.'

I converted the front field at home into a miniature track in March 2000, when I was recovering from the Valencia fall. I actually designed the track by riding my KTM round the field very slowly, leaving enough of a mark for the plant hire people to follow – the first time I had done anything like track design. It was built free of charge by a firm called Winstanley's; the proprietor's son races in motocross grands prix, so they knew what they were doing. It's a tight little track because I didn't want to make it so big that the neighbours would start to complain about the noise (and there's also the small matter that this is the same field which Michaela uses to ride her horse!). I ordered two Honda XR100s from America – they can't be bought over here – with the intention of finding someone to race round it and over the couple of jumps I had built in. Of course, within a month I had nearly killed myself in Australia and it wasn't used again until August that same year.

By that time I had bored myself rigid trying to build my arm back up in the gym. There was enough strength back in the shoulder to ride one of the XR100s for 15 minutes, but that was enough to completely knacker me out. But now that the arm is a lot stronger, I intend to do 30-minute sessions on my home track, which provides a really good workout. It's also there for Danielle and Claudia to ride their quads on. It's not the type of track that's going to test the likes of Jamie Dobb, who's leading the 125cc world championship as I write, and someone I used to go riding with. The fact that he was up there made me want to try a lot harder, and I'm a lot faster on a motocross bike now than I ever was when I was racing them. Even so, Dobby would come jumping over me on a double jump. Bastard!

OTHER TYPES OF BIKE RACING

COMPETITIVE

4: Speedway

It's quite simple: all speedway riders are mad! You have to be to ride a bike with no gears and no brakes. I was really impressed when I went to my first speedway event at the Millennium Stadium in Cardiff. There were 40,000 people there, about as many klaxons, and the atmosphere was amazing because the crowd was grouped in certain areas.

There are also a lot more tactics involved than meets the eye. For instance, the track changes throughout the night. The only way a track can alter during a weekend in road racing is as a result of a temperature change or rain, as well as if a bit of rubber is deposited during the week. The speedway guys told me that the track is more slippery early on, until the more moist gravel is thrown to one side. In Cardiff you could see that some of the riders were really struggling for grip, but all of a sudden, as the circuit changed, their wheels started to shoot up in the air. At one point the world champion, Mark Loram, was just on the balancing point of tipping himself over the back when he tried to take a tighter line.

Then the inside line began to get rutted, which can cause a few crashes and heart-in-the-mouth moments. So the riders started to move towards a wider line in order to get more grip. When it comes to the final, the guy who has qualified in first place is

Notice how world champion Mark Loram gets on the gas on the corner so that the rear of the bike is pulled round.

allowed to come out onto the track, test the dirt like a bull that's ready to stampede and decide from which position he wants to start on the line. I would have thought the worst gate to go for was the outside one, but that's not always the case. If the guy on the outside can get a drive on better out of that corner, he could still exit it in the lead. A lot is obviously down to the start, but it was also interesting watching the guys in second and third trying different lines to see if the grip was better on other parts of the track. Sometimes they worked and sometimes they didn't. I guess that kind of knowledge comes down to experience.

I suppose the main difference between riding speedway and road racing is that we shut off the gas when we go into a corner, whereas they get on the gas in order to bring the rear of the bike round so that they can turn the corner. Even in dirt track riding you throw the bike into a corner until the bike starts to come round and then get on the gas. Speedway riders don't seem to do it that way. They whip it round sideways while on the gas, almost to the point where the bike stops three-quarters of the way round the corner. That's how it appeared to a first-time spectator anyway, but obviously they are driving the bike forward and the wheel is spinning a bit.

Another way in which speedway riders differ from road racers is that they will regularly compete at two or three different meetings a week, all over Europe. And it's not the case that their mechanics load up the van and drive over there, the riders themselves do it. So I have every respect for them. At the end of the day they are just very fast and skilful guys on bikes.

I would actually love to have a go at speedway, just to see how hard it is – as long as they took all the fences away so that I could have loads of run-off! It looks really hard, but probably looks more dangerous than it is because at least they have air-fencing now. With other forms of riding, you get a chance to build it up gradually; with speedway it seems that it's 'drop the clutch and away you go'. There's no in-between. You either slide the thing round the corner or you're straight into the fence. It certainly doesn't look as easy as riding a motocross bike or a supermotard, where you can get faster and faster in your own time.

Having said all that, I came away thinking something could be done to the sport to make it better for the fans. There are so many four-lap races during the night to determine who goes through to the grand final. The crowd is going mad waiting for this final, but it is still only four laps long. Why can't the final be extended to eight laps?

I also think it can be a cruel night for the riders. I was doing some commentary for Sky Sports and I compared Loram's experience to mine at Brands Hatch. Everybody there was behind him and wanted him to do well, but one tiny mistake can leave you out of the A and B finals. If you make a small mistake in road racing, you might just run wide, lose a place and get it back; in speedway, though, it can put you out of the last eight. It's not right when the world champion, the one everyone has paid money to go and watch, is not even in the big two races of the night. I was also surprised at how unreliable the bikes are. For a four-lap race, they really shouldn't break down so often.

The rules are also very strict. If someone crashes the race is stopped, but that rider is not allowed to restart. If you're knocked off, the guy who caused the crash is disqualified. It's all down to the referee, who has tough decisions to make. It's just like a game of football in this respect, and that's probably why there are regular punch-ups. I don't think it would have been the sport for me. The riders just seem to accept decisions and get on with the next race; I would have lost my rag all the time.

OTHER TYPES OF BIKE RACING

COMPETITIVE

5: Trials

I have to admit I'm not a fan of trial riding, although the riders can make a bike do unbelievable things. I prefer to see the two wheels of a bike going fast. Having said that, I am a big fan of the world champion Dougie Lampkin, who has been on a few of our rideouts to the Lakes. I have said many times that he should be voted *MCN* Man of the Year. In my form of motorsport, there are many different classes and I was the best in my class. There are also many different classes for motocross, but there is only one trials world champion. And he has been the best in the world year after year after year.

I went to watch a world championship round a few years ago as it was being staged near my home at Hoghton Towers. An event like this is never going to attract thousands and thousands of fans because you have to wander around acres of land to watch it, and when you get to a particular stage there are so many people there that you can't actually see anything. It would be a different matter if you had all the trials in one arena and people could just sit there and watch it. Dougie hated it when I told him that I thought it was boring!

Trials riders need incredible balance, at no speed at all. The best can balance on a bike without putting their feet down for an

World champion Dougie
Lampkin sets the standard in
trial riding.

hour without any problem.
I wouldn't be able to do it
for five seconds. On the
rideouts Dougie is very professional and steady, while
I'm always totally out of
control. I was actually
quicker than he was on
most of the sections,
because it was a bit like the
TT and I was used to not
knowing what was round
the next corner. But when it
came to the technical sections where you needed a
bit of balance and a bit of thought, I didn't even see which way
Dougie went. He looked so stylish and effortless going up a big,
steep gully on a big CCM, while I was hitting rocks and falling
over every minute.

As I write this, I am sat in my back garden, staring at a five-
foot wall. It might seem impossible, but if you told Dougie to get
up onto the top of it, he would be able to. There are a few big
pebbles just at the bottom of the wall and he would probably use
those to get a bit of lift. It all comes from starting at a very early
age, probably around the age of five, because his dad was also a
very good trials rider.

My dad once had a go at a charity event on the outskirts of
Blackburn when I was about 14 and he couldn't even get down to
the start–finish area, which was at the bottom of a very steep
drop. I was stood behind him when he asked some guy, 'How do
I get down there?'

'You just ride down the hill, mate,' came the reply.

'You're fucking joking! I'm not riding down there!' he spluttered.
He had no idea what he had let himself in for and probably

thought it looked easy after watching the *Kick Start* programme on television. When he eventually arrived at the bottom, after ploughing into a load of bikes, the first stage was to go up a stream. Within seconds you could hardly see him because he had disappeared under the water. And from a bad start, it got steadily worse.

Then, a few years ago, I had a bit of go when *MCN* organized a competition between road racers, motocross riders and trial bike riders at Donington. Right at the start I was stood at the bottom of a hill, looking up and thinking, *For fuck's sake!*

'Just put it in fourth gear and ride up,' advised Steve Saunders, one of the best trials guys at the time.

'You're taking the piss,' I said.

'No, just stick it in fourth and you'll be okay.'

To me the hill looked vertical, while for him it was almost horizontal. But I took his advice and, because their bikes have so much low-down power, I shot up the hill as soon as I let the clutch out. I zoomed over the brow and just missed road racer Mick Grant, who was quietly chatting away in the spectator area, before squeezing in between two parked cars. How I missed them I will never know. Mick had turned away because he couldn't stand to watch what he thought was going to happen to his brand new car. Then I tried to go over a log, hit it full on and went right over the top. I thought, *That's me. I'm not doing any more of this shit.*

> **FOGGY FACTOR**
>
> 'I have every respect for the riders because they are incredible, but it's not a sport for me.'

Apart from falling, the bikes are really uncomfortable to ride because there is no seat; the riders just stand up all the time. And it can be quite dangerous, because if a rider gets it wrong he can fall a long way, although they do have minders there ready to try to cushion the blow. Each to his own, I suppose. I have every respect for the riders because they're incredibly talented, and I always follow how Dougie is doing in his world championship. But it's not a sport for me.

OTHER TYPES OF BIKE RACING

COMPETITIVE

6: Supermotard

This was meant to be my life after road racing! It was my new sport and was a lifesaver after my retirement – until the day in September when I snapped my leg in two places on a track in Anglesey.

It was a circuit that I was unfamiliar with and contained a lot of gravel, so obviously the CCM 640 was moving around a lot more than it does on tarmac. I had done 11 laps of 15 and felt pretty good as I went into a fast left that tightens up a little bit. Then everything locked up and I was sliding the bike in, speedway style.

It all happened so quickly as I thought to myself, *I'm not slowing down here...I'm not going to get round.* Then it gripped and fired me over the front. When I was up in the air I saw a bank of tyres. *I don't want to hit that,* I thought. So I must have put my feet out and landed flat-footed, and when you do that you usually break bones – I've always known that. My right leg snapped and I knew immediately it was broken. The first think that came into my head was that Michaela was going to go mad. Then I realised I'd ruined a good night out in Manchester!

Even as I was lying there in the grass I knew I would have to cut down the risks by not riding bikes fast around tarmac any more. I didn't have any choice. I could still get injured trail riding but it's a lot less likely. At the end of the day you can't go through the rest of your life wrapped in cotton wool, avoiding the things that you love. But I do now know that I have to calm it down and get off the tarmac.

Supermotard racing is a sport that's growing in popularity and manufacturers are making more and more of these bikes for use in and around towns. If that trend continues, it's the perfect sport through which to promote those sales. And I'm not just saying that because Michaela is a director of CCM, which produces supermotard bikes! It was with their team that I was testing in Anglesey for a one-off race in Belgium that I planned to do in October.

The supermotard bike is basically a cross between motocross and road racing on a motocross-style bike with superbike-sized wheels on a road racing style circuit. These tracks tend to be tight and twisting because the bikes, which probably reach 100mph, would seem too slow somewhere like Donington. In the countries where it's a big sport, such as France and Germany, tracks are split between half dirt and half tarmac. We have found that go-karting tracks are as good as anywhere for having a play around on. The two we use are at Three Sisters, near Wigan in Lancashire, and a track up in Cumbria called Rowrah.

FOGGY FACTOR

'I have to ride with my foot sticking slightly out so that, if I feel I'm going down, I can dab my foot on the floor to stop it.'

We also went down to the south coast to a place called Lydd, where a small crowd soon built up, not believing that they were watching me ride again. But these are just tarmac; I haven't yet been on a track that has some dirt sections. I'm really keen to do that because I think it will be even more fun than I'm having already.

One of the main reasons I'm enjoying it is that my arm doesn't hinder me. I do not have to tuck it in like I would have to do on a road bike. The other reason, of course, is that I'm getting pretty quick; I wouldn't be having fun if I was getting my arse kicked every week. I tried to race in the same way I did on a road bike,

Supermoto bikes are very tall compared to their road racing counterparts, and they suit the kind of rider who hits the brakes, front and back, and slides it into a corner. That was never my style.

carrying corner speed, and that meant I was always complaining about the bike because it was chattering all the time. I had a couple of days' testing with CCM and WP suspension trying to cure the problem, and although they made it better it was more down to my riding than any fault on the bike. They even said that in their experience of supermoto, guys who came from a road racing background always had this problem, whereas motocross riders didn't. That's because it's a very tall bike and it suits the kind of rider who hits the brakes, front and back, and slides it into a corner. They almost stop, turn halfway through, then squirt it out again. That was never my style in road racing, so I'm finding myself having to do exactly the opposite. And I enjoy it.

As a general rule, whenever I've been riding with the British champion, Warren Steele, I pick up time on him mid-corner while he's a bit quicker than me going into corners, because he's happier sliding it in. So I have learned not to ride with my toe on the footrest and my knee on the floor. I have to ride with my foot sticking slightly out so that, if I feel I'm going down, I can dab my foot on the floor to stop it. Although you feel as though you're going really fast, the corners are so tight that you're probably only doing 30 mph, so it's not as dangerous as it sounds. If you tried to do that on a road bike you would almost certainly damage your knee.

While it's great fun, there's no chance that I'm going to start racing seriously. I have been in a few races, though, at the Bologna and Paris Motor Shows. At Bologna I was third a couple of times against Grand Prix riders and other superbike riders. It's usually the superbike guys who win, which is quite pleasing. And that tells its own story.

I have been criticized for staying in World Superbikes rather than going to the Grand Prix circuit, but there is absolutely no doubt in my mind that I would have won Grand Prix races as well, had things turned out differently. I have only ever once rode a 125cc, in 1989 when I was third in the Isle of Man TT on a Honda RS. Basically, to do well at 125ccs you have to be 4ft 3in tall. I hated riding it because I was so uncomfortable and lost a few hundred revs every time I moved on the thing. But I was right behind Robert Dunlop through the tight, twisty sections and he is tiny and a lot quicker on the straights.

The 250cc are very similar, all about high corner speed. Guys who have done well at 125ccs seem to be able to jump straight on a 250cc and go very fast – Valentino Rossi for instance. I loved my Yamaha TZ in 1986, but after my bad leg injuries these smaller bikes were very uncomfortable and it made sense for me to move up to superbikes. I now think the 500cc class is suited to a 250cc style of rider, carrying lots of corner speed. There is so much rubbish still written and said about how hard these things are to ride. Nearly all the best guys now have come up from 250cc, and there's even some, like Garry McCoy, who have come straight from 125cc and started to win immediately. They became a lot more rider-friendly around 1998, and I remember Michael Doohan saying that the 500s had become too easy to ride because he could remember them when they were animals. The power used to be very aggressive and you needed tough guys like Kevin Schwantz and Wayne Gardner to handle them coming out of corners. But now people like Max Biaggi can go straight from the 250cc class, jump on a 500cc and win a GP. So the rule book is torn up and thrown out of the window.

But, as I've shown, I am the type of guy who has always been able to adapt to any kind of bike on any kind of circuit. Even in 1993 at Donington, when I was riding someone else's bike, I just jumped on and finished fourth, having been third until the bike ran out of fuel down the final straight. People who know me know that I would have been up there winning races had I made the switch. There would have been only one guy to beat – Michael Doohan. In my humble opinion, I cannot believe anyone would have carried as much corner speed as me once I had the bike set up right with the right team. That's from the heart. I don't care about other people's opinions, although I find them frustrating because I know what I could have done. But I suppose we will never know.

However, whether it's on a supermotard, Ducati 996 or a 50cc scooter, there's one place that none of the principles I've talked about applies...

OTHER TYPES OF
BIKE RACING

LEISURE

1: Roadcraft

Riding on roads is scary, there's no escaping that fact. The only way to make it safe is to take all the cars off the roads. In addition, the bikes made nowadays are fast but not particularly comfortable to ride. Machines like the Yamaha R1 and Honda Fireblade are, in my opinion, race bikes made for the race track. Some of the guys on them know what to do with them, some of them don't. And it's the ones who aren't so sure who are in real trouble.

They might get a corner slightly wrong, or not know how to react if they see a tractor pulling out of a side road. Sometimes you don't know how fast you can go on these things until it's too late. So the message is, *don't leave it too late*. The best way to minimize your chances of getting hurt riding a bike on the roads is to cut your speed. Sure, that might take some of the fun out of it, but I would rather have a bit less fun and live to tell the tale than lose everything in one moment's stupidity.

Of course, a lot of the time accidents are caused by people driving cars or trucks. It's a fact that bikes aren't that easy to see, but the biker has to be aware of this as well and must guess what a driver who's not paying proper attention might do. One thing a biker can do to limit his chance of trouble is always to leave the lights on. You could also wear something bright which will make you stand out against the road. This might sound a bit naff, but it's well worth the loss of credibility. A guy on a black bike in black leathers is not easy to spot.

If I had a choice and I rode bikes on the road on a regular basis, which I don't, I would go out on a fun bike like a Ducati Monster or an enduro bike, but not a superbike. It really worries me that someone who has just passed his test, which is designed to make road riding as safe as possible at low speeds, can go straight out on a superbike and onto the road.

You'll find that most racers don't ride bikes on the road. It's a bit like taking your work home with you, but we also know that these things need to be treated with respect. You also need to respect whatever is coming in the opposite direction. So, please, use any tips you've picked up from this book to ride fast under controlled conditions only, at organized track days, not to go faster down a country lane. Use your brake *and* your brain if you want to ride like a world champion on the roads.

FOGGY FACTOR

'The best way to minimize your chances of getting hurt riding a bike on the roads is to cut your speed.'

ACKNOWLEDGEMENTS

The Publishers would like to thank John Lawson for the circuit and telemetry illustrations; Daniel Balado and Cherry Ekins for their work on this project; and Dave Paterson and his team at Fylde Superbikes, Blackpool for their assistance and hospitality during the photoshoot.

Thanks also to Carl and Michaela for providing photographs for the book, with the exception of the following:

Allsport back cover
Ray Archer 314
Kel Edge front cover, 241 (x2)
Gold & Goose I, IIt, IIIb, IVt, IVbl, IVbr, Vt, Vc, Vb, Vit, Vib, VIIt, VIIbl, VIIbr, VIII, Xt, Xb, XIt, XIb, XIIt, XIIc, XIIb, XIIIt, XIIIb, XIVt, XIVb, XVt, XVc, XVb, XVItl, XVItr, XVIc, 31, 32, 68, 106, 113, 146, 213, 215, 234, 238, 273
Alwyn Morris 318
Double Red 8, 13, 26, 38, 41, 44, 47, 51, 52, 55, 56, 58, 65, 71, 80, 116, 122 (x2), 123 (x2), 134, 137, 139, 141, 173, 176, 188, 193, 204, 228, 231, 240, 242, 246, 254, 261, 294

Every effort has been made to contact the copyright holders of the photographs included in this book. Where there have been omissions, the Publishers will endeavour to rectify any outstanding permissions on publication.

INDEX